VILLAGE IN THE SUN

VILLAGE IN THE SUN

by Dane Chandos

G. P. PUTNAM'S SONS, NEW YORK

Designed by Robert Josephy

MANUFACTURED IN THE UNITED STATES OF AMERICA

To Abbie

CONTENTS

AJIJIC is real. The events related in this book are real. They happened. But, as regards the people, name and appearance, character and profession have been changed and interchanged, so that no person is directly portrayed, while certain houses described do not exist, but have been invented from parts of other houses. This is not a book about Mexico. It is a book about Ajijic.

VILLAGE IN THE SUN

JUNE

THERE were mountains all round the lake, but they were distant, they seemed low-lying, flattened like crouched animals. There was an immensity of sky, unfingered by any building. But it was the great lake itself, from the mirrored ash and sulphur of the sunset to the lilac hazes in the east, that dominated everything, as it dominates the lives of those who live around it.

"Is there any land for sale?" I asked. "On the lake shore, I mean."

"Who knows," said the fisherman. "From time in when somebody sells some land. A year ago Don Esteban sold some land of his. A very nice piece."

"And has he any more to sell?" I asked, with no idea of who Don Esteban was. "Or has anybody else any?"

"Pues, just recently he bought it back again. Of course, there's Amílcar. He is owner of that bit there."

The fisherman pointed out a long narrow strip running down to the lakeshore. It had some fine mangoes.

"And would he sell that, d'you think?"

"Oh, no. Surely that not."

There was a pause.

"In fact, it'd be difficult to get land here?"

"Oh, no. There's that Venustiano. He'd sell. That's his land, over there."

And the fisherman pointed to a little promontory which I had already noticed. I strolled along and looked at it. The lot ran a little way each side of the point before reaching the boundary wall. A lake frontage of fifty or sixty yards, I judged, in all. I could not tell how far back

I

it ran, but it seemed to be about a block. It was untidy, but it was full of fruit trees, oranges and bananas and mangoes, and coffee bushes. Then I turned my back on it and looked at the lake. The views each way were superb. I thought of a little house down here by the water's edge, a little house washed, perhaps, pale green outside, with a terrace in front of it and somewhere a balcony or flat roof to sit on, a little house with, on the lake side, as little wall and as much window as possible. On the rock beside me a gray lizard puffed his throat into a balloon of pink, just the pink I would like the inside of a veranda to be painted.

I went back to the fisherman.

"Does Venustiano live here?" I asked.

"Oh, yes. Over there. Go until the next street and ask at the house where the white turkey cock is."

I went up the lane that led past the land I wanted. Behind the low dry wall it was a jungle of vegetation. It wanted clearing and ordering. It stretched back the whole block. I turned the corner. The white turkey cock stood, immensely aristocratic, his head sunk in his wattles, under a mango tree while round him humbler fowl picked and pecked. I knocked at the door of the house next the yard, and after a while it was opened by a toothless woman with skin the color and texture of cocoa, wearing a flowered skirt.

"Can you tell me where Venustiano lives?" I asked.

The woman at the doorway pushed back three or four copper-colored brats who were trying to crowd out into the street, and said,

"Yes, how not. He lives over there."

"Where is that exactly?"

"Pues, you go straight on past the big mango tree, straight straight until that big pig, and there you give a turn to the right. A little way on you will see a house with a blue door. That's not it, pues."

The woman paused to draw breath and push back the children again.

"Then you go on till you come to the house with a table outside with tomatoes and lemonade on it, that's Pachita's, and there you give a turn to the left. Then you'll see a house with a new gate. Go and knock and ask if Venustiano lives there, and if they say yes then that's where he lives."

I had spent the whole day in the village. In the morning I had come down the lake in a leisurely little motor launch, passing slim-necked grebe that fixed their scarlet eyes on us disdainfully. The lake that day was yellow and a little broken, so that it glittered, it was like sandpaper. I think I came in the first place because of the four dots running. Ajijic. Say Ach-ich-ee, with the ch as in Scottish loch, and the tonic accent on the last syllable. By the rules of Spanish the final c should be pronounced, but when anyone pronounces it, we Ajijiquenses know he is a stranger hereabouts. The name used to be written Axixique, a Spanish corruption of a Nahuatl name that means The Place Where the Water Springs.

The village lies on the narrow strip of land left between the mountains and the lake. North winds never touch it. They fly over it to strike the south shore of the lake, where the climate is very different. It doesn't freeze in Ajijic, so that coffee grows there readily. All the narrow strip is abundantly fertile, and the hills, bare of all but brush, seem to plunge their feet into foliage—thick, tufty branches of mango, sharp green plumes of banana, glossy leaves of orange and grapefruit and tangerine, the discreet dull green of avocado, the feathery boughs of flamboyant or jacaranda. Above this billowing green rise a few palms and the church tower, new-painted and looking like a cake. You do not see the houses. They have no upper stories, and their adobe walls and tiled roofs are engulfed in vegetation. The mountains themselves are highly accidented, typically Mexican, the mountains of a country geologically young. From a serrated skyline, they sweep down in flutes and folds, in the dry months all pale gold, in the rains magically greened in a few weeks.

The first day I asked if you could go up to the top of the mountain. It did not look far in the clear air, but I was told that it was a three hours' walk.

"And up there is a spring called the Chupinaya, with fresh water that comes out cool cool. If you drink some water from the Chupinaya, you will never leave Ajijic again."

I was not prepared never to leave Ajijic again, but I was anxious to find somewhere to settle. I wanted, after years of hotels and furnished houses, to have my own roof. And so, since already the lake of Chapala

3

and the climate of Jalisco pleased me and Ajijic had charmed me, I began on that very first day to inquire about land.

But I didn't find Venustiano that day. He was away on business in Jocótepec, at the western end of the lake. I looked at his land again and watched from the small headland as the flame dimmed out of the sunset.

Then, in the little motorboat, I went back to Chapala. We chugged over a silky ripple of silver and lilac. It is an unusual lake. Its waters, heavy with silt, are never transparent, and reflect colors in curious half-tones. Often it is exactly like the shot silk that Victorians wore, dull-blue-and-brown or pale-blue-and-yellow. And I have seen it turn a vulgar Wagnerian sunset into the blue-and-red fuchsia shot silk that Victorian parasols were made of. It often has, in the evening, the qualities of old Chinese paintings on silk—a wash of amber over everything. Now that I know these subtly orchestrated colors I shall never again be content with the constant blue shout of a Como.

A few days later I went to Ajijic by road. On the way down from Guadalajara you pass many wheat fields. The wheat is harvested in May and June. In one field you will see a motor thresher, in the next everything is done by hand, and lunged horses, circling, trample the grain. That is Mexico. Everything is contemporaneous, today and yesterday and the day before yesterday all exist at once and side by side. A buxom young woman, delousing her child's head by the roadside, sang as I passed:

> "One day with another,
> The luck will surely change. . . ."

That is a current popular song. No wonder Mexicans are notoriously vague about the time, no wonder mañana is anywhen. How should it be otherwise?

It is only five miles from Chapala, but they are bad miles. Between Chapala and San Antonio, the village before you come to Ajijic, there were four bridges. All had holes in them, and two of them were impassable, so that one had to go round them, coaxing the car down a steep slippery bank, fording a narrow stony torrent, and climbing up the bank again on the other side. It was, and is, no road for a low car or a good car.

After going down the lake, it was an anticlimax to approach Ajijic by road, and I have always tried to arrange for newcomers to arrive by water. But the place itself I liked as well as ever, and that day I discovered it had good drinking water. Now this is rare almost to the point of nonexistence in Mexico, where everywhere you have to get electrically purified water or drink it boiled or bottled. But in Ajijic the water from a mountain is piped down to the plaza. At the foot of the mountain it springs from a place known as the Eye of Water. It is perfectly safe, and I always drink it. So that was an added attraction to Ajijic.

On this second visit I again failed to locate Venustiano, but I learned that he did not own the whole site I had seen. He owned only one-sixth and one-twelfth of it, in two separate strips, and the rest belonged in varying fractions to other members of his family. This often occurs among the Indios, and it is unusual for them to have their property legally registered and their titles in order.

I realized that if I were going to try to buy land in Ajijic and thereafter build on it, I should have to have somewhere to live meanwhile in the village. Most houses in Ajijic have one or at the most two rooms, with an earth floor and unplastered adobe walls, and usually one window permanently bricked up and one, unglazed, closed by a heavy wooden shutter. But I found a house that I liked. It lay a little way back from the lake, behind a huerta full of fruit trees. A huerta is an orchard, if orchard means somewhere where oranges, bananas, coffee, and mangoes grow. It had a roomy pale green patio, roofed by a vine, and just now great bunches of ripening purple grapes hung down from it everywhere and its thick foliage filled the patio with a green aqueous light. The house looked large, but it had only three rooms, on two sides of the patio. Two, flanking the zaguán or arched tunnel between inner and outer street door, were large, one very large, running nearly the whole length of the patio. The third side was a high wall, and the fourth was occupied by the kitchen on top of which was a covered terrace, whence you had a splendid view over the huerta to the lake beyond. The house contained practically no furniture. But it had a water closet. There was no water pressure, and the toilet had to be flushed by pouring water from a bucket. But in Ajijic earth closets are the rule, and plumbing was, when I first came to the village, unknown.

5

This was the house for me. The owner, I learned, lived in Guadalajara.

In Mexico, anyone you want to contact is usually the cousin of a friend or the friend of the cousin of the friend. And if he is not that, he is the cousin of a friend's wife. There are still plenty of families fifteen and twenty strong, and in a country with so small a population, and most of that Indio, the whites are inevitably widely related and acquainted. Back in Guadalajara I found that the owner of the house was the cousin of a friend. He was an old man who had once been very rich. He lived in the Avenida Vallarta, in one of those houses whose pillars and porticoes and pediments and portes-cochère recall the first decade of the century, the age of Porfirio Díaz and the capitalists.

Señor González de la Comarca received me in a stiffly brocaded salon, Bohemian glass on the mantel answering the ruby of the silk. He was as representative as his house of an epoch when the culture of Guadalajara was predominantly French. He himself had lived for years in Paris and he spoke French as readily as Spanish. One of his daughters was married to a French duke. Now he was ruined. That is to say, he had only enough left to live in this young mansion and keep one car. We talked Europe for a while. It was the Europe of my childhood, before 1914, for though Señor González de la Comarca had visited Europe since then, he belonged to the old days. I think I really got the house in Ajijic, which he had not thought of renting, because we established that my mother had known a number of people whom he had also known. But I did get it, renting it as it stood, though Señor González de la Comarca was anxious to send down "quelques meubles convenables." But I didn't want the rent to go up, and I didn't see French furniture in a house in Ajijic. There is a nostalgic charm to surroundings such as Señor González de la Comarca's, but I do not want to live in them, least of all in an Indio village. To me, too, Europe, and especially France, had always been the center of the world, but I do not like copies of it in the Americas. I wanted my house to be Mexican of today, not an echo of yesterday across an ocean.

For a few days in Guadalajara I shopped for furniture, glass, linen, household things, and got them sent down to Ajijic by the daily bus, which carried freight, livestock, and passengers impartially and mixed together.

"You know," said a man in the market from whom I had bought

6

several white wood tables and wanted some more quickly, "the only thing wrong with you foreigners is that you want everything done in such a hurry."

All the same, I got a lot of things done in a hurry. And I began to notice what I had noticed in Spain. At the beginning of any undertaking, it is prosecuted with enthusiasm, practically with fury. Then there comes a lull, sustained effort being out of the question. And until the next wave crest of energy comes along, you won't get much done. Once in Andalucía my workmen partitioned off a length of corridor as a bathroom, got the pipes in, and the tub standing in the room within three days. Six weeks later the tub was put in place and connected to the piping. You will find the same thing in Mexico, and, if you are going to enjoy yourself, you will find that this is an ancient rhythm of living which you aren't going to be able to change. It is a different wave length, and if you can't adapt or resign yourself to it, you had better leave Mexico. If you can stand it, you will find that everything can be done here, that it is still the land of unlimited possibilities. But what you need more than knowledge or energy or money in order to achieve anything is plain old-fashioned patience.

At this time I had not yet learned this, and gave myself a deal of unnecessary and unprofitable nerve strain. I remember being worried because the bus to Ajijic didn't give me any sort of receipt for my goods. They all arrived except for a big crate of china and a bundle of blankets. But these two packages turned up a couple of days later, unharmed. The driver had forgotten to unload them in Ajijic, and they had made the circuit to Guadalajara and back again. It is useless to make a fuss about things like this. Fuss will change nothing, and nobody will understand what you are driving at. You will be judged mad or grouchy, or at least just too pernickety.

At last the day came when I myself was to go down to Ajijic and move in. At that time practically nothing could be bought in Ajijic, and one had to take all such things as butter, flashlight batteries, medicines, and typewriter ribbons. So I set out with innumerable parcels and packages. On the way, in Chapala, I ordered my ice. This is sent out daily from Guadalajara, and small blocks are forwarded to Ajijic by the morning bus. By the time it reaches Ajijic, it has come about forty miles. It is wrapped in a bit of straw matting and keeps well. But in

7

Ajijic it is dumped at the corner of the street, and if nobody has heard the hoot of the arriving bus, there it sits and melts in the sun until fetched. At least once it was taken on to Jocótepec and returned in the afternoon about six inches cube.

At last I arrived to find the patio crammed with cases and bundles of all shapes and sizes. I had been lucky enough to have a cook recommended to me in Guadalajara. She was middle-aged and plain and rather deaf.

"Yes, señor, I have worked for foreigners before," she had said when I interviewed her. "They are the best masters. And I know foreign cooking."

"Not English, I hope."

"Oh, yes," she said.

My heart sank. I expected her to add that she was a good plain cook. But she noticed that she had not ingratiated herself, and added dubiously:

"I worked for one family that came from a place called Hamburgo, and another that came from Burdeos. They'd be English, wouldn't they?"

She had, it turned out, no idea at all where England was. And when, shortly after, I ate a meal prepared by her, I was pleased to note that Bordeaux had definitely triumphed over Hamburg.

She could not read or write. At the time, I did not realize what a disadvantage this could be. But in Mexico it is usual to buy everything day by day as you want it, in small quantities. That is the way of living the servants are used to, and to have a large quantity of anything in the house means that it is used up very quickly. Every day I had to listen while Candelaria did her accounts—so many centavos' worth of sugar, so many of flour, and so on. And if, as usually happened, she could not remember how a few centavos had been spent, she had to go through the whole list again and again. Then suddenly she would cry, "The little garlics! Eight little centavos of little garlics!" And another day's accounts had been brought to a happy conclusion.

Yet she could carry in her head scores and scores of recipes.

She had come down the day before and received me as if she had already been for years in my employ. I was her patrón, her master. She had got in some men and boys to help with the unpacking, and I had

8

hardly emerged from the car when they were all whisking my baggage and packages out of the rumble and from inside the car, with an energy that no doubt followed a nice long rest. In a moment everything was stacked in the patio.

I had bought a bed. Or rather, I had had made the wire bedspring and a Simmons mattress, and had ordered a bedstead, not only because I am too tall for Mexican beds, but because, given a comfortable bed, I can put up with other discomforts. In the last census of Mexico one of the questions asked was "Do you wear shoes or huaraches or do you go barefoot?" and another was "Do you sleep in a bed, in a hammock, or on a mat?" They were very sensible questions, and the answers revealed the way of life of any given community. At the time I filled in my form, I was actually wearing huaraches, but the censor insisted that I describe myself as of the shoe-wearing class. He was of course quite right. In Ajijic, many sleep on petates, reed mats laid on the floor, and there are many bedsteads laced with thongs and many others with bamboos laid across the bedframe. Mexicans of all classes often prefer planks to wire springs. So I had brought my bed with me. But naturally the carpenter had not finished the bedstead. In the end it was weeks before it was ready. But that first day, when we propped the wire bedspring on six chairs, three at the head and three at the foot, it seemed quite a temporary measure.

When we had arranged the furniture somehow, and unpacked the most necessary things, I sent away the men. The cook had already installed one of the main features of an Indio kitchen, that is a bunch of ripening bananas hung from a ceiling, probably from a hook designed to support a light, and hung at the height to bump the majority of heads. And now she went out into the village to get milk, bread, and a maid. She had lived in Ajijic at one time, and had many connections. On the flat stones of the patio her sneakers made a scampering sound. She walked quickly but dragged her feet, and this scamper, as of busy mice behind the wainscoting, became an accompaniment of life in Ajijic.

I had arrived after an early lunch, and the unpacking seemed to have taken most of the afternoon. It was late and I was tired. I went down to the bottom of the huerta, where there was a mirador, four pillars and a roof against the boundary wall, with a window and a door onto the beach. I opened the door and sat in the entrance watching the lake. The evening was still as glass. It was blue and gold. Very blue and very gold. From behind a great cloud to the west there fanned out great rays of light that swept across the sky like golden searchlights to fade and lose themselves in the east, where all color dimmed to a soft haze of lilac and wedgwood.

Suddenly the air was filled with clattering. I went out on the beach. The sky was loud with birds. I have never discovered what these birds are called. They are black and not very large, and one never notices them during the day. But often at sunset they emerge from the trees, in groups hundreds strong, and perform astonishing aerial gymnastics. There are thousands in the air at once, but when two groups meet they coalesce for a moment in fantastic whirling patterns and then separate without hesitation. Each member of the ballet is highly trained, and only once have I seen a lone bird lose its group. It flew hither and thither, peeping distractedly, every now and again trying to join a passing flight but retreating unhappily when it found it was not its own. At last it flew down the shore, but only when already most of the groups had retired to rest. For perhaps half an hour the wild dance continued, weaving a dizzy pattern across the glowing sky and filling the air with the clatter of wings and the high sustained note of cloven air.

Suddenly Candelaria came scampering down the huerta, carrying a length of string and accompanied by a young girl muffled in the dark shawl that the Indio woman never moves without. I asked Candelaria what the birds were.

"Who knows," she said. "They're birds."

"And why do they fly about like that?"

"Who knows," she said. "Because they like it. Señor, this is Nieves. She is the daughter of Valentina, who lives over there, down the street."

"Good afternoon, Nieves."

"Good afternoon, señor," said María de las Nieves, Mary of the Snows, who had certainly never seen any snow. She had the thin nose with the eagle bend that gives the purer-blooded Indios an aristocratic look, and skin the color of golden tobacco. She did not raise her eyes from the ground and she spoke very demurely.

"She has worked in Guadalajara," said Candelaria. "She knows how to work. She is disposed to work here."

While she was talking, Candelaria went to the dry wall, and chose with care a small rock. With its sharp edge she cut the string she was carrying to various lengths. Then she put the rock back in its place in the wall. This is no country to sell gadgets in.

"She knows how to sweep and dust and mop and make beds and wash the dishes," said Candelaria.

"And do you think you would like to come and work here?" I asked.

"Yes," said the girl, without raising her eyes.

"And what wages do you have?"

"Pues—you will know, señor."

In this part of the state of Jalisco good Spanish is spoken, and the people of Ajijic speak far better than the inhabitants of many villages in Spain. You can know those who come from Guadalajara by their constant use of the word pues. They say, "Pues yes," and "Yes pues," meaning different qualifications of yes, and sometimes they shorten it to pos, and they may say, "Pos yes pues." Pues is able to convey any shade of meaning, is quite untranslatable and great fun to use. And in the villages, where they have a trick of adding -en to words that end in s, one's vocabulary is further enriched by puesen and posen.

"What did you earn in the city?"

"Pos, who knows, puesen," said Nieves with a little giggle.

Meanwhile from behind the girl's back, Candelaria was making signals to me, holding up bunches of fingers and mouthing. It seemed to be twelve.

"I pay twelve pesos a month," I said.

The girl hesitated, then mumbled something which only Candelaria understood.

"She says, with assistance?" interpreted Candelaria.

"Of course I give you your board. When can you start?"

"Whenever you may like."

"I will show her your room and she can help with the supper, and then come tomorrow in the morning early," said Candelaria briskly.

"Very well, Nieves. Then that's settled, is it?"

"Pues yes, señor," said the girl.

11

All the time she had not raised her eyes from the ground. She turned and followed silently behind Candelaria's scamper.

I sat on in the open door of the mirador. Several cows came down on their own, drank out of the lake, and returned whence they had come. A man drove a herd of black sheep with white topknots down and watered them. Southeastward, over toward the snowy twin towers of Tizapán, a square sail shone like white gold. The color drained out of the sky and there was nothing left in the west but an even lemon-yellow sheen.

By day the air is so clear that it is hard to believe that the farther shore of the lake is a dozen miles away. Those with good sight can count the windows in the church tower of the village opposite. And often at night the mountains, looking as if they were cut out of black cardboard, seem only a little way off across the dark shimmer of the water. But at evening you have a sense of the long distances. Then you can believe that the lake is sixty miles long and varies between twelve and twenty miles in width. It lies at an altitude of about five thousand feet. Neither days nor nights ever become intolerably hot. In the morning blows the Mexicano, the wind from the east, from the direction of the capital. It has come over the Nevado of Toluca, and sometimes you can sense snow on its breath. In winter it can be a sharp wind, too sharp to let you sit in the shade. In the evening blows the Colimano, which has come up from the Pacific, over the lowlands of the tierra caliente and up past Colima, soft and balmy, a gentle scented wind. That evening I watched it come across the lake. A yellowish streak appeared on the pale blue water, widened, advanced, the yellow gradually engulfing the blue, till it reached the shore of Ajijic and suddenly rustled the willow trees and fanned my face.

But now darkness was almost here, and I went up to the house for supper. Candelaria had made a good omelet, in the Spanish style, streaming with tomatoes and sweet peppers. She brought it in herself.

"Nieves is too shy to bring it in," she said.

But eventually Nieves nerved herself to bring the coffee. She put the coffeepot to my left and the milk jug to my right, and when I asked for the sugar she gave a little spurting giggle and disappeared.

"Ay, what a girl," said Candelaria, bringing in the sugar and Nieves.

She held the sugar in her left hand and Nieves stood at her right, and she addressed them both impartially.

"And now go for the cheese, go you, hurry you," she said, and Nieves rushed out of the room again.

"You will see, señor, she will do better," said Candelaria. "She's very shy and for that she gets muddled. Will you believe in the kitchen I told her to peel the tomatoes and she peeled a potato, and then—"

"Could I have the sugar?" I asked, for Candelaria was still holding it in her hand.

Then Nieves came in with the cheese. According, no doubt, to Candelaria's instructions it was on a plate and on top of it reposed a sprig of parsley. But it had not been taken out of its wrapping paper, and the parsley looked extremely rakish.

That night it rained, the first rain of the year. When I went to bed there was lightning among the clouds, and above Cerro de García, the mountain with long restful curves on the far side of the lake, a great mushroom plume of cloud was climbing, a cloud that flashed carnation as lightning played in its heart. About two the storm broke, preceded by a very strong wind that lasted only a few minutes. For the half hour that the storm lasted you hardly noticed the thunder against the rush of water. Every spout and gutter of the house was rustling, the street outside was roaring. I looked out of the window and in a lightning flash saw that the street was a muddy rushing torrent. All streets drop toward the center. The drain of the patio could not carry off all the water, and its farther side, where the level was slightly lower, was a lake. From every vine leaf and every bunch of grapes poured little waterfalls. But in the morning everything was bone-dry. Only the clear washed air and the dustless leaves told that it had rained.

When I came out into the patio, there was a big bunch of flowers on the table. I had a variety of bowls and vases, but they were arranged in an oilcan, small white starlike blossoms, that smelled very sweet. A wild flower called the flower of Saint John that blooms up in the hills. They had been brought by Nieves. Her golden skin flushed apricot when I thanked her for them. I said I thought they were so pretty that they should be in a prettier vase, and Nieves bustled away with the oilcan. When I next crossed the patio the big bunch was wedged into a narrow-necked earthenware drinking bottle. These drinking bottles keep water extraordinarily cool, though when they are new they give the water the taste of clay for a while. If you keep drinking water in a big earthenware jar wrapped in damp cloths and standing in the shade in a draught, it will keep cool in the hottest weather. But they are unsuitable for flower vases. All Indios love flowers, and in the humblest hovel you will see a few flowering plants and a vase of flowers, and they have a knack of arranging bouquets in the most charming way. But they have no understanding of putting flowers in water. They always overcrowd them so that they cannot live, and I have seen stalks doubled up with their ends protruding out of the water. The flowers of Saint John were crushed and strangled, their slim stalks bruised. I feared to hurt Nieves' feelings by changing them again, but it seemed a pity to let them die so quickly. I put the larger part of the bunch into a wide-necked vase and left the rest where Nieves had put them. I told her I wanted to have some of them in my room as well, and that was why I had divided the bunch. I needn't have bothered, for like all wild flowers they only lasted a day.

Venustiano had sent to say that he would come at eleven, so I waited for him. But that day Venustiano did not come at all. He came two days later, punctually at eleven, and Candelaria fetched me from the beach where I was watching an old Indio woman lead a huge hog into the water by a string tied round its neck and bathe it with a small metal dipper.

We got down to business at once.

"You see," said Venustiano, "my grandfather left the land between all the family. So that my cousin Olimpio owns a third of it. That is, he would if he had not died. His third of it belongs to his son César. The third that went to my uncle Wenceslao belongs to his children Pedro and Rosario and Jesús and Rafaela and Lorenza. That is, five of them own that third. Now the other third belonged to my father, but I only got half of that, since we were two, but then my brother Ignacio died, and his daughter Lupita, who married a foreigner from over the other side of the mountain, sold me her half of the half of the third, but I haven't finished paying for it yet."

He stopped and mopped his head with a gaudy handkerchief. His face was filigreed with countless wrinkles and he had a ragged bristly gray mustache. He was sitting shyly on the edge of his chair, a dignified middle-aged man in white. He had the sharp-boned face of the Azteca, whose faces in repose look cruel.

"Are all the owners here in the village?"

"I am here, and César is here one day with another when he is not in Guadalajara, he is a rich man, he has many little businesses. And Chui, my brother Ignacio's son, who owns the other half of the half of the third that Lupita did not sell to me, is here, and so are Lorenza and Rafaela and Jesús. But Pedro had a deception with a girl a year or two ago and after that disgust he went away to Tampico, and Rosario is in Guadalajara."

"I suppose you have the deeds of the land?"

"Pues, I have the papers. And the receipts for paying the taxes, of course. Yes, I have some papers."

It was plain that he didn't understand much about his papers.

"But who knows about Chui, for instance, for he can't read," he added.

That was the beginning of being a landowner in Ajijic.

In the course of a week or so Venustiano, Chui, Rafaela, Jesús, and the girl Lorenza had agreed to sell their portions.

Chui turned out to be a loutish youth with a wide slewslung mouth. Venustiano and I found him down the beach, lying flat on his back under a tree with his sombrero over his face. He agreed at once.

"And when do you pay me the money?" he asked.

"When the legal transfer is made," said Venustiano, whom I began to suspect of being less vague about things than he pretended to be.

Chui accepted a cigaret.

"It wouldn't be possible to have something in advance?"

I thought not.

Rafaela and Lorenza sent their consent through Venustiano.

To find Jesús, whose house we had twice visited in vain, we finally went out to the gold mine where he worked. It lies under a knee of the hills, and the manager welcomed us very politely. An old woman appeared from somewhere with three hard straight chairs and arranged them in a straight row on the terrace of the little house where it seemed the manager lived. Mexicans always tend to arrange chairs

15

in straight rows. It is a good method for looking at the view, and Mexico consists almost entirely in splendid views, but it is unsuited to easy conversation. You are forever cricking your neck.

We exchanged politeness about our health, the weather, the climate, and the locality. Then Venustiano asked if we might speak to Jesús for a moment. Of course we might. The manager called a laborer, gave him the order, and we continued to sit on the chairs. Conversation languished, but we could always look at the view.

Time went on, and I began to ask questions about gold miniing. After about forty minutes Jesús came.

He was tall, gangling, and the dust on his dark skin made his face mole-brown. He had Venustiano's Aztec features. Everything seemed to amuse him, and he laughed all the time.

"I'll sell," he said. "How not? While the avocado tree lived I got about forty pesos a year out of the land, but this year the only tree that had any fruit, the old papaya, got broken one night when there was a strong air. I'll sell, that yes yes."

So that lined up all the owners in Ajijic except César. Everything had progressed with unnatural speed. To obtain the consent of Rosario it was necessary to write to Guadalajara. As I had to go into town myself I decided to interview her. She worked as cook at an address that was given me.

When I arrived there I climbed a musty staircase painted in crumbling liver color to a big iron grille. I could not see much except quantities of potted ferns, and above them numbers of bamboo cages containing small drab birds, many of whom sang sweetly. I tugged a mended wire and a distant bell jangled. A girl came.

No, she was not Rosario, but she would fetch her if I would pass inside. I passed, and was offered a chair by the ferns. Now I saw that I was in a huge second-floor patio. Its open center was partially roofed by a canvas awning, many of whose patches had given way, to flap idly here and there. All round ran a very wide covered passage, furnished with little groups of the stiffest salon furniture, and the roof of this passage was supported by twelve beautiful pillars of carved stone. Everywhere there were birds in cages and potted plants, including some camellias with fine blossoms. Afterward I was told it was a pension.

16

Rosario, having taken time out to remove her apron and wash her hands, came down the patio smoothing her hair. She was thirty-fivish, buxom and flashy-looking, with big earrings made of many small brightly colored enamel flowers. She had a highly social manner.

"Sell my land? Pues, maybe. But then what do I do about my friend Refugio? I told her she could keep her chickens there, because she has a very small yard herself, and she's got all her chickens there."

We discussed the various aspects of this question, and then Rosario thought for a long time.

"I know," she said. "You tell her that as I'm going to sell my land she can't keep her chickens there any more."

Meanwhile, a letter had been sent to Pedro who had gone to Tampico. And there remained César, who owned a full third of the site. He was, as Venustiano had said, a man of many little businesses. He owned a small mill where the women took their corn to be ground, he owned a cantina, he owned several plantations of tomatoes and papayas, and he owned an elderly truck. He would not be in a hurry to sell, but it was his third that I particularly wanted. It was better cared for and had the best orange trees. They were good trees, Valencians and seedless navels. They sell for four or five pesos a hundred, and one tree may bear more than a thousand fruit. Orange trees take about eight years to come into bearing, and I could not wait that long for a return on my investment. But César had to be handled carefully. Undoubtedly he would suppose all foreigners to be rich.

So there came a pause in the negotiations. And I got to know the beach life.

The beach rather than the plaza is the hub of life in Ajijic. The fishermen, of course, are at work all day long. So are the washerwomen, or rather the women washing, for every housewife does her own washing, rubbing the garments on the flat stones at the lake edge, regardless of the fact that the water there is not exactly clean. They have a sort of women's gossip club, no doubt an integral part of the village grapevine. Often, while at their grueling work in the sun, a woman wears a man's sombrero on top of her shawl, which gives her the surprising appearance of a medieval pilgrim, wide-hatted and wimpled. Beasts are driven down to water, and often cattle are left to consume cornstalk fodder, the herd of black sheep with white topknots appears twice daily, muscular hens earn a laborious livelihood, there are any numbers of dogs about, and although they represent a quite remarkable variety of mongreldom, it is possible to recognize family resemblances between many individuals living all over the village. Burros browse everywhere, their tails cut into graded fringes ending in a tassel. Men come down to the beach to sleep a siesta, to bathe, to chat, to husk coffee, mend fishing nets. The young men go in swimming, the older ones hardly ever. But the women of all ages go into the lake to wash. They wear shapeless slips of any material from calico to rayon satin. It is quite usual to see a woman, apparently attired in a yellow satin ball dress, march into the lake and start soaping. Having gotten thoroughly wet, hair and all, they stand there breast-deep in the lake for anything up to an hour, soaping repeatedly. Less than three soapings does not count as a bath. And they often choose the sunset hour, when a wind blows across the lake, and why, standing thus half out of the water and wet, they do not catch pneumonia is impossible to understand.

There is a mole. It is a small promontory of rock flung carelessly together, usually completely submerged in the wet season and often difficult to approach in anything but the smallest boats in the dry. Here the big sailing canoas that ply down the lake with freight to the railhead at Ocotlán tie up, loading and unloading mangoes or potatoes according to the season. Sometimes there will be half a dozen of these moored at the same time, and Ajijic seems to be quite a place. They are picturesque craft, with sharply pointed prows, a small iron-roofed cabin astern, and using big lugsails, usually decoratively patched. With a good wind, they spin down the lake. But I have seen one becalmed four days in midlake. That, however, does not matter. The men aboard make a little fire, heat their beans and tortillas, and there they are. They drink the lake water. Immune, no doubt from generations, to germs which would kill softer folk, they will drink from the lake's edge, where the water is fouled with soap and scum. Indeed, I have seen a peon, offered pure drinking water, prefer to take his can down to the lake's edge and fetch his drinking water from there. It is probably tastier.

I needed a mozo, a man to look after the huerta and to do the heavy work about the house. Indio servants, though they are ready to keep irregular hours, do not do a quarter of the work that, say, French servants do. But then they do not earn very much. My cook was to have thirty pesos a month and her food, the maid, as I have said, twelve. The mozo would earn the same as the cook. (Take the dollar as being about five pesos.) This sounds a large establishment. But actually it is not. In the first place, a patio has to be cleaned a number of times a day if it is to be well kept, and the swish of the trapeador, the square of cloth attached to the end of a stick, is a sound that I shall always associate with Mexico as inevitably as the pat-pat of tortilla making. At first I had a low opinion of the trapeador; it seemed to me that in every Mexican house any servant who wanted a quiet laze picked up a trapeador and meandered around with it, swishing feebly. I have learned better. There is probably nothing more effective than a damp trapeador for cleaning cement or tiled floors.

Apart from this incessant work and the routine house cleaning, in Ajijic everything has to be fetched. Nothing is delivered, not milk nor meat nor bread nor fish nor mail. All day long one servant or another is out on an errand. Buying fish may take an hour, waiting while the big seine net is drawn in. It may be necessary to go through half the village to find a chicken. Eggs do come to the house. One or two eggs will probably arrive every fifteen or twenty minutes. There comes a knock at the door, and there is a very small child, grasping in an anxious hand an egg still warm from the hen and saying, as he shakes his head doubtfully, "If you don't want to buy an egg of me?"

So, if you are going to do any work of your own, you need someone who can buy eggs. In addition, cooking on charcoal needs constant attention. The cook must be at hand ready to fan, to smother, to rearrange the coals. Candelaria was to look for a man, but as at this season labor is scarce since everyone is busy sowing his corn patch, until now she had not found one. Then one morning she told me that a candidate was there.

In the patio a man was sitting at ease in an armchair. He had about ten days' beard. His clothes were filthy and the big flat hat that lay in his lap had a grayish tone. When I came he got up, put on his hat, and took it off to me.

From the first I didn't like the looks of him. But he spoke civilly, and claimed to know how to do practically everything. And I could see from Candelaria's face that she considered I should engage him, and eventually I did. When he had gone, Candelaria launched into a discussion.

"You see, señor, it is very difficult to find anyone. Eugenio isn't good for much, I'll tell you myself. He's very drunken. Only last week he was in prison for a night. Since at once we must lock up all the drinks. He has always been the same, there is no changing him."

"Have you known him long?" I asked.

Candelaria smiled something between a simper and a leer.

"Oh, yes," she said. "He was my boy friend once. He was very good-looking. But he was never any good."

"And have you ever been married, Candelaria?"

"Pues—" she said doubtfully, and hurried away to attend to something in the kitchen.

Then Nieves came out of my bedroom with a coat of mine in her hand.

"Look, señor, look at what the little doves of Saint John have done," she said, and her face wore a look of real concern.

Under the collar were several holes, and, burrowed into one, a small brown creature like a legless ant. The little dove of Saint John has wide transparent wings and commits suicide readily in any flame. But his nature is to shed his wings and then to eat his way into clothes, preferring cotton but not really minding wool. For a few weeks there are quantities of them, and then they are gone. That is the way with most of the few pests of Ajijic—a short season and then they vanish.

"We must throw Flit," said Nieves firmly. Only she said Flee instead of Flit. For some reason, the Spanish tongue finds it very difficult to pronounce foreign words that end in a consonant other than n or r.

So Saint John brings his pretty scented wild flowers, and his unpleasant little bugs. His day, June 24, is also the fiesta of San Juan Cosalá, the next village westward along the lake from Ajijic. Most of the villages have a pre-Conquest name preceded by a saint's name added by the Catholic church, such as San Luis Soyotlán, San Pedro Tesistán, San Antonio Tlayacapam. Ajijic itself is really San Andrés Ajijic. On the Saint John the Indios bathe. Many do not bathe before it, and others do not bathe between one Saint John and another. The younger ones bathe all the time, but I once saw an old Indio, standing

20

on the beach watching them, shaking his head disapprovingly. "They say that certain evil spirits, the airs, are most likely to be met with and are most potent near water." And he really looked agitated. "These young people don't know anything—" He walked away still shaking his head.

The fiesta of San Juan Cosalá is notable for a result of the bathing. The village must have been the site of a big pre-Conquest settlement. Perhaps the culture was Tarasco, though whether that culture was centered at Pátzcuaro or Colima or at each at different epochs is quite uncertain. Mexican archaeology is all guesser's ground. In any case, at San Juan Cosalá there are quantities of pre-Conquest artifacts, usually made of clay, to be found, and on Saint John's Day numbers are fished out of the lake by the bathers. The commonest objects are small ollas, toy-size caldrons of clay with two pierced ears, which were perhaps thrown into the water to propitiate some god, maybe Tláloc himself, the god of waters. Then there are many small animals, impossible to identify, standing on four legs, with medium-length tails, sharp snouts, and very big ears. Maybe they were broken and thrown into the lake every fifty-two years, as was the custom at the ceremony of extinguishing all fire and waiting to see if the sun would rise on a further fifty-two years or if the world would come to an end. Sometimes there are seated figures, wearing swathed turbans or crowns. Most of these are small. In San Juan, any day of the year, you can buy strings of the little caldrons and plenty of the animals for a few centavos. The figures are rarer and sell faster. But in the days after the Saint John various Indios turned up in Ajijic offering small idols for sale.

"They're intic, intic of the Africa," said one old Indio to me surprisingly. For even when I had discovered that intic was the local variant of authentic, I could not see where Africa came in. It was merely an imaginative touch of exoticism.

I picked up twenty or thirty small objects that I was ready to buy, and asked how much they were. The man arranged them in groups, the figurines together, beads from a necklace together, animals together, little caldrons together. Then he went into a short trance, staring at them. At intervals he moved an object from one group to another, as if deciding that it more resembled a human than an animal figure.

After a series of rearrangements and long pauses, he said, "Pues—how much will you pay me?"

"No. You must tell me how much you want."

There was another long pause. Then suddenly he said, with the air of one guessing an impossible problem, "I'll leave them to you in twelve pesos. Or does that seem a lot?"

I said it did. I said it was far too much.

He thought again. After another long pause, he said, "The price, puesen, is six pesos—and at the least least, three-fifty."

JULY

AT THE beginning of the month there were violent rainstorms about every other night. And suddenly one morning I noticed that the mountains had ceased to be golden. As though the rain were some subtle blue wash mixing with the yellow hillsides, everywhere they had taken on a tinge of green. And the Cerro Colorado, the Red Hill, stood out sharply. It is a bare shoulder of mountain down toward Jocótepec, and it is in fact not red but ocher-colored. It was always said that there was much gold in it, and in the course of years thousands of pesos have been put into it, but very few taken out. Across its nakedness trooped a chain of burros, laden with straw from humbler, more fertile slopes.

Many people who know both countries see resemblances between Mexico and Morocco. There is a certain visual similarity, less, I think, of landscape than of coloring. There are the same parched golds and dusty pinks in the dry season, and in the Mexican rains and the Moorish spring the same intense greens, richer far for the time they last than any English greens. There are many cultural connections, naturally by way of Spain. Here you do not hear the cante jondo, which makes Spain echo with Arab tones, but Mexican music is not far from Spanish. You can find the same glazed tiles, in peacock and canary, that you have admired in Ronda and Fès, the patterns stamped on leather you have seen in Tetuán and Marrakech. And of course there is the burro.

All the donkey-using countries have a common aspect. From Syria to Mexico, there are the same processions on the roads, bulging panniers of basket- or network, the same little family groups—probably

23

with the man riding and the woman afoot—and from frontier to frontier, from dawn to dusk, you hear the clippety-cloppety of asses' hoofs. Somebody ought to write a history of the burro. The empires he has supported would make tame history compared to his.

In Mexico you are practically never out of sight of a burro and a mountain. The mountains, endlessly range upon range of mountains, strike one more than anything else in the country. On the central uplands, to climb a few feet is to discover, behind the farthest chain, other chains, more distant peaks, faintly blue against the faint blue sky. Down every street of a city, beyond the streetcars and the shop fronts, peer mountains. It is not a serpent and an eagle, it is a mountain and a burro that the arms of Mexico should bear. In Ajijic, both are ever present. The burros go alone about the streets; they are dirty, but decently fed and not badly treated. And there are few places where one sees so much sky as here across the great expanses of the lake. At sea and in the desert, yes. Yet sea and desert lack frame. There is only the bent bow of the horizon, only the arc of the world. Here the rim of the huge sky is serrated with mountains, distant periwinkle peaks that stand above the eastern horizon as if they were islands, cliffs that turn fluted gold at sunset, dark jagged spurs, and the long swooning curve of Cerro de García, the mountain opposite Ajijic, whose name is less romantic than it sounds, meaning, more or less, Mount Smith.

Now the lake began to rise. There are sluice gates down on the Santiago River at the eastern end of the lake, the river that leads to the ocean. They are tolerably well managed nowadays, so that there will probably never again be a flood as disastrous as that of 1926, when the adobe houses on the beach were washed down, and in Ajijic the waters reached a block up into the village, a flood which legend attributes to the fact that the governor of the state kept the keys to the sluice and he was away on vacation. But still the lake is subject to a pronounced seasonal change of level. In 1926 the highest known level, 5,003 feet above the sea, was registered, while the lowest known was 4,974 feet in 1914—a maximum variation of 29 feet. This year in a very short time it had invaded the rocks of the mole and swept across a flat stretch of beach to the foot of the outmost of the clump of willows.

There was still no answer from Pedro who had gone to Tampico. But César quite suddenly sent to say that he was willing to sell. He said that his third of the land measured 2,600 square meters, and he wanted two pesos a meter. But I had already taken some measurements of his land, and it seemed to be only a little over two thousand square meters. In addition, all along the lake, ten meters up from high-water mark is the federal zone. This has not long been so, and before, owners used to put wire fences right out into the water. Out beyond the village you can still find them, because nobody has been interested in enforcing the federal law. But along the beach of Ajijic there are white cement marking stones—or, I should say, there were, for almost immediately after their construction they became desirable targets for stone throwing, and nowadays you have to hunt to find their remains. It is best to calculate your land without the zone, just as it is best to see that walls on side roads are four meters from the center of the road. Maybe today it is a narrow lane. But if ever roads are made of them, an eight-meter width will be taken, and if you have not allowed for this you may have to move your whole wall. Taking all these things into consideration, I sent to say that it seemed to me very dear, but that I would buy half of it, the half that lay toward the lake, at one peso fifty a meter.

Some days passed, and then César sent a message to say that after all he didn't want to sell.

"Why not?"

"Because now he doesn't want to."

"I should like to see him about it."

"He's in Guadalajara."

So that was that.

But, if César and Pedro delayed, the hummingbirds did not. I had arranged several sugarwater tubes for the hummers to come to. Any small glass tube, wrapped in a bit of tinfoil or colored silk, will attract their attention. They like it attached to a small branch at an angle of forty-five degrees, and there should be another small horizontal twig on which they can perch between drinks. They say that hummers can fly across the Caribbean, but in that case they must make, as do other migrant birds, temporary adjustments of their alimentary system, for ordinarily a hummingbird must feed every ten minutes of his waking hours in order to live, and he doesn't want to stay far from his food. Plant this branch in a flowerpot full of earth and keep the sugarwater changed, and you will have plenty of visitors. It seems as if they cannot hear low notes, for I found that human voices did not disturb them at all, whereas the smallest movement did. Until, that is, they had become used to me. Then they didn't mind my typewriter. And it was not long before I could sit holding the branch in my hand for them to come to. At that distance one sees the long narrow tongue, shining and transparent as cellophane, as it licks down into the tube. There are not many or very gay types of hummer in Ajijic. There is the iridescent blue and green one, and another who wears a gray coat and a white waistcoat and who seems drab until the sunlight catches his poll, which is iridescent lilac. He is lazy, and instead of hovering, as he would have to do before a flower whose petals would be too weak to support even his small weight, he likes to claw the edge of the tube, fold his wings, and take his meals without effort. And he is a nasty-natured bird. He will perch a little away from his chosen feeding place, natural or artificial, and, at the approach of a blue and green hummer, rush forward and hover, beating his wings in a fierce whir, and frighten away the other. I have noticed this many times, in various places, and it is always the gray and white bird which scarces off the blue and green.

In Nahuatl the hummer is called huitzitzlin, and it is the most perfect name for him. It shimmers and it almost catches the whir and timebeat of his wings, which move so swiftly that they are always a blur. In Spanish he has many names, charming but less graphic, such as chupamiel, chuparosa—honeysucker, rosesucker—or sometimes picaflor—flowerpricker. But unfortunately he is more frequently called colibri, which is far less attractive.

"For the rosesucker?" said Venustiano, when I explained the tube to him. He remained quite silent for a while, his face blank of expression, and then he said, "How rare." And the hummer flew away to a banana tree.

He is very fond of the little pale yellow florets which bloom under the big purple petals of the banana blossom. That makes Ajijic comfortable for him, for here bananas grow almost like weeds. There is a great variety of them. There is the guinea, which is very common, and the creole, which is good eating too, and there is the ruatán, which is coarser and grows prodigiously down in Tabasco. Then there is the red banana, small and with a delicious flavor. And the apple banana, which doesn't taste of apple, and the pear banana, which does taste faintly of pear. There is the dwarf, and there is the even smaller one which produces a quantity of tiny fruits in a bunch and which is called hundred-in-the-mouth. All these grow readily in Ajijic. But take care when you walk under the trees, for banana-leaf stain is quite indelible.

My hummers amused me while we were still settling into the house and getting used to one another's peculiarities. I became so accustomed to the interminable metallic drone of Candelaria's voice in the kitchen that I hardly heard it. And I became fond of the pat-patting of tortilla making. Of all sounds there is none that suggests Mexico so much as the endless pat-pat of palm on dough, coming from the other side of the patio, or from down below the veranda, an interminable accompaniment to the singing, the laughing, the barking, and the crowing that are the themes of the village song. But tortilla making is the bane of a Mexican household. Nowadays most villages have mills where the corn is ground, so that no longer do women have to work for hours, as formerly, grinding the corn by hand. But the process of mixing the meal and patting the tortillas is also very lengthy, and I have long since insisted that they be bought ready-made, otherwise most of the morning is spent preparing them. Personally, I cannot eat tortillas. One tortilla will stay like a lump of wet lead in my stomach. But when they are toasted they are superb, and bear about the same relation to ordinary tortillas as toast Melba does to bread. Off one side of the finished tortilla the skin is torn, and this is toasted, till it browns and curls up as crisp as a lettuce leaf. Candelaria does them excellently and always brings them into the dining room herself, smiling benignly and saying, "Here come your little toasteds."

Gradually Nieves lost some of her shyness, held her head up, and even dared to hum quietly at her work. Her thin pointed tobacco-gold face is at times almost beautiful, and her eyes, very small and black, have the dull gleam of dark sequins. She began to have some idea of timing a meal, and of giving me long enough to eat one thing before bringing the next. For in Mexico you wait a long time for meals, and then they are served in a rush. Often in restaurants I have had three dishes to come waiting on the table beside me at once owing to this

27

overzealous service. It is not unusual, also, to serve a table individually. That is, when the first person has finished his soup, he is brought the next course at once. By midmeal, no two people are eating the same thing, and chaos reigns.

Eugenio was to fetch from the plaza the pure water piped down from the Eye of Water.

"Then you must buy me a she-ass," he said.

"Whatever for?"

"To carry the gasoline cans on," he said. "You have the cans."

But just then Venustiano came in and explained that a she-ass is the wooden shoulder yoke on which a peon hangs the cans.

"How was the señor to know you didn't mean a real she-ass?" he said very grandly to Eugenio. "The señor didn't learn Spanish in a little ranch."

I also put Eugenio on to painting doors and windows and furniture. But this was a mistake. Not only did it not occur to him to paint underneath a chair or table, but he often left one leg unpainted and then ran out of that particular color. And he managed to spatter everything within reach. Candelaria, continually untidy and apparently without method, served excellent meals and kept her kitchen spotless. But it was not until now that she announced to me that I had forgotten to bring any dusters or dishcloths. In Spanish a duster is called a shaker, and a very apt term it is, for here dusting does not mean wiping, it means shaking, flicking, flipping, and getting the dust well dispersed into the air. Sometimes it is done after and sometimes before sweeping.

"But what have you been using?"

"I found myself some little rags," she said.

"Why didn't you tell me before?"

"I would have told you, señor, if you had been going to Guadalajara."

"But I'm not going to Guadalajara, so why tell me now?"

"Because Doña Porfiria, she of the cheap stuff, is here in the village today. She comes from Chapala. Do I tell her to come to the house?"

Doña Porfiria was middle-aged and ample, very respectably dressed in black and carrying a large worn leather bag heavy with quantities of small change. She was followed by a boy, shouldering a huge bundle of bolts of material and leaning on a chipped wooden meter measure, and by a number of customers and would-be customers, all of whom came into the patio, where the stuffs were laid on chairs. Everybody fingered cottons and calicoes and sprigged silks and rayon satins. The Indio women not only love these satins, they love them in the most brilliant colors, in cyclamen and magenta, in biting lime and poison green and acid mauve. And they are perfectly right. Colors that are terrible against a pale northern face are superb against the ambers, coppers, cocoas, mahoganies of the Indio skin. In the doorway of a near-by house there sits every day a beer-brown old woman nurse-maiding some shiny black piglets. She wears a frayed satin blouse in shrill peacock, and the little scene glows like a Byzantine mosaic.

In no time the patio looked like a dry-goods store. Candelaria fingered her way through the cottons suitable for shakers. A young woman bought a dress length of startling magenta rayon satin, which they call mirror cloth. It was going to cost her nearly ten pesos, and she paid one-twenty-five down.

Candelaria flirted with some emerald-green satin and draped herself in a very unsuitable sprigged muslin. But she put it down again in a minute, and began to look through the calicoes.

"Aren't you going to get yourself a dress?" I asked. "To go to the fiesta in?"

"I? Oh, no," said Candelaria. "It gives me much laziness to go to fiestas, they don't call my attention. In any case, I like a turnsun silk, silk that changes, and there isn't any. But what I would like is a new shawl, with a nice long beard."

She handled several shawls of dull sham silk, a dark blue, a speckled black, a deep purple, an amber brown. The last had a very long silk fringe, plaited for at least fifteen inches and hanging free for another fifteen. By the length of its fringe you judge the distinction of a shawl. It was expensive, fourteen pesos. Candelaria launched into an interminable bargaining with Doña Porfiria. First she found a minute flaw somewhere. Then she said it was very dear anyway, in her native village she had bought a much nicer one for less. Then, when agreement seemed on the point of being reached, she suddenly put the shawl down.

"At the finish and the end," she said, "I don't really need a new shawl at all."

I was called away just then by Eugenio, who had run out of linseed oil. A big tin had vanished very quickly.

"Can you buy it here?"

"Oh, no."

"Then you'd better leave that table. I don't want it painted till the wood's properly oiled. Instead you'd better—"

"You can buy oil in Chapala," interrupted Eugenio hopefully.

"Well, what's the good of that?"

"Pues—I could go with the bus and get it. And I could get anything else you want of one time. I´could be back by four. Or by three. With all security."

"But I want to clear all the ground down beyond the grapefruit trees today."

"Pues," said Eugenio. And the conversation died of inanition.

In the patio I found that Doña Porfiria's customers had thinned. On the chair by the kitchen lay the shawl that Candelaria had decided she didn't, at the finish and the end, really need.

"So you bought it after all?"

"Sssh," hissed Candelaria, nodding and almost winking in a way that I took to mean that she had driven a good bargain. "Now look, señor, at this little calico. Now if I get four meters, I calculate I can make six little shakers. It's forty centavos a meter. And with four meters of this thicker stuff I can make driers for the kitchen."

We decided on our purchases, and Doña Porfiria, putting down her huge black bag, measured off the meters while Candelaria watched every centimeter. This was still going on when Eugenio appeared in the patio.

"Look, señor, I've found another tin of oil," he said, grinning with satisfaction.

"What a good thing," I said bleakly, and he hurried away to his work.

As soon as we had paid for the goods, Candelaria briskly turned everyone out of the patio and went back to preparing lunch. All afternoon she and Nieves sat on low chairs at the entrance of the zaguán, hemming busily.

Something fell on my bed in the middle of the night. The blanket had slipped off and I had only a sheet over me, and the beam of my flashlight discovered a scorpion crouched on my knee, facing me with its tail up. I couldn't remember ever seeing a scorpion before except once in Egypt, and I felt very doubtful as to what to do. It was small comfort that he seemed as puzzled as I. Outside the curious night bird that hisses, sounding exactly like a Spaniard calling a waiter, hissed loudly and made me start. I gave the sheet a violent shake, and heard the scorpion land on the tiled floor. Scorpions, though they obligingly stand still waiting to be killed, move with great rapidity, and in a moment this one had hidden under my wardrobe trunk, whose bosses raised it just sufficiently from the floor for him to get under it. I found a shoe, rolled the trunk round, and forced the scorpion out. He ran up the wall and stayed still while I squashed him. This room had a ceiling of bamboo, and in the interstices armies of scorpions could have hidden. The next day I bought myself a mosquito net, which I never closed but which served as a secondary ceiling. Since then I have seen Indios approach a scorpion and pinch off its sting between thumb and forefinger, and then playfully fling the live but harmless creature at a friend on whose bare brown chest it could find purchase as easily as on a wall. In comparison with Egyptian scorpions, those of Ajijic are not poisonous, though they may be dangerous to children and animals. In other parts of Mexico, in the tierra caliente and in Durango, the scorpion is very dangerous, but here I have since been stung with no ill effects. I took a few drops of ammonia in hot water every half hour, and don't even remember feeling unwell. On the coast an Indio remedy for scorpion bite is to take a cup of coffee, charged with lard and some human excrement.

During the rains there are fewer scorpions, and I didn't see another till the fall. I cannot say that I have ever come to regard them with anything but repugnance, though their shape is graceful and might well inspire a goldsmith.

"All scorpions are very dangerous," said Nieves. "All little animals are dangerous, such as this, and this, and this."

And she vigorously exterminated several house spiders, a wood louse, and an earwig.

"Very dangerous," she said, murdering a moth.

31

The cat went with the house. Candelaria already behaves, however, as if the cat were her personal property. She is called Mariposa, though what could look less like a butterfly than a cat I cannot imagine. She is a terrific huntress, and in general opinion has had up to date well over a hundred kittens. She seems to be permanently gravid. But that does not interfere with her very efficient ratting. In the grape seasons she preserves the crop, since rats will run out on the branches of the vine and consume all the fruit. Her last batch of young were, I was told, born in the garage, the ones before that in what is now my bedroom. I told Candelaria to see that this time Mariposa gave birth in some suitable place.

"I'll make the struggle," said Candelaria. Effort is a really big thing to the Spanish genius, and when you try, you make the struggle. "But I never knew a cat better at fishing little mice."

A few days later, when I was working down in the mirador at the bottom of the huerta, Candelaria came scampering down to say Mariposa had caught a rat the night before and had seven kittens in the morning and to ask whether I wanted to buy any sarapes.

I didn't think I did.

"They're very pretty," she said. "They're from Jocótepec and you can't usually get them unless you order them specially."

So I told her to send the man who had brought them down to see me.

He was tall for an Indio and dressed in spotless white pajamas, the trousers ironed into countless small squares which is the modish way of pressing them. He carried two sarapes. On a ground of oatmeal color they had end borders and a small center design in fuchsia pinks and mauves. They were simple and dignified and well woven. He wanted thirty pesos each for them.

"That's cheap, señor, most cheap, really. I couldn't make them for less than thirty-five or forty."

"Then why are you selling these cheap?" I asked, for I could find no flaw in the weaving, and they were obviously new.

"Pues, you see, señor, it's like this. A young gentleman ordered them some time ago, and when I went to deliver them I found that he'd been killed. And as he didn't give me anything in advance when he ordered them, I need the money, puesen. In Guadalajara I could get more, of

32

course, but I heard that there was a foreigner living here, and for-eigners often buy things like this, and if you buy them I needn't go to Guadalajara."

"The young man had been killed? Why?"

"Who knows. They killed him in the street. They say he had eleven dagger thrusts. That was over in San Pedrito, they're bad people over there. But they say he was very drunk." In Mexico it is never the village you are in, but always the next one, where the people are bad people.

The sarapes were attractive. Finally I bought the two of them for fifty pesos.

Eugenio was very busy with the papayas, which were in season. The papaya tree has only an eight-year life, and bears for only five of these eight. You have to be planting all the time between existing trees to keep up a plantation. Sometimes it is a decorative tree, with its wide fringed leaves springing from the top of the bare silvery trunk. But often, leafless, the pointed trunk top-heavy with a dozen or more big green melons, it looks extremely silly. Eugenio, every now and then, brought me a little money, earned by selling papayas. But there was no doubt that he was taking a rake-off.

However, at present he was the only available man. Indeed, so busy were they all with their corn patches that you noticed a dearth of men about the village. In all countries accustomed to civil unrest, it has been and is the habit to live in villages and to go out to the fields to work. Only in settled countries can the farmer live in an isolated house on his land. Elsewhere he must return each night to the safety of numbers, to the enclosed village. In Mexico that is always the practice. Here men will sometimes toil a couple of hours up the mountain to some tiny upland corn patch and work there all day. So there was nothing to do except to wink at Eugenio's failings and get as much work out of him as possible. As Candelaria observed: "We couldn't find anyone else. It results that there's no remedy."

I had not completed the purchase of the available parts of the land I wanted. I had instead paid the owners varying sums that gave me an option.

33

Chui went off on a spree to Chapala with his share, and returned some days later without a centavo and with a headache. Rafaela and Lorenza, Venustiano told me, bought very gay dresses, and Lorenza decided to go on the annual pilgrimage to Talpa in the following March.

"If she can keep the money that long," said Venustiano.

And Jesús, who lived in a one-room hut with his wife and eight children, bought a bicycle. Rosario, I am sorry to say, soon wrote from Mexico City where she had gone with a man she described as "young, handsome, and all a lady," which hasn't got a sissy sense, but means that he had very polished manners. "And," she added, "about a year ago he worked for a time as a barman's help." Since she was to get six hundred pesos for her share of the land, and she had only had one hundred in advance, no doubt she felt she had bought herself a bargain.

As for César, I was marking time, not wishing to seem too eager, and giving him time to change his mind. For in Mexico, no does not mean no. It means no, today. Tomorrow is another day. But it was an annoying time for I was still determined to have that land and no other, whereas I could not afford to pay a fancy price for it. And being so determined, I was anxious to start improving the huerta, to make plans for the house I meant to build. I became crotchety and nervous, and I welcomed the cloudburst.

First there was the waterspout in the lake. It was an afternoon of especial sultriness and the sky, piled everywhere with billows of dark wadding and white whipped cream, was almost too highly colored as the sun sank to the mountain ridges. Then suddenly there was the waterspout, linking the gray-blue waters to the blue-gray clouds. It was not a very big one, and it spun loosely, now vertical, now strung out in a loping curve, as flexible as if it were a streamer of ribbon. There was great excitement about it. It is called a snake.

"You see, the snake sucks in the lake, and then stings somewhere. If it stings in the village, that would be bad. Ojalá that it stings in the mountains." In Spain, where there are Moorish traces everywhere, it is not surprising to hear Allah called upon in the traditional Castilian phrase for God grant. But whenever I hear ojalá, may Allah grant, on the lips of a Mexican Indio (which is about a dozen times a day), it rings strange.

34

I have not heard that a cloud thus charged has ever burst in the village. There is a superstition that this can be averted by a young virgin who makes the sign of the cross, and thus "cuts the snake." This time, the waterspout spiraled thinner and thinner, till it was a mere thread, till it was nothing, leaving a lowering black cloud over the lake. The cloud moved slowly toward the village, over the village, and beyond to the mountains. And there it burst.

In less than half an hour after bursting nearly at the top of the mountains, it was all over. In that time the waters, pouring down an arroyo, had all reached the lake. And in that time they had covered several large papaya plantations with boulders that smashed the trees off short like matchwood, had scattered the rocks of dry walls before them in all directions, had crossed the main road and torn it up, had knocked three adobe houses to flitters, and had flooded a dozen more. Several of the families whose house had been flooded had all their few possessions ruined by water, but fortunately nobody was hurt. It would certainly not be at all pleasant if the snake stung in the village. On the mountain, where the cloud exploded, there is a long red gash in the undergrowth, a gash that will not heal for years.

Otherwise the damage was quickly repaired. The families whose houses had been destroyed found shelter with relatives, those who had been flooded put everything in the sun to dry, the main road was cleared of boulders, but remained with its potholes unfilled. The ruined houses could not be built up again until after the rains. You cannot even cut adobes during the rains. And gradually their walls melted a little and lost their sharp outline. An adobe house will take some time to disintegrate, in the worst conditions, but it is part of the earth, an extension of the earth. And if you leave a house roofless and unplastered, or a wall without a coping, it will gradually dissolve and return into the earth. As easily the brown Indio people are born and die. Families are huge, infant mortality is huge too. It is as if the people too were merely an extension of the fertile earth.

Nieves was ironing in the veranda of an outhouse. Like most Indio women, she irons well. She had a little brazier full of glowing charcoal, piled with irons, and there was a sheet spread on the table. As I went by, she picked up a little earthen pot, filled her mouth with water, and spat it over the sheet.

"Is that the way you always damp linen?" I asked.

"Oh, yes," she said.

I asked if she couldn't sprinkle the water with her fingers.

"It's not good that way," said Nieves.

I explained that spitting was unhygienic, and, casting about for a suggestion, asked whether she could use a Flit gun.

"But the water's quite clean, and it's really no trouble," she said, and, gulping a mouthful, spewed it strongly and efficiently over a large area of sheet.

I consulted Candelaria.

"What about this?" she said, as she came back with a big metal flour sprinkler.

So that was what Nieves used.

The mangoes were just beginning. Ajijic is full of mango trees, though the first ones were brought here no more than fifty years ago. Their glossy ivy-green foliage, with tufts of coral-brown leaves where a branch is renewing itself, dominates the deep green. A branch that has fruited one year will not fruit the next. The mangoes of Ajijic are quite famous, but I do not care for them. Here, they do not like the Indian mango with its flavor of petroleum. The Manila mango was tried here, but did not prosper, and the Ajijic mangoes are disagreeably fibrous. You need about four toothpicks to a mango. Quantities of them are sold and taken in trucks to Guadalajara, in sailing canoes to the railhead at Ocotlán, and I have heard that they are sent as far as the United States.

Perhaps I owe to mangoes the fact that César felt inclined to sell me his land. As I have said, he owns a truck, and though he has not himself many mangoes, he does quite a trade trucking them. One day, coming back from Chapala where I had been to buy oddments unobtainable in Ajijic, I found his truck bogged. There is a place where a stream crosses the road, and any heavy rain will turn it into a difficult passage. Like most vehicles in Mexico, whether they carry people or freight, César's truck was invariably overloaded. It was usually piled ten feet high with half a dozen Indios perched on top and hanging on the sides. Today it seemed to be more than usually bulging and top-heavy and was surmounted by a double bedstead. It was stuck at a perilous angle, its off back wheel sunk deep in the mud. Eight or ten men were hauling on a rope in vain, and as I drove up César was resigning himself to send for a yoke of oxen, which would take an hour or so to arrive. I pulled his truck out. He thanked me elaborately, but land was not mentioned. It was five days later when he called on me, and after a little general conversation worked round to the question of the land.

César is very different from the rest of his family. He has not the Aztec bones of Venustiano and Jesús, nor the flabby features of Chui, and he is whiter-skinned than any of them. He is corpulent and ruddy and in spite of his sombrero looks like a townsman. He has not Venustiano's lofty dignity, but he has the assurance of the successful businessman. You can see that to him Ajijic is not the hub of the world.

We spent a long time working round to agreement about the precise area of his land. There I felt at an advantage, having measured it out myself. And when César finally agreed with my computation, at 2,150 square meters, I was convinced that all along he had known perfectly. I felt quite elated.

"But two pesos seems to me dear," I said. "It isn't on the center of the beach, it's even quite a long way out."

"I was going to say," said César, "that Amílcar, who has that narrow strip of land next mine, has been offered two-fifty a meter for it."

Silence. My elation died. Having yielded on area, César was going to make a stand on price.

"Well, I shouldn't think of paying two-fifty," I said.

And that was as far as the conversation went that day.

I don't know how the servants knew it was my birthday. I had had a couple of cables the day before but they had been in English—and, telephoned from Chapala letter by letter, a very strange English it was. Perhaps somebody in Chapala understood enough English to get the drift of the cables. In any case, in the morning while it was still dark I became aware of tiptoeing outside my bedroom door, and then suddenly, after a short portentous silence, two voices were raised in song, starting not quite together. I could recognize the voice of Nieves, and the other I realized must be the voice of Candelaria, though one would not have expected her to have a thin but pleasant soprano. They were singing the mañanitas, traditional greeting for a birthday or a saint's day, and in the traditional way they began to sing very quietly and sang gradually louder with each verse and chorus, a chorus which ends: "Get up, my friend, for morning has come." After several verses, when the light was coming up, I decided that I might now be presumed to have been awakened, and, climbing out of bed, opened the door. The doorway was blocked by two deal tables, and on the tables stood zinc buckets and in the buckets were huge bunches of bougainvillea, plumbago, and jasmine, spiked with tall flamboyant cannas and brilliant zinnias, a flower show so exotic that the buckets were infinitely grotesque. Behind the tables stood Candelaria and Nieves, by now smiling so broadly that the song died. Candelaria's eyes snapped and Nieves' splendid teeth flashed very white. I passed the barrage of blossom and shook hands with each.

"Congratulations. We desire you many days of these," they said.

Then they both started singing again, as loud as they could this time, and I stood there, feeling a little chilly, while they sang. As abruptly as they had started they stopped and Candelaria scampered off to the kitchen, emerging after a moment with cups on a tray. The cups had weak tea in them, and the tea had been laced with tequila. It was a tepid and rather nauseating drink to take before seven in the morning. They drank my health and I returned gratefully to bed.

But this was merely a faint echo of what happens when your friends celebrate your day. Then the music is a band, and it starts outside your window as softly as brass can, and when you finally emerge the patio will be full of people, and the band comes in, and there is no question of going back to bed again, because the band goes on playing and everybody has a nice warm drink and probably more people arrive to felicitate you. Maybe toward nine there is a lull, and everyone disperses, those who are staying in the house to dress, for they have appeared in night clothes. But after that callers may arrive all day long. A birthday is exhausting, and a saint's day is about ten birthdays.

I was sent a present of some early avocados. They grow plentifully in Ajijic, of several varieties, none as big as the monsters you get down in Vera Cruz or on the Pacific coast, but they have a very good flavor.

The best of all are small with satiny black skin, a skin so thin that you can eat it with the fruit, to which it adds a pleasant tang of bitterness. I never tire of them and as long as they are in season have them on the table as inevitably as salt. I don't think they are ever better than when served plain with a dash of lemon juice, but Mexicans make them into a delicious cream with onion, cheese, and vinegar, and I once concocted an amusing salad of avocado, mango, string beans, and orange, with French dressing.

Outside the house, in an angle formed by the garage and the boundary wall, is a passion-fruit vine. It is the only one here, or anywhere near here, and I have never seen passion fruit on sale in the market at Guadalajara, a market which is crammed with good things. And I have met many Mexicans who had not tasted passion fruit. But here in the huerta it does very well. It is trained over a pergola, shading a square of about ten feet. And now it is covered with fruit. I am very fond of them myself, but there is such a crop that I can make presents of basketfuls.

They are especially welcome since oranges are almost unobtainable. Even in Guadalajara I found only bad and expensive ones, and there will be no more until the fall. The trees in this huerta have not been properly looked after, and I have never had to do with orange trees before. In addition, we were now much plagued by ants, which are a pest in Ajijic, practically the only one. I asked Venustiano what to do about them, and he came over to see the damage I had sustained. I showed him a tree which had been stripped of every leaf.

"Oh, they'll finish with a much larger tree than that in a night," he said.

Ants were still milling around the base of the tree, picking up the leaves which the larger ones, the warriors, had cut for them. We followed the busy procession nestward, as far as the dry wall. They came from the next huerta, and we climbed the wall and found their nest by an old well. It was a good hundred yards from the tree. The ants do not eat the leaves, as I had supposed, but drag them underground where they put them in layers, forming a sort of mushroom culture on which the young ants feed. This, when it has thoroughly rotted and been thrown out of the nest, makes good manure.

"Do they always work at night?" I asked.

"Only in summer. In winter it is too cold and then they work during the day. In summer, they are not so bad. They come because of the rise in the lake. You see, the water pushes them inland."

My own impression is that in summer there is more wild green stuff for the ants to eat, so that they attack garden plants less. But Venustiano may be right.

All the citrus trees in the huerta had been bound with pochote, a kapok-like natural cotton which is found in the hills in December. This is supposed to present an impassable entanglement, but it didn't seem very effective.

"It works in the dries," said Venustiano. "But, you see, when it rains the pochote gets wet and mats. Then the ants can climb it easily. Look at this one here." And he showed me one that was negotiating the entanglement quite effortlessly. He picked it off and crushed it in his calloused fingers.

"What can I do about them? I can't let them eat a new tree every night."

"Eugenio should have told you. It is quite simple. You must get some of the refuse from a distant anthill and put it round the part of the huerta where the fruit trees are, or, if you like, round each tree —you needn't bother about that tangerine tree, they won't eat that."

So Eugenio spent a whole day collecting ant refuse. It doesn't matter from how far away so long as it comes from a different nest from the one that is attacking your trees. I had to ring each tree individually because they were so scattered about the huerta. I left the tangerine tree to its fate, and certainly ants never touched it. In fact at the time I had no faith in the operation, but it worked. The ants did refrain from crossing this foreign and presumably hostile rampart, and I can only conclude that ant refuse has an individual smell.

I went round to tell Venustiano how successful the experiment had been and to thank him.

As I was going, he said to me, his wrinkles set in solemn lines, "Will you keep this key for me?" He proffered a key about ten inches long.

"Certainly."

"And you'll take great care of it?"

"Yes, of course. What does it belong to?"

"I don't know."

After all, a key that belongs to a known lock is a drab thing. You know exactly what it will lead to. But a key of which you do not know the lock may lead to anything, it is an object of romance and a gate to fantasy, and as such should be taken especial care of.

I still have the key. Sometimes, when Venustiano visits me, I fancy I see him eyeing it where it hangs on the wall, envisioning perhaps (for he has a romantic side) that one day it will prove to unlock some treasure. For that is the common explanation here of how somebody became rich.

"Oh," they say, "he found a treasure in the mountains."

I am getting to look at the key myself as if some special quality were inherent in its plain iron shape.

THE July rains have changed the landscape. The mountains behind the village have greened and in the valleys wild flowers are beginning to come into bloom, all orange and chrome and gamboge, for this is the season of predominantly yellow flowers, though the rose-lilac of the wild gloxinia, which the Indios call cat's claws, shows in the crevices of the rocks. There is the double frilly marigold, the sempaxochitl (Xochitl is the ancient Indio flower goddess), in all sizes from tiny untidy florets to big rosettes. This is the flower that went from Mexico to North Africa and thus came to be called in Europe the African marigold. There is the little dusty orange star-shaped flower that must be the ancestor of all the zinnias. There is the yellow cosmos, offset by drifts of the pink. There are half a dozen others, whose names, even in Spanish or Nahuatl, I have never been able to find out. Now that the tawny earth is greening the flowers sustain the note of yellowness. Over the other side of the lake the parched golds have all been hidden by thick green, and in a flat hollow near the summit of the range appears a paler patch, shrill as the green in a flame, where a high cornfield is springing. From the top of the church tower you can see, way down beyond the twin towers of Tizapán church, the bright green of the great valley of silt where corn and sugar cane grow richly. And the little hill of Tuxcueca (which means The Place Where They Make Petticoats of Rabbitskin), crowned by its chapel, shines like the clear jade of China.

Now every evening Cerro de García grows a plume of cloud. It pillars up high into the air, then mushrooms out, spreading at the same time farther and farther across the lake toward us, until at last the whole sky is dominated by a top-heavy alp of whitish purple cloud shot through with lightning. The storms come at night, in a frenzy of rain and a fury of thunder. And in the mornings the air has a wonderful translucency, as though the world stood under a bell of polished glass. There is no trace of cloud, except that Cerro de García wears a billowing foamy garland of it, which will dissolve by noon.

There are three principal kinds of fish in the lake: the whitefish, the catfish, and the charal.

"The whites are rich, savory, exquisite, unbetterable," said Candelaria firmly the first time she bought some. And undoubtedly it is one of the world's great eating fish. It has so delicate a flavor and such firm soft flesh that it really needs no sauces or condiments. Lightly fried in a thin envelope of beaten egg and with a squeeze of lemon juice, it is superb. But it lends itself too to soufflés or any treatment you wish. It is good cold, pickled in vinegar with sweet basil.

The catfish, though it shines magnificent black and gold in the sunlight, has soggy flesh and tastes of wet serge. It is used for the local bouillabaisse, Caldo Michi, a sloppy mess in which big lumps of fish and onion and tomato drown slowly in dishwater heavily seasoned with coriander. Caldo Michi is often also made with carp, of which there are a good many in the lake, preying, unfortunately, on the young whitefish, and assisted in their ravages by the popocha, of the bream family, and remarkable for its superabundance of bones.

The charal is tiny, a sort of fresh-water whitebait, and if fried exactly like whitebait and served dry enough to be eaten with the fingers, charales are excellent. Dip them in mayonnaise, or tartare, or white sauce stung with English mustard, and see. But they give a lot of work, since each tiny fish must be beheaded and cleaned, because the charal often harbors tapeworm. Twenty centavos will buy enough for three or four people.

They say that only in the lakes of Chapala and Pátzcuaro in all the world does the whitefish exist. Unfortunately in Chapala it is getting scarcer every day. All round the lake, night and day, every day of the year, fishermen fish with big seine nets, with hand cast nets, with hook lines moored in deep water. And they never by any chance throw back the small fry. I asked a fisherman, an alert-looking cedar-brown man I had often spoken to, why he didn't.

"At this rate, in five or ten years there'll hardly be a whitefish in the lake."

"Yes pues," he said. "Can you lend me a bit of cord, to mend my hook line for tonight?"

The grammars will tell you that the word "I" is very little used in Spanish. It is quite true that you do not usually employ it with verbs, the first person singular having a distinctive form which makes it unnecessary, unless for emphasis. "Who did it?" you ask, when you find, as I did, a rhubarb plant thrown on the rubbish heap. "I was he. I thought it was a weed," came the answer. Nevertheless, apart from the emphatic usage, it must be one of the hardest-worked words in the Castilian language. Listen in any café, and note how often you hear the monosyllable "I." But then the Spanish character is one of the most individualistic there is. It is a strong strain. In Ajijic there is hardly such a thing as a full-blooded Indio, but Indio blood predominates heavily over Spanish. Yet here too, at every turn, you meet an Andalucían independence, a Castilian pride, an Asturian obstinacy. And do not imagine that material profit will be the determining factor in any decision.

There is a little one-room house down the huerta that nobody uses. I offered it to Nieves' mother, who lives alone with her daughter. I said I would have the roof repaired and the walls whitewashed and they could have it rent free. This would have saved them five pesos a month or more. Nieves was earning twelve.

"But then what can my mamma do with her pigs? They couldn't run about the huerta," asked Nieves.

"Has she many pigs?"

"Six, and three little ones, which will render much later, and one we are going to kill next week," said Nieves.

"Why don't you give up pigs and keep chickens? They could be in a corral, that I would arrange for you."

"My mother likes pigs," said Nieves. "And I ask myself, next week, when we've killed the pig, if I could have the day off, to help take out the lard?"

And that was the end of the idea of putting Valentina and Nieves into the house in the huerta.

"Does any of you know how to open oysters?" I asked the servants, as I looked at a sack of Guaymas oysters sent me by friends.

"I," said Eugenio.

"And who left the huerta door unlocked last night?"

"I," said Nieves.

"And which of you forgot to put out the lamp in the patio?"

"I wasn't she," said Candelaria.

There was a knock at the door. Candelaria asked: "Who?" And a very small voice, the voice of a five-year-old hoping to sell a small egg, answered:

"I."

To make sure I really liked the land at Ajijic, I decided to go and take a look at the next village, San Juan Cosalá. But the road was said to be very bad. Several arroyos crossed it, and had piled big stones over it. Eugenio suggested we go by boat. He hired one of the smaller canoas from a fisherman, and we set out. It was a great mistake. For one thing, the seats in these canoas are level with the gunwales, so that you sit precariously poised on a hard board. I sat in the stern and Eugenio rowed. We started in the morning, and took lunch with us. The morning wind was behind us, and we seemed to be making fine headway. But about noon it dropped, and our progress became slower and slower. We stopped and drifted awhile for Eugenio to rest. But by two o'clock we were still a long way short of San Juan. I said we would land and have our lunch.

"Yes, how not," said Eugenio, with alacrity, and at once turned in toward the shore.

We lunched at leisure, in the shade of a mango tree on a small sandy bay. I had given up all hope or intention of reaching San Juan. Eugenio was cheery about it.

"It's often like this," he observed. "One sets out for somewhere and one doesn't get there after all." And indeed in Mexico you will often hear people say, "We'll start on Monday," rather than "We'll arrive on Tuesday."

"But you were so sure we could make it easily," I said.

"We might have. If the wind had been stronger. If the wind hadn't dropped. As it is, by afternoon we shouldn't have got to San Juan, nor much less. One never knows," answered Eugenio, and as I seemed unresponsive to his philosophic viewpoint, added: "I have a friend here who has a very nice plantation of papayas. He has some melons too. Wouldn't it be good if I went to look for him? Then we'd have something to take back."

I told him to go, and waited in the shade of the mango. The small bay was quiet and manless. A bevy of grebe swam into the shallows and fished hard. Soon they were joined by some ducks, who also liked charales. At the horn of the bay two blue herons were wading. In the neighboring field big sparrows and pink-footed ground doves walked busily about. Up the remains of an adobe wall ran a wall creeper, who is a great insect hunter, balancing himself with his long wide copper-barred tail. Then a big zopilote, the bald Mexican vulture which is a fine scavenger, landed at the head of the beach. I remained very still in the shadow and watched him. He advanced inch by inch, stopping after every step and staring from right to left, suspicious, cowardly, and repulsive. At first I could not make out the object of his advance. But I had field glasses with me, and at last, between the stones at the water's edge, I saw the corpse of a bird, about sea-gull size. The zopilote took twenty-five minutes to cover the ten yards between himself and the corpse. Then he began to eat. He proceeded with the same exaggerated caution, pecking and then raising a bloody head to stare all around him before having another peck. I don't know what he feared. He was easily the largest bird about, and there seemed to be no possible enemy. I looked away from him, above me in the mango, where several burriones, plump and pink-breasted, were fluttering about. Some orioles, black-backed and yellow-breasted, were searching diligently between rows of growing tomatoes in the field behind me. Hummingbirds were swooping and fussing about. All the birds ignored me.

Then Eugenio came back, and the zopilote flew away, bloody and frightened. Eugenio had some large earth-colored roots in his arms and three or four small melons, cantaloupes of a sort which, though they do not have the flavor of French cantaloupes, are good eating.

"Look, señor," he said, grinning and proud of himself.

"And what is that?" I asked, pointing to the roots.

"Root of the hill," he said. "It's very good."

And so it is. Boiled and allowed to get cold and cut into thin slices, it makes a salad very like potato salad, but more translucent than potato. I prefer it to chayote, which grows on a pole-supported vine in the huerta, and which is extremely dull, though its root, chinchayote, is better and can be prepared like root of the hill.

"Very nice," I said. "And how much are they all?"

Eugenio looked hurt.

"They're a present," he said, "from my friend. I brought them for you."

It was impossible to be cross. We took three hours to row back to Ajijic. But the going is always beautiful. The narrow belt of highly cultivated land is now, in the rains, as thickly green as a cabbage patch, and every little bay has its own character. One is rocky, one is sandy, and on a third the Indios, reclaiming land as the lake goes down, have planted chili or peanut to the water's edge. The lakeside must have changed aspect greatly, for, in the old days, before the revolutions, Ajijic was one big hacienda. The principal crop cultivated was mezcal, for making tequila. All the hillsides were covered with mezcal plants, whose soft green-blue and orderly alignment must have been very different from the dense disorder of lettuce-sharp and spinach-deep greens of today. But after the revolutions the hacienda was split up into many small holdings, and all mezcal cultivation ceased, for each mezcal plant needs seven years to come into maturity, and only large estates can afford such acreage devoted entirely to growing plants.

Tequila, when it is good, is one of the purest hard liquors you can find. It doesn't tend to hangovers and it isn't bad for the digestion. But most tequila you meet is bad. Then, not only does it have a disgusting smell, but noticeable aftereffects. Good tequila is excellent with grapefruit juice. The best brand I have come across is La Herradura and it is made outside Tequila at an hacienda called San José del Refugio, where they use the ancient methods of distilling, and circling oxen still move the stones that crush the mezcal.

"Yes, it is of the most smooth class," the manager told me, proudly. "Unbetterable for making monkeys." A monkey is a cuba libre with tequila instead of Bacardi. "I give you some to try." And he handed me

47

a horn of his best thrice-distilled tequila. You can't put a horn down till it is empty.

There is a legend that the Indios are stupid. It is rubbish. But you must teach them one thing at a time. This I have learned in the household. When you consider the one-room house from which Nieves comes, and the paucity of utensils with which she lives and sleeps and eats, it is really extraordinary that in so short a time she should have learned to do housework, to set a table, and to wait as well as she has. Perhaps she leaves the Flit gun on my turned-down bed to indicate that she has really flitted the room, but I think it is because using a Flit gun and putting it back in its place are two processes that must be learned separately.

"Where is the key of the beach gate?" I asked Eugenio one day. "It isn't in the door."

"No. You told me not to leave it in the door."

"But it isn't on its hook either."

"No, it isn't," said Eugenio, gazing at the empty hook. "It's hanging on the orange tree, the little fellow by the well."

So in this case using and putting back had to be learned in three steps.

But this slowness is due more to the survival of the slave mentality than to stupidity. The less you learn, the less work you will have to do, the fewer things you will do wrong, and the less you expose yourself to scolding. The same attitude is noticeable whenever anything untoward happens, from murder to breaking a plate. "I didn't do it, I wasn't there, I saw nothing, who has been killed, is there really a plate broken?" That is the Indio reaction, and it is natural enough in people accustomed for long centuries to live as slaves without rights and without defense. Long before the Conquest, most Indios probably lived in slavery, either to the Azteca imperialists or to their own tribal chiefs. They cannot forget all this, and the period of peonage to the Spaniards, in a year or two.

Nothing in Mexico, in fact, can be changed or reformed in a moment. It is a fact which often makes progressive Mexicans impatient, but it is a fact. The charcoal burners, for instance, have done incalculable damage to the forests of Mexico, and it is only in recent

48

years that the government has concerned itself with their depredations. Charcoal is the national fuel, and I do not know what could take its place. Wood is generally scarce, and though there is oil in plenty the majority of the population could not at present afford oil-burning stoves. In the dry season charcoal is cheap, about five centavos a kilo. But during the rains the charcoal burners cannot work, and the price rises anywhere up to twenty centavos. It is advisable to get in a supply of charcoal in May, and Candelaria was much pained because, since I had arrived too late to do this, she had to buy it by the kilo, a few centavos dearer every day.

"This girl," she said, pointing at Nieves, "has a cousin in San Antonio who might have some charcoal. Wouldn't it be good if she went to see?"

This was good news, because ordinarily nobody has sufficient capital or storage room to buy charcoal when it is cheap and sell when it is dear. One notices throughout Mexico that most people have no capital at all, and insurance is an infant business. You cannot insure against theft and I don't know anyone who is insured against fire. Small and moderate capitals were wiped out during the revolution, and most people in all grades of society live from month to mouth. The Indios are generally even less well off. And not even the charcoal burners can afford to hoard any of their produce against the seasonal rise in price.

"Imagine to yourself," said Nieves when she got back. "There weren't enough centavos to pay my cousin Chucho for the hire of his yoke of oxen so they gave him some loads of charcoal and a little basket for his daughter Bartolita. And last night he shot a badger!"

I looked out this morning onto an entirely new view. Forty yards from the shore was a solid bed of green plants and all round as far as you could see the lake was covered with islands of greenery. They are water hyacinths which escape from the river at the eastern end of the lake. Some of the floating meadows are in full mauve flower and one is at once reminded of the chinampas, the floating gardens on which the Azteca used to bring their goods to market and which, gradually sending down roots below the matting on which the earth was piled, have formed the rich gardens of Xochimilco. But our islands are natural, depending on the interlacing roots of the hyacinths. They will eventually pile themselves all the way down the lake shore to Jocótepec. The flowers do not last indoors, but out there in the lake they are extremely beautiful. There is one immense island right off Ajijic, more than a quarter of a mile long, and on it stands a white heron surveying with aristocratic disdain the villages past which his flowery raft slowly takes him. Previously, before there were sluice gates on the river, there used to be even more hyacinths, and once a cow, drifting from Chapala, came safely to land at Ajijic, and behind the bridge at the mouth of the river the hyacinths piled up so thick and so deep that a man could ride on horseback across them. Others escape down the Santiago River that goes to the ocean and are pounded to liquid dust going over the waterfall at Juanacatlán.

A few yards from the water's edge some little Indio boys were bathing, splashing about, stopping and bombarding each other with handfuls of mud, intensely enjoying the stickiness and the sliminess of the hyacinth roots. On some rocks that were not quite submerged cormorants were standing. They remained motionless, their wings outspread to dry in the sun, looking like battered American eagles. Their wet plumage glistened as brightly as the wet naked brown bodies of the Indio boys against the tulip-leaf green of the plants. The boys tumbled and spluttered. One of them pulled a mauve hyacinth flower and offered it to a cow.

Now, after fifteen days of clear and almost rainless weather, it has started to rain again. This is said to be due to the change of the moon. A great many things are said to be due to lunar influence in Ajijic. In England I have been told that mushrooms grow with the full moon, and in France I have been given instructions for bottling wine "by a south wind and decline of moon." It is hardly surprising that the natives of Honduras insist that mahogany must be cut during the rainy season by moonlight. And in Ajijic, when you ask what is the season to transplant any flower, you always get the same answer: "By full moon."

Moon or no, the rain is back, and the sky fills with huge black clouds every afternoon. The first plume rises from behind Cerro de García by lunch time. One notices here that clouds do not seem to move much. They condense and they dissolve, but they very seldom travel, and they never scud. Usually they hang for hours in the same

50

place, I suppose high above the wind, swelling or diminishing but static. The low rainclouds, when they burst, come racing across the lake, though often, halfway to us, they turn west or east or divide, leaving us in sunshine, while gray curtains are drawn across the view, toward Chapala or toward Jocótepec, behind both of which are open valleys. When these rainstorms advance at sunset time, the color effects are fantastic. I have seen the whole lake and all the empty sky blazing with fuchsia shades, from violet to magenta. And sometimes the water is gun metal, glinting with deep metallic reds and greens, like carborundum in its crystal state. Such a sunset usually means that the storm will reach us in the middle of the night. Then the evening is black, moonless and starless, as the sky fills with cloud, and the still air gets stiller and hotter and more vibrant. And everywhere it is aglimmer with fireflies. I caught one in my hand, and watched the light flash on and off in the neat little bulb of its tails. It has no constant period of flash, but makes its amorous signal at caprice. In Spanish the firefly is called luciérnaga, a name gracefuller far than ours. There are glowworms here too, much less showy than the fireflies, which soar and plane, stitching the night with tinsel.

I met Chui coming down the beach. He was carrying a willow branch strung with a few whitefish, slivers of milky silver among the pointed leaves.

"Have you been fishing?" I asked. Chui seldom does anything so energetic as fishing.

"No. It's a friend of mine. He caught them and as he's owed me fifty centavos for much time he gave them to me."

"Don't you want to sell them?"

"Pues, I was going to have them for supper. How much would you give me?"

"Well, they look like a kilo more or less, I'll give you the usual price. Sixty centavos."

He grinned, pleased. "Here you have them."

I gave him the money. "Now you've got back what your friend owed you."

"It's true," said Chui. "And ten centavos more. I can have supper for that."

51

We walked on in silence, and the whitefish shimmered as the willow branch swayed in my hand.

"You know," said Chui, "I don't think my friend was paying me. He was just giving me the fish because he couldn't pay me.

"He's not a very great friend of mine," he added.

Today, August 19, is the feast of Saint Louis, celebrated by the village immediately opposite on the other side of the lake, San Luis Soyatlán. Now San Luis, though quite a big village and, since the completion of the Mexico City highway which passes through it, ever more prosperous, has not got a band. Traditionally San Luis hires the band from Ajijic. The musicians get paid, and they have a wonderful outing. Yesterday they set out in a big sailing canoa. Half the village saw them off, and they played gaily as the wide sail was spread and the canoa got under way. For a long time we heard the music sounding faintlier across the pale blue water.

All day we have heard the explosions of the firecrackers from across the lake, and seen the little puffs of smoke above the village. Mexicans generally demand of a firecracker only that it shall make a nice big bang, and so they let them off all day long, in bright sunshine.

The evening was very still, and the sunset was less spectacular than usual, as if to avoid competition with San Luis. And indeed, as soon as it was darkening, colored fireworks began to shine across the lake, the sound of the explosions lagging far behind the flame. The mountains behind San Luis were a deep plummy blue, with the bloom that a damson or a sloe has, and against it sprang fountains of white stars, fountains of rosy stars, fountains of white stars again.

"What a lot they must have spent," said Candelaria, her mouth and eyes wide open with marveling. "They'll all be poor for a long time after this."

Till ten o'clock, in the rich blackness of the night, the colored stars streamed up. Then there were no more. San Luis had not been so extravagant as that. But for long afterward flashes of fire and nice big bangs scarred the quiet night.

The next day the Ajijic band was due to return. Sometime in the afternoon the sails of the canoa were sighted across the lake, and a welcoming crowd gathered by the mole. The boat came very slowly, and its big patched sail hung at a very rakish angle. Music, strangely distorted over the water, came from it. The canoa held a wavering course, and seemed to be making for a point some distance from the mole.

"They've certainly put themselves a tremendous drunk," said old Venustiano, who was accompanied by a cow, as if to suggest that he had had to come down to the beach anyway, and had not come to watch the band return.

Then the canoa halted, and the men aboard began to lower the sail. It stuck, and then slithered down in a shapeless heap, one end trailing in the water. A shout came from the boat. It was still some way out, but they were going to pole in. The lake is shallow for its size, nowhere, it is said, more than sixty feet, and one can pole out quite a distance from the shore.

Propelled thus, two men planting poles at the prow and walking slowly back to the stern, the canoa's course was even more curious than when an uncertain wind had guided it. It was the first time I had ever seen a boat weaving like a drunk. And the sail, which nobody had retrieved and which still trailed in the water, added a touch of crazy gala, reminding one of those rich stuffs that trail from barges in paintings of the headier Renaissance festivals. And now too it became plain that, whatever distortion passage over water may give to music, the band was making very strange sounds. Not only were all the musicians playing their loudest, but, if any two of them were playing the same tune, they were not in time with one another. The audience on the mole laughed and called out and jeered by name at now recognizable players.

"There's Nacho! Look, he almost fell in, waving that trumpet of his! Listen, Nacho, do you know how to swim?"

So at last the canoa sidled uncertainly alongside the mole and the musicians, prudently passing their instruments to friends, reeled or were supported down the narrow plank slanted from a rock to the deck of the canoa.

There could be no doubt that San Luis Soyatlán puts on a good fiesta.

Don Bernabé came to see me. He is the oldest master mason in Ajijic, and he was going to build my house.

In Chapala the subsoil is unstable, and houses acquire cracks soon after being built. Even a house built on a concrete raft was not proof against the shifting earth. But in Ajijic the earth is firm and solid, and houses are built on very shallow foundations. Don Bernabé feels himself competent to undertake the whole construction of a dwelling. Once he built a two-story house, but it was on the shore and unfortunately it was washed down in the great flood of 1926. Now, to show what he is capable of, he has added an upper story to his own abode. He is a little old man, always with several days of white stubble, but with very elegant manners. He carries a blood-red sarape from Michoacán over his shoulder. Here the sarapes are black or dark brown with narrow floral borders and Don Bernabé's gaudy red is conspicuous. His hat doffings are models of grace. He likes to use dollar words and sometimes lengthens such as are unnecessarily short with an extra syllable or two.

"For what purpose, señor," he said, "could we need an archichitect? If you make the drawing of the plan of the project, my son and I will execute it. I have worked in the metropolis, doing work so fine that you could not put a straw between the bricks. I repaired the church and the Señor Cura was amiable enough to say that I had in places improved on the original design. Between an educomplished master mason and an archichitect there is no differentientation."

He sat gingerly on the edge of his chair, his big dingy sombrero in his hand, and after a small glass of tequila his words got longer and longer. Eventually it was decided that we should do without an architect, and that I would draw the plans of the house. Don Bernabé was to work by contract, and be responsible for hiring his assistants. At last, with many repetitions of "With permission," he rose to go. As I was showing him out, he said, "My brother-in-law has a field that is very good to cut adobes from. And my wife's cousin over in Ixtlahuacán makes tiles. In case they should be able to be of assistance to you, señor, I tell you."

I thanked him, and with several superb waves of his sombrero, he hitched up his old blue trousers and went.

As though she had been waiting for him to go, Candelaria came

54

into my room and said abruptly out of the blue, "You know, señor, that Lupita? Pues, today I saw her."

I was baffled. "Who?"

"Lupita, the niece of Venustiano," said Candelaria. "What shall I say to her?"

"What did she say to you?"

"Oh, she said to me to tell you that her uncle hasn't finished paying her for her land yet, and all the same he's selling it to you."

I said nothing, and there was quite a pause. It irked Candelaria and she went on:

"Of course, I don't know anything about it. I met her at Don Vicente's, no more. She was buying some boiling meat, and she asked me to say that to you. He'd sold both steaks, and I only got the kidneys, though I could have had the lungs. It was a bull. Do you like testicles?" These are also eaten in Mexico, and by some they are even considered a delicacy.

"No, I don't. And I don't like lungs either. But I wish you could find out what those other things are, that I described to you and don't know the Spanish for."

By which I meant sweetbreads, which I can never get in Ajijic, probably because they never kill an animal young enough to have its thymus gland. Your meat has always done a reasonable life's work on the hoof.

"I was going to say," answered Candelaria, who is unsympathetic to the idea of sweetbreads and who had become deaf, "what shall we do about the cooking oil?"

Now that olive oil from Spain has become unobtainable or fantastically dear, we cook with peanut oil, which is odorless and pure.

"What about the oil?"

"Already there isn't any."

It is useless to hope that Indio servants will warn you when something is running short. I had often tried to persuade Candelaria to use a little foresight, and I suppose I looked angry. But happily just then the rain increased suddenly in violence, and Candelaria, already scampering to the door, cried, "I've never seen if that Eugenio put in the chickens! I'll tell Lupita I told you what she said, and what you said."

"But I didn't say anything."

"Exactly, that's what I shall tell her."

Although it was raining very hard this morning, Eugenio actually came to work. It was impossible, of course, to do any work in the huerta, so he sat in the patio by the kitchen door and talked to Candelaria. He came wearing a china, a rain cape made of palm leaves. Tier upon tier of dried palm leaves is all it is, and water runs off it exactly as off a thatched roof. You do, in fact, walk about carrying your own thatch. Whether the name, china, really betokens that it derives from the East, where such straw waterproofs are also used, or whether Mexican Indios thought of them for themselves, I do not know.

It was the sort of day, cold and gray, sad and wet, when one doesn't like an open house. One thinks of houses that shut up securely, where one doesn't have to cross a patio to a bathroom. And I sat down to draw plans for my house. It would have to be small, but, like everyone who thinks of a house, I wanted it to have everything.

I spoiled a lot of squared paper. But eventually I decided that it should have two big rooms facing onto the lake, with a wide veranda in front of them, a bedroom, and a sitting room. Perhaps if I hadn't started to plan the house on a rainy day I wouldn't have thought of a sitting room that could be quite closed. Behind the sitting room, the kitchen, not so wide as the sitting room, behind the bedroom a garage, not so wide as the bedroom. And in between them room for a tiny patio, which could be enclosed by a wall on its fourth side, and of which the bathroom, opening from the bedroom, must occupy one corner. That way I should have more or less everything—veranda twelve feet wide, big enough to live on in good weather, and inside room for the bad days and evenings, and a patio. By making the rooms twenty-four feet by twelve I would get a wide view.

I was so pleased with my efforts that I sent Eugenio to ask Don Bernabé to come round, and we spent most of the afternoon modifying and redrawing. I decided that the sitting room should have a fireplace, not because it is really necessary here, but because a fire is companionable sometimes.

56

"Certainly," said Don Bernabé, "I have built many chimneys. And their functionment was perfect."

In the late afternoon Nieves' cousin arrived with the charcoal loaded on two donkeys. Each donkey carried two big sackfuls. There was prolonged flurry while it was unloaded, weighed, and stowed away, and while Candelaria insisted at every minute that I should not forget to deduct a kilo from each sackful for the weight of the sack itself. One of the donkeys ate most of a geranium. At length they were driven out of the patio into the street, and the boy was about to depart when Valentina, Nieves' mother, came puffing up the street leading a big pig by a thin string. Valentina has the outline of a blimp, but I think that, under that upholstery of flesh, her nose has the same aristocratic aquilinity as her daughter's.

"Listen, Chucho, as you're going, don't you want to take this pig? I owe it to my compadre." She gasped out this sentence and then collapsed abruptly and sat panting on the curb. The pig lay down in the dust and appeared to go to sleep.

"Yes, how not," said Chucho, grinning. Chucho and Chui are both diminutives of Jesús. This Jesús was a cheerful lad. He called to several young men who had been propping up the houses at the corner of the street, and between them, while Candelaria, Nieves, and Valentina (now slightly recovered) shored up one of the burros, the young men hoisted the pig onto its back. It reposed with it head behind the burro's head, one forefoot and one hindfoot hanging down on each side. The feet were then roped together under the burro's body, and further lashings were passed right over the pig's back. During the whole process the pig remained motionless, still apparently asleep. The burro lurched and stamped a little, but, once the pig was secured, seemed content with its new load. I have often seen a donkey giving a lift to a dog.

Chucho said good-by to everybody, Valentina called out streams of thanks and instructions. And then Chucho jumped on the back of the other burro, called to the pig's mount, and set off up the street. Chucho rode on the burro's rump, the only possible way to ride a burro bareback. The spine of a donkey makes the position amidmokes very uncomfortable, and the way to ride is aftmokes. We watched them out of sight. The pig still seemed to be asleep.

I was still at the door when a woman came along carrying a fowl. "Don't we want to buy a little hen?" asked Candelaria. "I think we do because of those that were drowned. When you've no chickens, they make much lack."

Four small chickens, not properly enclosed for the night, had been overcome by a flood during a storm. Candelaria had used them for frying.

And that was how I made the acquaintance of Tiburcia, the village wisewoman. In some ways she is a disappointment, for instead of going up into the hills, collecting simples and compounding brews and unguents of her own, she often buys things from a pharmacy. But she has, they say, a good hand for massage, and I am told that she performs an abortion for thirty centavos. Poison is a little dearer, it costs you fifty centavos, but it is guaranteed effective.

She herself is now elderly and ample. But it is easy to see that she must have been pretty and attractive, and there is a roving gleam in her eye, which makes village gossip say that she will still go behind the hedge with a man. She has a charming speaking voice and her skin is that Indio shade which is like amber with apricots behind it, but it is crossed with several scars, legacies, legend relates, of knife fights with female rivals. She has several children, and is a devoted mother, adding to her other earnings a little gained by doing washing.

We bought the fowl, which was then tied by the foot to a table leg until Candelaria had time to take it down to the hen run. And just then Nieves, who had been back to her house for the afternoon, came in.

Her face froze, and she passed rapidly and haughtily by Candelaria and Tiburcia, without greeting them and holding her shawl up to her face. Tiburcia, though she gave no sign of having noticed Nieves' behavior, prepared to leave at once. She said she had to go to see a patient.

"Poor woman, she hasn't enough milk for her baby. He's thin thin. I recommended her to eat the placenta, cooked, to make sure she'd have enough milk, but she didn't."

When Tiburcia had gone I heard Nieves crying in the kitchen.

"Whatever is the matter?" I asked.

"You see, pues, it's like this," said Candelaria. "Dispense me for mentioning such things. But the father of Nieves last month left his house and went to the house of Tiburcia. So Nieves is very sad about it. He is a man old enough to know better, and of course he no longer brings his money home nor much less. He is quite infatuated, and Nieves thinks perhaps Tiburcia has bewitched him."

Candelaria started to go to comfort Nieves, but a few steps away an idea struck her, and she turned back.

"Wouldn't it be good if Tiburcia didn't come to the house since she has this disgust with Nieves? She sells good eggs, but I could go for them."

The big seine nets are stretched on poles on the beach to dry. When one is drawn in and gathered up, it is piled, carefully arranged on the stern of the canoa, which rows round to the spot where the drying poles begin. Two men crouch and the heavy yoke on which the net must be carried is slid onto their shoulders. They stagger erect, and walk slowly down the line of poles, while other men hook the net into the forks. For this operation to go smoothly, the net must have been piled on the stern of the canoa in even folds. The wet seine is very heavy, and I have seen two men who had gotten the yoke a little off balance on their shoulders fall flat beneath the weight.

A seine net represents quite a capital. It is worth from three to four hundred pesos, and is seldom the property of an individual. It may belong to a family, or to partners. Often five or six partners jointly own a net. But also there are capitalists, who own one or more seines and pay a foreman who is responsible for his helpers and the catch. There are middlemen who buy all the catch in advance for sale in Guadalajara. I have seen basketfuls of whitefish caught, and been unable to buy one. And sometimes in Holy Week, when Guadalajara demands more fish than usual, the people of Ajijic and the lakeside villages can get no fish for the fast days.

The nets are delicate and tear frequently. No doubt they are not made of good material, and the lake bottom is in many places rocky. Often a net catches, and an Indio, all white shorts and mahogany torso, has to swim out and disentangle it, or even row out in a boat and spend half an hour groping with a pole or an oar. Every day you can see the fishermen mending their nets. And it is not unusual to meet an old man who is netting as he walks along the shore or about the village. The floats are not made of cork, which is scarce and dear, but of light porous wood. It is illegal to have nets that end in thick mesh-less stuff. But there is not much control, and many nets do in fact end in calico.

The circular cast net, which they call atarraya, is very different. It is hard work to use one, but independent. A man is his own master. I talked one evening to a fisherman who used an atarraya. He was the man I had talked to on my first visit to Ajijic and I had often seen him wading and flinging his net. He was noticeable because, though not young, he had bronze legs as well muscled and proportioned as those of an antique Hercules. He waded ashore and threw a few small fishes into a basket.

"Not much luck," I said.

"No, they're not coming out," he answered.

"Bad everywhere, isn't it?"

"Maybe. But it's worse here. Though I've had my little nephew throwing stones with his sling all afternoon to keep the ducks away." Here all waterfowl are called ducks. They are the fishermen's rivals. "But there's a good reason for it," he added.

"Oh, what's that?"

"You see, I always fish this stretch of shore. And the other day a compadre of mine, from over in San Pedrito, came down here. He was talking to me on the beach in the afternoon and he asked me whether it would disturb the fish if he bathed. I said that not. So he bathed."

The fisherman stopped and sighed deeply. "And he didn't tell me—"

He broke off and threw a pebble at a duck.

"He didn't tell me. He ought to have told me that just two days before his sister-in-law had died."

He threw another pebble.

"So what?"

"Posen, that's bad luck puesen. The fish know a thing like that."

SEPTEMBER

IN MEXICO, just when everything seems impossible, where there seems to be no solution at all, suddenly a door opens, everything gets arranged quite quickly, and everybody behaves as if there had never been any difficulty at all. That applies to minor or major problems. For weeks now the purchase of my land had been hung up because Pedro who had gone to Tampico had not yet replied. Then quite suddenly he did. I heard from my lawyer that he had agreed to sell, and that he had even signed the documents sent to him in the right places and remembered to enclose them with his letter of acceptance. Now we had clear going, apart from the delays incidental to transferring the land to my name, before which I must get permission to own land in Mexico. But that was lawyer's business and not Ajijic business.

This was really heartening, and I began to hatch quantities of plans, many of which I should be able to realize only gradually. However, it was pleasant to sit in the evenings and look at the daily different color show of the lake and think how nice it would be to have a seat of Moorish tiles in such a corner, and a lily pond in another, and a workroom up on the roof with glass almost all round it and a wide built-in table running all round the room and a guest room and another bathroom.

The month opened with delightful weather, cool, rain-washed, and fine. Everything was growing, thrusting up greenness with every handful of dirt. Usually, if the rains are mild, they will be long, perhaps starting early and going right on into October. If they are violent, then they are of shorter duration, and September will see them out. We have had fierce drenching storms this year, and now there is a little lull. Whatever the weather is like, it will probably go on being the same for ten days or so.

One evening I was sitting wish-thinking about my house in the open door of the mirador, when I noticed a young Indio edging gradually nearer to me. To save him trouble, I said good evening. He answered promptly, taking off his hat and advancing. Then he sat down beside me. I made some remark about the sunset.

"Very nice," he said. "Much very nice, and the huerta is very nice too."

I agreed.

Pause.

"It's a pity puesen that it has so much grass. Such a lot of weeds."

The huerta, which when I had come had been bare earth and fruit trees, was now thigh-deep in all kinds of grass and weeds. To clear it was more than one man's work. It needed two or three men working for several days to make a good job of it. I had been conscious of this for some time, but I had been putting off doing anything about it.

"Yes."

"They grow very fast during the rains."

"Yes."

"Wouldn't it be good to have it cleaned?"

"Yes. But my mozo can't do it alone."

Pause.

"I could do it, señor."

"But you couldn't do it alone either."

"Oh, no. But I could get a couple of peons and between us we could do it in two days. Three of us could do it. I know how to so-much a job like this. I could be responsible for the peons. For nine pesos I could arrange the whole thing."

It is unusual for Indios to make such definite and concrete offers.

"You're very young," I said, "to be contracting like this."

He smiled grandly. "Oh, I've been in charge of a big seine net, with four men under me, for whom I was responsible."

"So you're a fisherman?"

"I have been. I know about that. But I have worked a lot in the fields too. And as a mason."

62

I didn't say anything for a time, for just then the sky changed from a dusky orange to the color of Persian lilac. The boy was watching it too.

"How pretty," he said.

I agreed that it was beautiful, and we watched in silence as the mountains wrapped themselves in grape-purple velvet.

Then the boy got up. "With permission, señor," he said. "Good night."

"But what about cleaning the huerta?"

"I thought perhaps you didn't want me to do it."

"Oh, yes, if you're serious about it."

"Yes, how not, señor."

"All right then. As you said, nine pesos, and you arrange it all. Two days' work. Understood?"

"Yes, señor."

"When can you start? Tomorrow?"

"That yes no. Tomorrow I should have to find the peons. The day past tomorrow."

"Good. What's your name?"

"Cayetano Flores Pérez, to serve you."

"Very well then, Cayetano. Until the day after tomorrow. Good night."

"Until past tomorrow. In that we stay. May you pass a good night, señor."

In the dim light, as he stood with his back to the sunset, his coppery face was dark and featureless. Only there flashed in it the typical splendid white teeth of the Indio. His hat was in his hand, and he made a very elegant bow.

Opposite me, above the hills to the south, the constellation Scorpio shone out of the deepening evening. It is visible here from June through September, and its great swinging inverted S is one of the most graceful forms in the sky. The night hid the poverty, the crudity, the dirt. There was nothing left but the shimmering blacks of the landscape. And Cayetano's bow and Scorpio's sequined swoop were courtly things in a world of elegance.

"What shall we do, señor?" said Candelaria. "We have nothing for

63

dinner. I went to try to get some fish, and I sent down this girl again, and there isn't any. Not one little whitefish have they caught. And there's no meat. Don Federico hasn't killed, and Don Vicente hasn't killed, and Don Amílcar hasn't killed."

There are three butchers in Ajijic. Here, as in Spain, the butcher who has killed hangs out a red flag, which is why Spanish communists had to adopt a red and black flag. The three flags are always out on the same day. It would plainly be to the advantage of the three butchers to decide on which days they were going to kill, and for no two to kill on the same day. But no. They argue in a different fashion. If one kills, the others want to kill too, so as not to leave the third a monopoly of the market.

"Don Vicente promised always to send and tell me when he was going to kill, so that I could order what we want. So did Don Federico. But what shall we do today?"

"Well, why not make—"

But Candelaria wasn't listening. She didn't really want suggestions. She wanted to work off her annoyance with the butchers. She went on telling me how difficult it all was, and then was diverted by the arrival of an egg. She did not come back. But for lunch she had made a soup of cream and beet, and she had stuffed sweet peppers with mashed sardine, and she had made a salad of red cabbage, and she had cooked some very tender white string beans.

The following morning I had hardly awakened when she came scampering in to hold under my nose a dish laden with a pound of steak, kidneys, and a tongue.

"Look, señor, Don Vicente killed this morning. And without that I said anything, he sent this. Now isn't that nice?"

I said it was, and she stood for a few moments turning the dish round before my face, admiring the juicy red flesh.

Then she went, but hardly was she outside the door before she put her head in again to say, "And he's kept us the brains. But he won't take them out of the head till we send for them."

Cayetano had come to say that it was impossible to start cleaning the huerta on the day he had promised, since he hadn't managed to find two peons. But the next day he would start for sure. He did.

64

"Wouldn't it be good," suggested Candelaria, "if you were to sit up on the roof terrace instead of down in the mirador today?"

"Why?"

"Because then you could see over the huerta and you would be able to see whether that Cayetano and his men were really working or not. Even if you don't watch them, they'll know you're there."

So I sat on the roof and watched the hummers at the sugar tubes. Cayetano and his two peons were hard at work in the far corner of the huerta. At intervals I looked up, and they were always working. They were never resting. It was like that all day. And by the evening they had, it seemed to me, done more than half the work.

Cayetano appeared on the terrace about six, his face glazed with sweat, his white teeth flashing, and a pleased smile on his face.

"Good afternoon, señor."

Then he said nothing, waiting my comment.

"Well, you seem to have done a lot today, Cayetano," I said, wondering whether the same effort could possibly be sustained the next day.

"It appears that yes," said Cayetano, hardly containing his pride. I gave him the money to pay his men. He refused to take more than their pay.

"You can pay me when the job is done, señor."

I told Candelaria to give him some supper if he wanted it, and the kitchen was loud with chatter.

At supper Candelaria said, "He's a good boy. And he works much very hard."

Candelaria is on in her forties and Cayetano is a handsome youth. The supper party in the kitchen went on quite late.

The following day I heard Cayetano's voice soon after it was light. They had made good progress. Now there was enough clean ground for the weeds to seem invaders. All day the work went on with the same intensity. At last Cayetano came for his peons' pay.

"Finished?" I asked.

"Not quite," he said. "But these companions don't want to work any more. They're not used to directing things, you see, just to working by the hour. So I shall finish alone. Of one time I want to clear away the evil eye from the guamúchil tree."

65

The evil eye is an orange-flowered tree parasite, looking very like a wild bignonia, and the guamúchil bears a small tasteless nut which the Indios like.

And he did it all. It was after dark when he came in from the huerta and propped his mattock against the vine. He had borrowed my flashlight to cut away the evil eye.

"Ready," he said proudly. "Now it's all as clean as you could wish. Now it hasn't got the face of the huerta of a widow."

He had supper again, but he needed persuading to take the extra fifty centavos I gave him for having finished on time.

That night the sky was clear and blue-black, more blue than black, of that luminous intensity which in German is called a satisfied color. Every few minutes a meteor dissolved on a shining path. I stopped counting them. One of them reversed and sped upward and turned out to be a high-wheeling firefly. Perhaps it was a good-luck omen. Under cloudy northern skies, it is held to be good luck to count thirteen stars on each of thirteen successive nights, or to count three meteors on any given night. Such superstitions would be ridiculous here. But perhaps a firefly giving a gallant imitation of a shooting star is lucky. For the next morning I was told that César was here to see me. He was in town clothes, and looking more than ever the successful businessman. This time there was no delay.

"If I sold you the land you want," he said, "would you pay in effective?"

In Mexico almost any sum over two or three thousand pesos is paid by installments.

"Yes, I'd pay cash."

He frowned at an ant that was carrying a large green banner of leaf proudly across the tiles. He swallowed hard. Then he looked up and said, "If you would pay at once, within eight or ten days, I'd sell you the land at two pesos a meter."

I felt there was an angle to all this that I didn't know.

"One-seventy," I said firmly.

And at one-ninety we met. After all these bickerings, suddenly everything was agreed, and we even made a date to meet at my lawyer's in Guadalajara in four days' time to settle the matter.

66

As César went out of the door, Candelaria approached, leading a small boy by the hand.

"This is Julián," she said. "He is the son of Don Amílcar, who sends to say, if you didn't put yourself of accord with Don César, he has a piece of land which he would sell you, it is nearly at the mountain and it isn't a very good piece, I know it myself."

I was working hard in the mirador when suddenly Cayetano appeared from the beach. He had on a very decorative shirt of pale pink, nicely faded.

"Good afternoon, Cayetano. I'm afraid I haven't any work for you today."

"I know, señor. But there is a man in the village who has two equipales for sale."

An equipal is the Mexican chair made of untrimmed wood and leather.

"They're well made and he's selling them cheap. I thought you might like them."

"What's he asking for them?"

"Five pesos each."

Now this was cheap. There couldn't be much rake-off for Cayetano, if the chairs were any good at all.

"Why's he selling them for that?"

"Pues, you see, he's on the way to his sister's wedding in San Juan, and he thought he might bring some chairs of one time to see if he could sell them on the road. And nobody here wants any now. Nobody, that is, who can pay for them. So he's lowered the price puesen. I bring him, señor?"

"Very well."

Cayetano was gone like a flash and came back in a surprisingly short time with a man, each of them carrying an equipal. They put them down, and the man, an elderly dirty Indio with a straggle of gray beard, sat down in them very hard and then invited me to do the same.

"You see, it doesn't undo itself," he said with a high cackle of laughter.

They were sound chairs and cheap. I bought them and paid the man, and Cayetano went up to the house with the chairs. He didn't come back. Later I asked Nieves where he had gone. I thought he deserved a tip.

"He brought the equipales and went out by the street," she said. "His mother is a widow and sells cool waters of many flavors."

I heard that there would be further delay about my land, because it turned out that Venustiano's holding was not properly registered. This was remediable, but meant more time. And it was about now, as I watched the great thunderheads roll up nightly and splash deep rich tones across sunsets that were too shrill, that I made up my mind that I wanted to be in my house before the next rains. This was ambitious. Of course, if you employ a contractor from Guadalajara, you can get work done rapidly. But at much greater cost. Also I preferred to give all the employment possible in Ajijic. I knew it would be a race against time, since I must calculate that the rains might come at the beginning of June, we were already almost halfway through September, and I could not even start digging foundations yet. All I could do was revise plans, and purchase necessary materials, since it was now reasonably certain that there would be no unsurmountable hitch in the land purchase.

The following day in Guadalajara everything went almost incredibly well. César was fairly punctual at the lawyer's office, the documents of his land were in order, he understood the papers offered him to sign, he signed them, and our business was dispatched with efficiency and speed.

When I got home in the evening, Candelaria, after asking how the day had been to me, inquired, "And did you see poor Don César?"

"Oh, yes."

"And how is his wife, the poor thing?"

Candelaria's forehead was puckered, her eyes seemed ready to fill with tears, she was almost at the funeral.

"I don't know. Is she ill?"

"Ill?" said Candelaria, forgetting her look of grief in one of astonishment at my ignorance of current events. "Pues, the other day, no more, the day before Don César came here to talk with you, she was taken terribly ill, and they sent for the doctor from Chapala, and he said she must go at once to Guadalajara to be operated. He took her the very next day. How strange that he didn't tell you anything about it!"

I said nothing, thinking how César had needed cash down and how I had paid it and how these facts I knew completed Candelaria's information.

"They say," said Candelaria, "they say that he sold you his land because he had to have centavos for the operation. Did you say that with the artichoke I should give you the mayonnaise or put little capers in it?"

With big rooms, a big patio, and terraces there is an immense amount of sweeping to do, not once but several times a day. Hitherto Nieves had been doing all the washing, scrubbing away down at the lake edge on a special flat stone that she liked. These stones are precious, and as the lake rises or falls they are moved to appropriate positions. Washing like that, in cold water, takes endless time, and ironing with irons on a brazier of charcoal takes a long time too. So, though drying is very quick, even in the shade, where all colored things must be dried in case of fading, and you need do no bleaching of white things because the sun will do it for you, the whole process of washing is very lengthy. So we had decided to have somebody else do it.

"My comadre's sister-in-law, Aurora, washes very nicely," Candelaria had said, so Aurora came to see me.

She looked sixty and was probably forty-five or less, a little shrunken woman with a wrinkled face, the color of potato peel, dusty wispy hair, gnarled hands and arms, and a slight limp. She smiled perpetually, with the look of a dog that cringes for fear of being kicked. She had been abandoned by her husband and had five children. She had a thin whining voice.

"Yes, of couse I know how to wash and starch and iron, but who knows if it will be done the way you like it. We can only see."

"And I want you to do the drying in the huerta and all the ironing in the house."

That is better, for clean washing may arrive from an Indio house with a bedbug in it.

"Just as you may wish."

69

"And what wage do you want?"

"Pues, you will see, whatever you think right, you will see what you will pay me when you see my work. Maybe you will like it and maybe you won't, but what shall we do pues?"

A little later, still smiling ingratiatingly and sighing despairingly, she limped out of the house with a big washing basket on her tousled head.

Venustiano came in to see me, ostensibly to ask for the loan of a brace. When I had brought it, he hung around, looking at my bookcase.

"A lot of books," he said. "Have you any in Spanish?"

"Look and see if there's anything you'd like."

He scanned the books for a time, his wrinkles corrugating yet deeper as he concentrated. Then he said, "You wouldn't have any of the works of Carlos Marx?"

I hadn't.

"Are you a communist?" I asked.

"Certainly not," said Venustiano. "But you never know."

On the sixteenth, the day of the Fiestas Patrias, I went up to the plaza. In the loggia of the comisaría there was a large picture of the president and another of Hidalgo. There were also some chairs and a table, and everything was decorated with a lot of red, green, and white paper. Don Pedro, the comisario, fussed about. He was a little wisp of a man with a little wispy mustache. Once upon a time he built himself a tower on the beach, not to live in, but to entertain his friends in, to sit in and contemplate the view. He kept chairs there and a cupboard with drinks. He loved his tower. But in the flood it came crashing down, for it was all adobe. He never built it up again.

Don Pedro was proud of his village. Now he fussed over the other side of the plaza, arranging the procession. It was, as usual, made up of the band and anyone who had a horse. But this time too there were the school children who were going to act a play, a sort of Mexican version of Moors and Spaniards such as you see in Spain, only here Conquistadores and Indios.

The boys had on paper cocked hats, with wooden swords buckled on their belts, and some of them had paper breastplates, and some had very large sham mustaches. The girls had various garlands and sashes of the national colors.

At last they were all formed up and set off in a ragged column. Some of the children carried arches, cardboard centerpieces on poles, with patriotic mottoes all in green, red, and white paper. They went all round the village and came back to the plaza.

From the loggia the comisario made a speech and everyone applauded. Then, in front of the loggia, the children began the play. It was interminable. I sat on a bench and watched the bees in the zinnias. The zinnias were very fine. Don Pedro had had them planted in time to flower for the feast and he had calculated well. He had had them well watered, and now they were four feet high, a drift of rose and yellow bloom. The bees had made a number of journeys to the hive and returned before the play was over.

The afternoon was waning, and now there was nothing before us except the usual illuminations in the plaza, the walking round, the firecrackers, and the old tune by the band.

Don Pedro came up to me, a glow of gratified pride on his little wrinkled face.

"Of course it's a very humble village," he said deprecatingly. "Nothing really. But still, it was rather a nice procession, wasn't it?"

Eugenio didn't come to work. About the middle of the morning I asked Nieves if she had seen him.

"He's going about drunk," she said.

Candelaria had warned me, and there was nothing to be done. But later that afternoon I heard from Candelaria herself that the comisario had arrested him and put him in the lockup. The lockup is a one-room building, closed by a door made of wooden bars. The prisoner's friends come and talk to him, give him cigarets, and bring him food. But Eugenio, it seemed, had passed quietly out, once in the lockup, and was in no need of anything.

The next day he didn't come either.

"Is Eugenio still the lockup?" I asked.

"No. Not today."

"Then why hasn't he come to work? Hangover?"

"Pues, perhaps he's crude, perhaps he has a hangover. But also he has shame."

"Well, if you see him, tell him not to be a fool and come to work or else he'll lose his job."

But Eugenio remained ashamed all day, and in the evening he felt so ashamed that he went on the drink again, and got locked up quite early. I thought that was enough, and told Candelaria to let him know that he needn't come back.

But in the morning he did come back. I heard his voice quite early. He sounded angry, perhaps still drunk.

"Where's Eugenio?" I asked Nieves when she brought my breakfast.

"He went," she said. "He said he was going to his country. That's over in Tizapán, across the lake. He came for his things."

So for several days we had no mozo. Nieves brought the ice down in a bucket, and the drinking water in a big earthenware jar which she carried most picturesquely on her shoulder. We all of us, with the help of a small boy who had come in to sell an egg or two, watered the more delicate plants. And Nieves remembered the sugarwater for the hummingbirds, who come to feed a lot now, for though there are plenty of wild flowers of which the bees are making honey, the rains wash out so much nectar that a hummer has difficulty in finding his meals.

"You see, I told you to do nothing about Eugenio," said Venustiano, whose advice is always moderate. "You're well free of him, that Eugenio. He wasn't any good. Even to me he tried to sell some grapefruits, and everybody knows there aren't any grapefruits except in the huerta of you."

"Oh, he was stealing things, was he?"

"Where more are there grapefruits?" asked Venustiano. "If you'd found out, you might have been annoyed and fired him. But it would have been difficult to prove, and he's just the sort to claim three months' wages because of dismissal."

The result of that law has been to make bosses who want to fire an employee behave so unpleasantly that the employee is forced to give notice himself. Or else he takes advantage of an absence without permission and not explained by illness to regard the employee as fired.

"Laws," said Venustiano, pulling at his ragged mustache, "should be obeyed. But then, they change quite often, and meanwhile one has to know how to get along."

I was in the patio repotting some young geraniums when suddenly Cayetano walked in. From the yoke on his shoulder swung the two big gasoline cans in which drinking water is fetched. He said good day, unloaded the cans, and emptied them into the big filter of porous volcanic stone. Then he drifted into the kitchen and I heard him talking in low tones to Candelaria. After a little he came out and went down the huerta. I called Candelaria.

"What made Cayetano fetch the water?" I asked.

Candelaria shrugged. "He came in and asked whether, as we hadn't a mozo, he shouldn't fetch it," she said.

Just then Cayetano came back from the huerta. He had a lettuce and some onions in his hand. Candelaria met him at the door of the kitchen.

"Señor," said Cayetano, on a rising note.

"Yes?"

"I think the bananas want cutting, if not they'll throw themselves to lose."

"Yes," I said, "I've seen them."

"And there's a lot of room down there where you could sow carrots. I gave myself count that Candelaria is buying them very dear."

"Yes, I'd thought of sowing some."

"Of course, it would be very good," said Cayetano. "But that's heavy work, the ground needs digging over."

He was standing with his big hat in his hand, his eyes fixed on the floor at his feet.

"Supposing you were a mozo in the house," I said. "Would you be prepared to do housework too? Or is that something you'd think was woman's work?"

"I know how to sweep," said Cayetano. "And what I would really like would be to do work that wasn't so rough, work that I could do and keep myself clean, and indoors, out of the sun."

Sheltered by his big sombrero, the Mexican peon can work long hours in blazing sun, but it is a great recommendation of a job to say, "It's in the shade."

"You see, I expect to have many visitors, and I like things properly done. If you were my mozo, I should want you to learn all sorts of things—to wait at table and mix drinks, and know how to receive people, and wear a white coat, and keep your hands and nails clean, and still be able to fetch the water and to look after the vegetables and flowers."

There was a little pause. Cayetano's eyes were still downcast, but there was a smile playing round his mouth. Suddenly he looked up. "It would please me much to wear a white coat," he said. "I could start tomorrow if you like."

So that was how Cayetano came to work for me. He had to wait for the white coat until I went into Guadalajara again, but the next morning he was on the job good and early. Soon after breakfast he came in and, plainly remembering what I had said about receiving people, announced formally: "A gentleman desires to speak with you." Then he added in conversational tones: "It's old Bernabé, no more."

Don Bernabé was waiting in the patio dwarfed by the huge sombrero he was holding in his hand. He put it on when he saw me coming and took it off with such a wide sweep that when he bowed it dusted the floor of the patio. I noticed then that there was a large hole burned in the brim.

I invited him to sit down, and we started to talk about the house.

"Of course, señor, you will surround your land with a wall?"

A wall is understood to be built of adobe or brick properly mortared, usually reared on a rock foundation, as opposed to a foundationless dry wall. I said I thought it would be too dear.

"But you are rich, señor," said Don Bernabé. "All foreigners build walls round their properties."

I explained that I was not rich.

"Couldn't I have one of those loose stone walls that I have seen round here?"

"Oh, you mean a surround, señor." Don Bernabé shook his head, and went on to tell me all the disadvantages of dry walls. "And you know they fill themselves with capulines."

Now this happens to be true. Between the stones you often see the untidy web of a black widow, and, peering into the cranny, you can

74

distinguish the spider's shiny black body and red markings. But black widows will not attack, and here their bite is not very dangerous.

Eventually we compromised. I agreed to corner my land to the northwest with a real wall, because, as Don Bernabé pointed out, if a freshet were to break away from the main arroyo and come down the lane which borders my land, it might be powerful enough to knock down a dry wall and destroy my garden with boulders.

"Will there be enough stones for the surround with those which we clear off the property?" I asked.

"That will not matter, señor. There are plenty on the beach or in the street behind, and if that should result not sufficient, in the arroyo are quantitaties of them."

Then we started to talk about the entrance. Venustiano has a field surrounded by a dry wall, but it has no entrance. When he arrives in the morning with his yoke of oxen to plow, he undoes a sufficient section of the wall to enable the oxen to enter, and, when they are in, does it up again. In the evening he repeats the process. But I did not intend to plow and I wanted a permanent entrance on the street for the car and another that would open onto the beach.

"In that case," said Don Bernabé, "we can make a gate with a small roof of tiles."

Later that day Merced, Don Bernabé's son, came to me, and, after going over everything I had discussed with his father in the morning, braced himself to ask for the loan of seven pesos.

"That's quite a lot of money."

"Yes, señor, but you see, my cow was lost or stolen, and I had to offer a reward for it, and now it has been brought back, and I have to pay the reward."

"Very well." I gave him the seven pesos.

It was less than a week afterward that we were needing some manure. The strongest and best local manure is goat manure, and it costs fifty or sixty centavos a donkeyload. But we didn't know anyone who had any. When I was round at my land, Merced was not there, but his brother was, and I asked whether he had any goat manure to sell.

He shook his head. "No, señor, I'm sorry, I haven't."

"You don't know anybody who has? Your father? Your brother?"

He shook his head again. "No, we haven't any," he said. "You see, none of our family has any animals at all."

"Not even a cow?" I asked.

"Oh, no. I wish we had a cow."

Probably Cayetano had never seen a table properly set. He himself no doubt ate with a knife and a tortilla and his fingers. There is an ancient Mexican tale about a foreigner who was boasting that he was accustomed to have clean forks of silver for every course, to which a Mexican replied, "But we have a fresh fork for every mouthful," and, wrapping some meat skillfully in a tortilla, swallowed it and picked up another tortilla for the next mouthful.

I took Cayetano into the dining room and showed him all the things, and how they should be arranged, and then I told him to set a table for four people. When I came back half an hour later, he had done pretty well, and was standing with his chin in his hand and a heavy frown on his forehead, staring at his handiwork. There were no glasses.

"I knew something lacked," he said, with a happy grin. "Without glasses, what joke is a meal?"

The next thing was table waiting. Having explained the rough idea, and the appropriateness of left and right, I made him sit down, and then served him an imaginary meal. This amused him considerably, but it really made him notice, and that evening he waited quite nicely. There was one detail that was eccentric. I had left my typewriter on the dining table and, rather than move this sacred cow, he had laid supper all round it. Dali would have been pleased.

I had a good many visitors, and if only a few of them come into this book, it is because the book is not about Americans or Europeans or for the most part even white Mexicans, but about the Indios as you meet them every day. Because of the visitors, Cayetano had to learn to wait. And I explained to him that whereas in Spanish he is called a tableman, in English he is called a waiter and he has quite often just to wait about while keeping his eyes open. In a country where waiting about has become an art I felt that ought not to be too difficult for him to grasp. Nor was it. But Indios hate boredom more than anything. They would sooner be kept up half the night serving food and drinks for a party than have one day follow in the image of another. I eat too little for their liking. They would enjoy serving long meals. They would like me to have every day wet soup, dry soup (that is, rice or spaghetti), meat and vegetables, salad, beans, and dessert and fruit. They like me to have guests, and they would not mind in the very least if lunch were at four and supper at eleven. Nor do they mind carrying chairs and tables about all over the house and huerta. This is not a country where each room has its own chairs which stay in it. You have, perhaps, a dozen chairs, and these are moved about according to the exigencies of the moment.

One evening, sitting down as usual in the mirador at sunset time, I had the idea that it would be pleasant to have my supper down there. The air was as soft as milk. There was no breath of wind, and the fireflies were doing decorative gymnastics among the willow branches.

Tentatively I said to Nieves, "I'd like to have supper down here. Would it be a great trouble? Just a tray."

"Nothing of work, none at all," said Nieves, with her lively smile, and hurried back to the house.

About a quarter hour later a procession came down the huerta, Cayetano carrying a table, Nieves another, Candelaria with a chair, and Valentina, who happened to have called, with the cocktail tray.

In no time at all they had brought a third table to serve from, and had set supper with everything, even a bowl of zinnias. The meal was served as usual, but by all of them, everything being brought fifty yards from the house, not only without complaint but with obvious enjoyment. There had been no visitors for some days, and, as I had not given a party, they had made one.

They had all said good night and gone home when Aurora came to deliver the washing. I told her to leave the basket by the kitchen and come back in the morning, when Candelaria could count the things. In Mexico you pay for washing by dozens. A large object, such as a sheet, counts many handkerchiefs, or several towels. I have never understood exactly how it all works, but any Mexican servant can count in a moment how many dozens a pile of washing makes.

Aurora edged the basket off her head onto a window sill, and thence lifted it down to a chair. As she was near the icebox I asked her to bring me a beer.

"I can't, señor, I can't," she said.

I thought she didn't know how to open the box.

"It's quite easy, you just push that handle."

"But I've been ironing. I'm hot. I can't. I would like to, but what can we do pues?"

It is quite true, as I have found, that if your hands are hot and you put them in cold water for more than a moment, you get rheumatism. No Mexican servant who has been ironing will consent to wash the dishes, and one who has been bathing won't stay very near the fire. But a superstition has grown up around this fact, exaggerating it. It hurts nobody who has been ironing to open an icebox and take out a bottle. But often you cannot get an Indio to do it. So I fetched the beer myself, and Aurora brought a glass. She didn't go away.

"Is there something you want, Aurora?"

"Pues, señor, if Candelaria is going to pay me tomorrow, could you let me have some centavos today? I want to buy my little one's supper."

She is a grumbler. But I know she has several small children to support. I gave her the money.

"She lives very badly, in the most ugly conditions," Candelaria had told me. "Each night all the night she was moving her bed from place to place for the water was entering in streams. And her leg is always much swollen."

When Aurora had gone I glanced at the basketful of washing. On top were my shirts. I have seldom had them so well ironed.

After several days of rain today was fine and I went out to the Tepalo. This is a big arroyo to the east of the village, and it has a clear fall of about forty feet, which is a pretty sight when there is any water. But usually a few hours after a heavy fall the water has gone by and there is left a narrow ribbon and no more. Once before I had seen it in this disappointing state, but today the heavy rains of the last days of the month promised better. Today indeed there was a fine rush of water, roaring down and foaming into the rock basin below. There half a dozen women in colored slips were sitting being buffeted in the cold water and screaming.

The arroyo to the other side of the village, the Tempisque, often does damage to the lands and houses that lie between it and the lake shore. It was down the Tempisque that the cloudburst came. It was the Tempisque that might endanger my land. But you never hear of the Tepalo doing any damage. An old man was sitting on the edge of the rocks watching the women in the pool below. I asked him why it was that the Tepalo was inoffensive.

"Pues, you see," he said, "it did do much damage at one time. And then, some years ago, the comisario of Ajijic called on the men of the village to come and build walls along its course. No paid work, you understand. So of course it could only be done on Sunday. I worked at it myself. We did it in two Sundays. But that is a long time ago, and I wouldn't be surprised to see the wall give way any time now."

"And is anybody going to do anything about it before it gives way?"

"Who knows," said the old man. But it was plain he thought my question absurd.

I had some friends with me, and, after looking at the Tepalo, we went on further, eastward at the foot of the mountains, scaling dry walls and climbing steep banks, to another arroyo, which lies behind the village of San Antonio Tlayacapam. It is called The Tubs, and consists in a series of three or four natural basins that staircase up a narrow rock gorge. Trees and shrubs crowd close around, grasses thrusting up through bushes, branches pushing down into grass, and in any open space there are drifts of Victorian pink cosmos and feather-fine coral-pink grasses. Under arched green, the water spills down from tub to tub, netted with shade and dappled with foam.

We had taken a picnic lunch with us. This is a form of entertainment which in most countries combines the maximum of trouble with the pessimum of comfort and the minimum of enjoyment. In Mexico it is no trouble at all. Cayetano carried a huge and very heavy basket on his head, Nieves lugged a couple of string bags and assorted oddments. Arrived at the clearing at the foot of The Tubs, they made their kitchen. Cayetano collected big flat stones of suitable size, and set them round a hollow, in which a fire was lit. From the basket came earthenware pots and ollas of all sizes. Candelaria had sent salad and dressing, and various other things already cooked and in need only of heating. And she had sent halved spring chickens which had lain all night in orange juice. Cayetano, having made the kitchen, created a dining room, with more flat rocks as seats, around a big rock on which he arranged a tablecloth. When we were nearly ready, Nieves started frying the chickens in a wire basket and Cayetano attended to heating the tortillas. We ate extremely well, and after that Nieves and Cayetano ate extremely well too. To my certain knowledge Cayetano ate at least thirty tortillas. He deserved them.

It is when I see an Indio like this, all energy and invention, that I become most bored by the contention that he is feckless and lazy. Some people say that this is so because of sheer cussedness. There is another school of thought which attributes it to the weakening effect over generations of malaria. A third favors the enervation caused by living at sea level in the tropics, or, alternatively, by living at an altitude of four thousand odd feet, where oxygen lacks. And those who think in terms of social significance blame it on oppression and lack of education. All the above theories are rubbish. The Indio is not lazy and feckless.

He is not lazy. He can work as hard as anyone, and often harder. Watch an Indio spend eight hours a day drawing water from a well with the help of a rope, a crossbeam, and a bucket. Consider the huge weights an Indio porter will carry on his back, taking the strain on a forehead band, and moving in a little half-run. Remember that before there were corn mills an Indio woman would spend six hours grinding the grain for her family by hand on a slab of volcanic stone, and that still tortilla making is a long and arduous process. Look at an Indio plowing his land all day, with a wooden plow that only scratches the earth and a yoke of oxen attached to the shaft by yards of leather thongs that have taken an age to bind round the horns.

He is not feckless. He has never had many possessions or many rights. And happily he has few needs. As for those he has—well, centuries have trained him to be a master of going without, and poverty plus inventiveness have made him a master of making do. When you can go without and make do, you will own very little, and be able to save practically nothing. You are certainly very independent. But you are not for that feckless.

The factor that has given the Indio the name for laziness and fecklessness is that of time, or unpunctuality, or lack of time sense, or whatever you like to call it. Anyway, it is what is meant by people who gibber about Mexico as the Land of Mañana. These bribbling dopes have never even tried to understand what they bribble and brabble about, doubtless because they are too busy peering bug-eyed to catch

80

sight of flashing señoritas and muy hombre bullfighters and embroidered charros and all the rest of the phony phooey in night-club novels about Mexico, ever to get an Indio into focus. The Indio is much too sensible for such fripperies, and there isn't any fancy dress about his time sense either. But he does live on his own rhythm, and on a time plane of his own.

The past is real, it happened, we all saw yesterday, there it was. To-day is real too, it is cold or it is hot, we have eaten or we have not eaten, anybody's flesh and stomach can decide that beyond cavil. But tomorrow is imaginary, it is nonexistent, it is quite unreal, and things that are unreal do not have exact dimensions and precise seasons. "I'll come tomorrow," says an Indio, and arrives four months later—or maybe five. But he hasn't lied, he hasn't deceived or wished to deceive. All he has done is launch his thought into the unreal. How in the world can you define exactly something that does not exist?

OCTOBER

THIS is in some ways the most beautiful month of the year. Everything is still green, richly green, and, unless it is a year when the rains drag on, the air is dry and crystalline. In the mornings, the Mexicano sometimes blows chill, so that you cannot sit exposed to it in the shade. But by noon it has dropped, and the afternoons are still and silky. The oranges that flowered in May will soon be ripe, and in the horizontal evening light they shine like lamps, and the thick foliage, still fresh and full of chlorophyll, burns with deep greens, two-dimensional as a theater set. There are morning-glories everywhere, the hedgerows are strips of sky. They are just now so popular with the bees that one day, wearing a shirt of that blue, I was so bee haunted that I had to go and change. It is a sort of second spring. Flowers bloom, buds shoot, some animals breed again. I had no animals except the cat, but I was sent two ducklings.

"Now you're living in the country, I'm sure you ought to have these," said the card on the basket. I don't like poultry, but the ducklings were engaging. Typically, as it later turned out, the larger was standing on the smaller one's head.

For some days they waddled about in a corner of the huerta, and, as they did no harm, we got into the way of shutting them up at night in the poultry run but letting them wander about the huerta at will in the daytime. They did not like the cold and huddled together under a bush when the morning wind was blowing.

It was such a beautiful season and had come so suddenly when the last clouds were blown away, that I grudged days spent in Guadalajara. But I had many things to buy both for my present and my future houses. On the way home I had to leave the car in Chapala, because it was, as the Spanish say, decomposed, so I was glad when César appeared and offered me a lift in his car. The car is a very old Maxwell with a stertorous engine and the upholstery disintegrant. There were two people, a man and a woman, in the front seat beside him. I got in behind where there were already countless bundles, and, after we had waited for a little, two men, a girl, and a small boy wedged themselves in with me. Still we waited.

"Venustiano's coming," said César brightly.

"Where will he ride?"

"Oh, on the running board," said César. "Or inside, and the boy can ride on the running board."

We waited for a long time. Then at last Venustiano appeared. He had a pig with him. Nobody was surprised. With the help of friends, the pig was bound to the right-hand fender, grunting but not much upset. Then Venustiano hoisted himself onto the running board, and various friends handed him an assortment of packages. There were three or four brightly striped bags of the woven fiber they call ixtle, and these were hung on the door handles. I was the only person who was surprised that the car started and that it went and that we all got to Ajijic.

I was watching the shimmer of a huge hatch of yellow butterflies when Candelaria arrived, bringing the kitchen account book. When she does this in the middle of the day, it means she has spent all the money and wants some more. I took the book and wrote down the day's items as Candelaria recalled them.

"And fifteen eggs," she said. "But I only have centavos for four."

"But whatever do you want to buy so many eggs for? Haven't the chickens been laying?"

"Not one did I find. Not one."

"Is this a season when the hens don't lay?"

"They ought to, they ought to put many eggs. Do you know what? The Hungarians took them, those gypsies who were here the other day. They took a little duster I had left out to dry on a thorn bush.

83

The Hungarians took them. What are we going to do about the little pig?"

I had been expecting the visit of some friends, who had put off their visit, leaving us with a sucking pig, purchased especially since I knew their partiality for it. Now that they were not coming for some weeks it seemed probable that he would grow beyond the optimum stage of tenderness before their arrival. I could not have a sucking pig killed for myself alone.

"We can have it cut," said Cayetano. "Then it will be all right."

"Yes," said Candelaria, putting a diminutive ending onto practically every word, "then the little pig's little flesh will be little tender."

"And can you do that, Cayetano?"

"No, señor, but there is a señor here who can do it."

So it was decided that the pig should be castrated, and two mornings later the deed was done, with a great deal of squealing.

"The señor is asking for fifty centavos," said Cayetano.

"All right."

"It's very dear, señor. But we didn't make our contract first. It's very dear. That's a gringo's price for castrating a little pig."

Nieves didn't come this morning. Her uncle had died, and she had been up all night, watching the corpse. Today was the funeral. He was an old man, with a raggedy white beard, whom I had often seen about. When Nieves came in the afternoon I asked her what he had died of.

"A pain struck him," she said.

The horse here is still an integral part of life, not an extra. It is possible to hire a horse for about sixty centavos a day, provided that one is available and is not working out in the fields. It isn't much of a horse when you get it. Probably you have to work harder than the horse, kicking. And sometimes it is as well not to look under the saddle. However, there is really nowhere to ride, since the beach is rocky, the mountains too steep, and the road bad. There is nowhere else. It is said that a custom-made Mexican wooden saddle is comfortable. It may be so. Certainly a ready-made hired or borrowed one is an instrument of torture, in my experience. All Indios can ride, but there

84

isn't a young man in the village who wouldn't prefer a bicycle to a horse any day. There are two or three bicycles in the village now.

"You see, a bicycle doesn't eat anything," said a young man. And that finished the argument for him. He could not project his mind sufficiently far into the future to realize that tires wear out and bicycles need spare parts and various sorts of attention. A bicycle does not eat, that is incontestable. Therefore, although a bicycle is expensive to begin with, it costs less than a horse.

"And," added the young man, "you don't have to take it down to the lake to drink either."

"They are idiots," said Don Bernabé of the bicycle crazy. I was taking him to Ixtlahuacán de los Membrillos, The Place of the Lords of the Plain of the Quinces, over the pass from Chapala. They make tiles in Ixtlahuacán and we were going to order some from Don Bernabé's wife's cousin who had some kilns. "Idiots. What do they want with bicycles?"

"Quite," I said. "And such bad roads everywhere. Much better to have a horse."

"Horse?" said Don Bernabé. "What I want is a little automobile."

On the way back I saw that they were repairing the roof of the church in San Antonio.

"Don't we ask whether they would be disposed to allow us to purchase some of the tiles they are taking off?" said Don Bernabé.

"Why?"

"Because they are old," he said.

I drove on in silence, negotiating a passage between several square yards of peanuts put out to dry, a large pile of cornstalks that were being nibbled by a cow, and two sleeping pigs, and awaiting enlightenment.

"It is not easy to acquire old tiles," he said.

"But aren't new ones better?"

"That yes no. It needs two years for a tile to become impermiermable. For the first two seasons of the waters new tiles will let the rain penetrate and will remain humidous."

"All right. Then shall we go back and ask whether they'll sell the tiles?"

"If you wish to stop here," said Don Bernabé, indicating a house distinguished by a recent coat of whitewash (San Antonio is a poor village), "I will ask my compadre."

We stopped, and Don Bernabé disappeared into the house. After some time he emerged again, accompanied by an old white-haired Indio. The hair of Indios seldom goes white, but when it does, it goes white as snow. I was presented. The compadre, it seemed, was the contractor for the repairs to the church roof. He said he would sell us the old tiles.

"At what price?"

He looked at Don Bernabé in a puzzled way. After a pause Don Bernabé rescued him.

"My compadre," he said grandly, "will have to make his presupposition. Then he will advise us."

So now we had ordered tiles. Adobes were being cut in Ajijic. Don Bernabé and I had been over the plans a dozen times. And he could start digging foundations.

He began with the raised terrace on which the whole house will stand. This is squared out and surrounded with a stone wall to the required height. The inside, with due respect for foundations of party walls, is then filled with big rocks and earth pressed down between them. Finally, on top it will be cemented or tiled.

Building in adobe costs less than building in brick. In Ajijic, so long as you calculate that your adobes are well above maximum possible flood level, with a brick or stone base, your house is all right, but if water reaches the adobes they will crumble. Provided you have plenty of ground, the thickness necessary for adobe walls, anything from forty to fifty centimeters, doesn't matter. Thick adobe walls are soundproof and resist the cold and hold the heat. Long after dark in winter I have found outside walls gratefully warm to the touch. But there is one great disadvantage to adobe. A brick wall can be plastered in a moment, but if you plaster straight on to adobe, as it stands when finished, your plaster will flake away in chunks of any size, any time. To make the plaster stick you have to surface the adobe with broken brick.

Bricks are not made in Ajijic, and there is quite a lot of ground suitable to cutting adobes from. I decided finally on a compromise, using

86

adobes for main walls that had to take weight and brick for light dividing walls.

"Put that adobes are well laid," said César, puffing at his cigar, when I asked his advice, "they will last many decades and I have nothing against them. But my own house I am going to build of pure brick."

"There's no milk, señor," said Candelaria.

"Why? What's happened?"

Candelaria didn't know. She hadn't tried to find out. There was no milk and no prospect of there being milk.

"Chui hasn't sent it," she said.

I had not been satisfied with Chui's milk. It often happens that cow and goat milk are mixed, which is not only unpleasant but dangerous, for more goats than cows can give you Malta fever. In any case, it is inadvisable to drink unboiled milk. I was suspicious of Chui's milk, and went to see him myself.

"That yes no," he assured me. "It isn't mixed at all. Look, it's liquid cow's milk, pure pure."

"You didn't send any milk at all today."

"Pos, the cow had gone up the hill, puesen."

"Can't you shut her up?"

"Yes, how not, it's very easy. Only then she goes out alone."

When an Indio tells you something is very easy, almost invariably he doesn't do it. I felt inclined to tell Chui I would get my milk elsewhere, but you don't do that in Ajijic until you are sure there is somewhere else to get it. And by the time I got home I had calmed down and didn't do anything more about it.

By now the sun was going down, and there was a tang in the air, the sort of tang a Swiss mountain village has in the summer only muskier. I decided to have my drink down in the mirador.

"Señor," said Cayetano, when he came with the tray, "didn't you see Mundo as you came through the patio? He was waiting to see you."

"No. Who is he anyway?"

"Oh, you know, señor. Edmundo. He comes from Chapala and sells things."

"What does he sell?"

"Many things," said Cayetano.

I told him to send Edmundo down to see me, and in a few minutes there came a young man, very neat and clean and well shaven.

"I thought you might like to buy these, señor. I heard there was a foreigner living here and I know foreigners often buy curious things." He produced from various pockets about a dozen glass bottle stoppers of varying shades of blue and green. "You see, señor, I received a parcel of these bottles from Guadalajara and they were badly packed and on the way they broke themselves, they were made pieces, that is to say, all but the stoppers. I leave them you all in a peso."

"But what should I do with them?"

He looked at me as if I should have known.

"Pues, I don't know, señor. I thought, puesen, foreigners often do buy things."

Eventually I did buy them, on the theory that if a stopper of mine broke I would have some spare ones. In fact the stoppers never break but the bottles do.

It appeared that Mundo spent his time buying and selling oddments, and judging by his appearance he does well. He said he had been doing it for years, many years, and as he looked very young I asked him his age.

"Pues, who knows, señor?" he said. "Between twenty-five and thirty. My sister says I'm twenty-eight, but then how should she know? She's younger than I."

He had just left when Candelaria came ascamper, carrying the big covered can we use for milk.

"Look, señor, Chui has sent the milk!"

"What happened? Did the cow come back?"

"It appears that yes," said Candelaria, no longer interested in the milk question. After all, the cow might not go up the hill again for months.

"Whatever have you got in your pocket, Cayetano?" I asked.

Cayetano giggled. "A dog, señor."

"A dog?" There was a bulge in Cayetano's trouser pocket and I thought I had seen the bulge move, but it was a very small bulge.

88

He fished in his pocket and produced a tiny white pup that sat easily in the palm of his hand.

"Where did you get it?"

"A friend of mine bought it in Guadalajara and gave it to me. He bought it from one of those men who go round the streets with ten or twelve puppies in their arms selling them. He paid one-fifty for it."

By this time the puppy was in the palm of my hand. He was white, except for one dark brown ear and cheek, and a neat circle of black round a very small stubby tail. He had pointed ears disproportionately big for his size. He was shaking all over.

"He's very frightened still," said Cayetano, "so I take him everywhere with me. He doesn't give war."

"Of course he's frightened. He can hardly be two months old, Cayetano. Don't you think that to sit in the dark in your pocket is likely to frighten him? A puppy that age ought to give war, you know."

"Pues yes. But I didn't like to leave him alone. And he doesn't eat. I bought some meat specially, steak, but he didn't seem to like it."

I considered the pup, which just then licked my finger. He looked as if a very small terrier had paired with a large Chihuahueño and he was the result.

"Listen, Cayetano. Why don't you keep him here? Because, you see, he's too small for meat. He needs milk and a little soft bread and things like that. And when puppies are taken too young from their mothers, they often get nervous and remain nervous all their lives. You mustn't do anything to frighten them. You have to give them confidence."

"But of course," said Cayetano. "He's yours."

"No, I'm not asking for him. Just to keep him here and see that he's looked after properly."

So that was agreed, and while Cayetano went about his work, I coaxed the pup to eat some bread and milk, and after that it went to sleep inside my coat, with its head resting on the one button that was done up.

For a boy of his age, Cayetano was very well off indeed. He was earning a peso a day, living and eating in. Many an Indio in Ajijic pays house rent and keeps a family on a peso or a peso fifty a day. But he never had any money. He always wanted his wages in advance, and by the end of the week there was usually nothing left. In a way it was understandable, because he had never earned so well before, counting his free food, and because he was very pleased with himself, boasting to his friends and cutting a dash in the village. I heard he spent quite a lot of money on the jukebox at the cantina. But it seemed particularly stupid since he could do with some new clothes, such as trousers, for which there was, as things were, little chance of his ever having enough money to pay. So, to give him an incentive to save, I proposed a banking system to him.

"Look here, Cayetano, if you will try to save up your money, I will keep it for you, and I will give you interest at the rate of ten per cent a week up to ten pesos. What about it?"

This was too quick for Cayetano, and I had to explain things in detail and very slowly. When Cayetano finally grasped the idea, he obviously still had no notion of the enormous rate of interest he was being offered, but he was enchanted.

"Then tomorrow," he said, "which is the day you pay my wages, please don't give me the one peso sixty—isn't it?—that's left."

"All right. You'll get along without any money at all."

He hesitated.

"Pues, give me fifty centavos, señor, and keep the rest for the bank."

"Very well."

"Or perhaps it would be better to give me the sixty centavos so that a round peso is left."

So that was what we did. And in the first week Cayetano managed to save four more pesos. Almost every day he asked me, "How is the bank?"

Perhaps he thought it grew like a plant or an animal.

Aurora came for the washing, accompanied by her smallest child, a little girl of about seven. She was not very clean and she was dressed in pathetic rags. I found a few old clothes out of which Aurora could make her something to wear. Looking them over, Aurora decided to keep for her own use a checked tweed sports coat. She never altered it to fit her. She turned up the sleeves and fastened it at the breast with a big safety pin.

"Thank you, señor," she sighed. "Of course, I lost everything."

"When?"

"With the snake, the cloudburst," she said in a martyred moan.

Hers had been one of the houses flooded. It had not fallen, but the water had risen to a meter and a half inside and everything she possessed had been soaked and much of it spoiled. I thought it would be Aurora's house that was hit. She is that sort of person. Disaster crowds upon her and she sighs resignedly. But a note in her voice and the crooked smile on her potato-peel brown face persuade you that in a masochistic way she likes it all, and she certainly never wastes a chance to complain.

"That's too bad. And how's your back?"

"Pues, my back's been a little better. But last night I couldn't sleep because I suddenly had a terrible pain, just here." And she ran her hand over the whole of her body from shoulder to hip. "And then there's my leg."

"What's wrong with your leg?"

She pulled up her ragged cotton skirts and showed a calf bulged by a nasty varicose vein.

"And have you seen a doctor about it?"

"Pues, some time ago I was in Chapala, and I went to see the doctor, and he didn't think it could be operated, though my cousin Amparo was operated for the same thing and got quite well, but of course mine, the doctor said, can't be operated."

It seemed useless to tell her that she should rest and not stand about or kneel. Her work is to kneel at the water's edge on the beach and rub linen on a smooth stone and then to stand and iron it. I wondered if I could rearrange the work, and put Nieves onto washing while Aurora kept the house tidy. That might be less bad for her. I said nothing at the time, and when later I suggested this to Nieves she flatly refused to wash.

"Pues, what can we do pues?" said Aurora, with an agonized smile. "Allah grant that you are keeping well, señor. How good. May you go on keeping well. With permission, señor." And she smiled and limped herself away, sighing gently.

She is pathetic and unfortunate. And she is fulsome, servile, and insincere, none of which is probably her fault, for she has never had a chance to be an individual. She is pathetic, but she is also repugnant.

I was told there was a gentleman to talk to me. In the patio I found a man, small and timid-looking, dressed in a neat dark suit but without a tie. He told me his name, which at first meant nothing to me.

"It's about my land," he said. "You see, my family told me you were paying a peso a meter, and that made my share four hundred pesos, which they've sent me, but now I hear that you really paid one fifty, and so they should have sent me a lot more, they should have sent me six hundred pesos."

I realized that this must be Pedro who went to Tampico.

"But," I said, "it isn't anything to do with me, you know, if it's as you say. I've got all my papers in order, the ones you signed too. You take up the matter with your family."

I thought I saw a trace of tears in Pedro's eyes.

"But, señor, they have taken advantage of my absence, and now they just tell me to go away again. My own brother did. They have cheated me in a barbarous way."

"Well, if they have, that's very wrong of them. But what can I do? The whole thing's settled up, as far as I'm concerned."

"You wouldn't give me anything?" he said, shaking his head, expecting a negative.

"I'll tell you what I'll give you," I said. "I'll give you a drink and then you'll feel better and be able to tackle your family."

After one or two glasses of tequila, he became much more cheerful with me and much more aggressive toward his relations.

"Now they'll see," he said. "I expect they think I'll put up with anything, but that yes no, I don't put up with things. Thank you very much, señor. Now they're going to see."

He rose and stood very straight. He looked like a bantam rooster. At the entrance he turned.

"A gentleman I worked for in Tampico, a German señor, who was very authoritative, always said—he told me it was a proverb in his own language—'One must be hammer or anvil'! Yes, señor, and I will not be anvil."

He strode out, and I half expected to hear of violence in the village. In fact, I never heard another word about my visitor from Tampico.

For some reason I started calling Cayetano's very small dog Cuauhtemotzín. It is really a bad plan to give dogs names when they are very small. As they grow, they usually develop some characteristic or habit that gives rise to a name for them. And Cuauhtemotzín was obviously a very bad calling name. Tzín is a Nahuatl suffix denoting respect, so that Cuauhtemotzín is, more or less, the Great Lord Cuauhtemoc. Now Cuauhtemoc was the last of the Aztec rulers, nephew of Moctezuma, and the last to rally the Mexicans against the Spaniards before the final fall of Tenochtitlán. The Spaniards tortured him to death, asking foolish questions about hidden treasure. He is a Mexican hero. Dogs are of course superior to human beings, and in Anglo-Saxon countries where their superiority is recognized, if from confused motives, it is a compliment to Caesar to call a dog by his name. But in Catholic countries it is unsuitable to give a soulless dog a name used by human beings who have souls, and here it is unsuitable to call a dog by the name of an historical hero. It gives offense.

"Why don't you call him Palomita?" said Candelaria.

Now nothing could look less like a dove than this dog, even if he is small and white. But Palomita is a name often given to dogs and cats and I know an elderly very large white cow who comes home every day on her own from the lake to her owner's yard and positively answers to the call of "Palomita! Come on, Little Dove!"

To change the subject I asked Candelaria why we were using so many oranges. Sometimes she is very economical, and then all of a sudden she will throw the vegetables which should last a week into an excellent but extravagant soup.

"It is because they're only just ripening, so they're still green and they have very little juice. I'll put them into boiling water if you like."

She explained to me that if she did that they would be juicier. She did and they were, I have no idea why. But climate and latitude make strange changes. Here roses lack scent, and onion and garlic are also much weaker. Large onions, raw, are no stronger than a tender spring onion. Instead of a smear of garlic round the salad bowl, you can put in two or three cloves.

The dog had followed us into the kitchen to observe the experiment with the oranges, and was snuffling round Candelaria's feet.

"Go away, quit yourself, Moursi," said Candelaria, who handles names in her own way.

But that settled it, and the dog's name ended in a shortened form as Motzín, which seemed to offend nobody.

It was a village like any other. A long street of adobe houses, not many of them painted. In front of several doors, tables set with tomatoes and chilis and onions, or jugs of lemonade and slices of watermelon. Halfway down the street, a small plaza with ramshackle seats (each inscribed with the name of the donor, usually a commercial house), bedraggled jacaranda trees, a bandstand, and a white church. I inquired for Don Estanislao Pérez. After several misdirections, I was informed that he was at home certainly because it was his onomastic, his name day. A small boy guided me.

Some doors off I heard the noise. A four-piece brass band was screeching. On arrival, I found the entrance hall, the room, the veranda beyond it, and the yard beyond that crowded with people. Some were sitting and some standing, and all chattering. The children were the quietest there. They stood against the walls, upright, motionless, and demure. Out in the veranda the men were grouped round some tequila bottles.

I stood in the hall between half a dozen elderly seated ladies, all of whom politely said good afternoon to me and then equally politely refrained from staring or even looking at me. The small boy who had guided me plowed through the room and out onto the veranda and plucked the sleeve of a big burly man who was the center of the drinking group. In a little silence I heard him say, "They speak to you, Don Estanislao."

It is very difficult to get Mexicans to be more precise than that. "They speak to you," they say, or, bent on exactness, "A señor speaks to you," and the señor may be anybody at all.

Don Estanislao threw a glance in my direction and then, saying, "With permission" to his friends, approached me. He was weaving somewhat, but he looked bonhomous.

He invited me in, accepted my congratulations on his saint's day, led

94

me to the veranda, introduced me all round, and made me sit down on a chair which had been hurriedly vacated and brought up to the table. Then he offered me a drink.

I was doubtful as to how soon I could introduce business into this jolly social atmosphere, or whether it would be any good, considering the uplifted state of mind of my host. But at last, when there was a pause in the healths and backslappings, I said, "I'm afraid I've chosen a bad day to come to see you. But as a matter of fact, I saw some very nice equipales at the house of Don César Ramos of Ajijic and I was told that you manufactured them, so I came to order some. But then I'm sure it would be better if I came another—"

I was not allowed to finish. Don Estanislao was enchanted. He looked very grand, made a gesture that spilled his drink, and said, "Would you not like to see my factory?"

We all crossed the patio. Don Estanislao threw open a door on the far side, and a boy ran to open the heavy wooden shutter that closed the only window. The walls were unplastered adobe and the floor was earth. There were four or five finished or nearly finished equipales in the room, two or three benches, some smelly hides, and very little else. But I complimented Don Estanislao on his factory, and then we went back for another little drink.

"I should like to order six equipales," I said hopefully.

"Delighted, delighted," said Don Estanislao. "You won't be disappointed in them. Another little drink of tequila. I use the very best leather."

"That's fine. How much will they be?"

Don Estanislao frowned, glanced at me, frowned at the table, produced a stub of pencil and made some very uncertain and wavering marks on the oilcloth tablecover, and then, focusing with difficulty, said, "Nine pesos each."

"I'm sure they're worth it," I said. "But César Ramos told me you made them for six pesos."

"Everything has gone up so much, señor. Everything. Pues, eggs are ten centavos, what a barbarity! And as for leather—"

"But still, you know," I went on, "I came here because they told me it was the only place I could get really well-made equipales that weren't at the prices of the shops in Guadalajara, that weren't at gringo prices."

Don Estanislao considered, and somebody filled his glass. Then he smiled broadly, and his ruddy beard-blue face curved into deep folds. "As you are a friend of Don César's, señor, I'll make them for seven pesos fifty."

"Seven, and I pay the freight," I said, wondering if I had gone too far.

"It's good," he said. "Salud, señor," and he drained his little glass. It was at least the twelfth little glass since my arrival, and one's saint's day begins at dawn.

"And when can I have them?" I asked.

"In four weeks' time? The end of the month that enters? Would that be good? As you have seen, my factory has much work just now."

"And you'll send them to Ajijac?"

"Yes, how not, how not. Another little glass for the señor, Anita."

And before I could say no, a woman had refilled my little glass.

Business concluded, everyone was ready to go on celebrating, and I wondered whether I should ever get away without discourtesy. Visions of an all-day session appeared to me. But then in Mexico all difficulties have sudden and unexpected solutions, and the original small boy who had guided me appeared and said that perhaps I had better be going, because he thought it was going to rain and the road was very bad.

Half the company at least saw me to the door, the elderly ladies who were still sitting in the hall all said good afternoon, everyone shook my hand and crowded round the car and wished me good journey, but before we had gone fifty yards the street was empty and from Don Estanislao's house came the sounds of the four-piece band, now most drunkenly out of tune, blaring out "Jalisco no te rajes."

Suddenly one morning Cayetano, instead of Nieves, brought my breakfast. There was a knock more determined than that of Nieves, who merely taps. The double doors were thrown open and there stood Cayetano with a hand on either wing. He bowed, and wished me good morning. Then he advanced to the bed and extended his hand. I extended mine. And he took it and kissed it.

In the old days, Indios kissed the hands of the priests and of their patrón, the patrón being their permanent as distinct from a casual employer. I suppose Cayetano now views me in this light, and, Ajijic being behind the times (for you won't get your hand kissed by servants in Mexican cities), was behaving accordingly. I was considerably startled the first time this happened. But Cayetano was plainly determined to perform the ritual, and I have gotten used to having my hand kissed every morning, as well as on special occasions.

After the hand kissing, Cayetano goes out and returns with the bed table, which he adjusts over my knees, and then goes out again for the breakfast tray. Having put the tray on the table, he tests the table's equilibrium. I think he must have seen this on the movies, for bed tables are not usual adjuncts of village life. And then he stands back, surveys the arrangement with a swift searching glance, and asks me if anything lacks. All the fancy details of this procedure Cayetano has thought up for himself. I'm afraid he has a flunky's disposition. And he also thought up for himself the thing he does first of all when he comes to my room.

The house is an old house, and has suffered many changes. The doors have had their locks and handles changed a number of times. The doors of my room once had a vast lock, opened no doubt by one of the vast keys which are still used in Mexico. But the lock has gone long since, and in its place there is a hole three or four inches in diameter. One day I happened to remark to Aurora that my breakfast always arrived just when I wanted it.

"It's that Cayetano," she said. "He always throws a look through the keyhole to see if you're awake. Of course I did tell him perhaps you wouldn't like it, but what can we do pues?"

Some mornings later, however, I heard the timid tap of Nieves, and got my tray without the Cayetanan ceremonial. I asked where he was.

"He's helping Candelaria," she said. "Just think, a little chicken has broken its leg."

I went out to investigate and heard Candelaria saying, "There's none here, but that Venustiano has some, go you and ask him."

I saw a small chicken propped up on a dishrag in the sink and looking very forlorn. Candelaria was scampering about all over the room, chattering in an undertone to the chick.

"Ay, señor, the poor little one!" she said, when she saw me. "He's broken his leg. I found him this morning, caught in the wire. Such a strong little bird too. That old white hen always makes strong chicks."

Cayetano came in carrying a root, and Candelaria, picking up an earthenware bowl, rushed across the room to meet him. Cayetano had brought a round stone and together they began to crush the root, Candelaria holding the bowl while Cayetano ground the stone. It was a whitish root, something like a potato, but, as they pounded, the color changed to pale rose and it dissolved into a gelatinous mush.

"What is that?" I asked.

"Zacasil, señor," said Cayetano. "You know the creeper on Venustiano's wall? Pues, it's the root of that."

"What are you going to do with it?"

"It's for the chick, señor," said Candelaria authoritatively. "To mend its leg, the poor little one." She turned to Cayetano. "Fetch the oil from over there. You know what happens if there's no oil."

"You forgot it yourself once. You told me, don't you remember?" said Cayetano.

"The oil. Go you, hurry you," said Candelaria. "And don't forget we have to be early in the morning to kill the little pig because the señor's friends are coming. Yes, señor, if you forget the oil, then the zacasil sticks to the leg, and if it's still there when you eat him he's tough. Don't you remember that so very tough chicken we had, pues he was hatched from the brown hen's eggs and she usually puts very tender ones so I always thought he must have broken his leg and had zacasil on it."

Cayetano smeared the oil—the best cooking oil—on the broken leg. Then he and Candelaria plastered the zacasil on thickly with the back of a kitchen spoon and then Cayetano blew on it and Candelaria bound it lightly with a shred of banana leaf.

"When it dries it keeps the leg stiff," said Cayetano. "But it must be dry."

The chick was beginning to peck at the banana leaf and Candelaria held its beak in her hand. Already the zacasil was beginning to set like plaster of Paris.

"I shall have to watch him," said Candelaria. "He can stay in this old box in the corner and within a little he will be running about like the others, the poor little one. And you, Cayetano, go and kill one of his little brothers for the señor's supper and be sure you pick a little cockerel."

Cayetano went off, quite unsurprised. I, amazed, said to Candelaria, "But why in the world do you kill a healthy chick and try to cure this one?"

Candelaria gave me a look of horror. "Ay, señor! With a broken leg? Break himself the leg and be killed, all the same day? Ay, no, my poor little one!"

The next morning, very early, I was awakened by strident squealing. I went into the patio. That was where they were killing the pig. The paving streamed with blood. It didn't seem strange to anybody but myself to kill the pig there, and plainly only I felt queasy. Perhaps it was I who was not realistic about it. There was the pig, they were going to kill and eat it, and why not do both of these things conveniently near the kitchen? Here, blood is no shocking thing. Less than five hundred years ago, the sanctuaries of the gods of Mexico were never cleansed of human blood, the priests of those gods went with blood-stiffened garments and blood-matted hair. Why should the Indios of today mind a pool of pig's blood in the house?

"But when we kill a little kid, señor," said Candelaria brightly, as she wiped a blood splash off a plate, "I will serve him with a rich sauce of his own blood."

NOVEMBER

THE month came in with a high wind from the east and a sudden squall of rain—the last, I hope. The squall came swirling across the lake and the waves rose high. They were really noisy as they broke on the shore. Even the heavy native canoes can be damaged on this rocky beach, and light boats smashed to flitters. Some boys were bathing, jumping the maned waves.

If you are hardy you can bathe in Ajijic practically the whole year round. The Indios do. The young men used always to bathe in their white cotton drawers, which are cut nearly knee-length, and wrapped over at the waist, being secured by tapes that tie round the middle. On the outer beaches they bathe naked. Sometimes they ride their horses in to the water, romping and trying to shove each other off. The horses, rearing and plunging, make a picturesque scene, and I have seen a bay carrying a bay-colored young man, so that you could see a centaur and think yourself in Greece and not in Mexico.

But some time ago Javier, the village's most elegant youth, appeared in a pair of bathing trunks, and since then Joaquín of the post office has acquired a pair too. Progress is setting in. So I have given an old pair of mine to Cayetano, who would now, I feel sure, lose prestige if he didn't follow the new fashion.

The little storm wore itself out with the morning, and by noon the wind had dropped and the sun was shining on the remaining white horses that rode a yellow-green lake.

On November 2, the Day of the Dead, here, as everywhere in Mexico, the living go to the cemetery and leave flowers, as well as candles which are lit in the evening. The Ajijic cemetery is a very dismal place. So often in Catholic countries the cemetery contains the best buildings in the village. When, at one time, I was considering settling in Corsica, I thought it would be best to ask any local architect to design me a very roomy tomb with plumbing, so magnificent are the houses of the dead and so mean those of the living in that charming island. But in Ajijic a roughly walled enclosure holds unevenly arranged mounds and one or two broken-down monuments and that is all.

For a long time Ajijic had no resident priest. Every second or third Sunday a priest from Chapala came over and said Mass. But several years ago a permanent cura was appointed. Beside and around the church are various buildings, remaining from a time when Ajijic and the church were more important, and the cura has plenty of room in his house.

I had seen the priest often since my arrival in Ajijic. Every morning and every afternoon he walked up and down a certain stretch of the beach. He could not wear any religious garb, since this was forbidden to all sects in Mexico. He wore the black suit and soft black hat of the theological student. But had he worn dungarees or a grass skirt you would have known him for a priest. He had the look. He lived in the priest's house with a sister and the sister's daughter. The village said that he was very learned, that he had studied in Rome, and that he spent three hours every day at table. He was afraid of air in motion, and he always wore around his neck a woolen scarf which he held to windward of his face.

I said good-morning to him and he asked if I had any news of Europe. I wanted to talk about Ajijic. The priest is the one person who can enter every house. The priest is the person who above all has the opportunity to teach the people a little elementary hygiene. I knew a village priest at Mazamitla up in the high forests who had taught his flock many things, how to graft fruit trees and how to use better methods of extracting turpentine from their pine trees, which is the principal industry up there.

The Ajijic priest did not think his people were good people.

"Until a man can command in his own house, how can he do anything else?" he asked. "How can he be worthy to vote, to govern himself, if he cannot control his own family? Why, last Sunday I preached on Rerum Novarum to the village, but I doubt if they knew what I meant."

I doubted it too. But the priest went on talking about Leo XIII and his encyclical. When he paused I asked him something about Quadragesimo Anno. But he was not interested in this later encyclical, designed to bring Rerum Novarum up to date. He continued to talk about Leo XIII, a conversation which I sidetracked by saying something about my land.

"Ah," he said, "a nice piece of land. In a few years it will be worth all of sixteen thousand pesos. The other day I sold a little place of mine, outside Guadalajara, for eight thousand pesos, and four years ago I paid only five thousand for it."

I remembered how it was said in the village that from the pulpit the priest had announced that it was proper that the village priest should receive for his own consumption all produce of the village free, gratis, and for nothing.

"It is a pity that the people here do not know how to extract the best from their properties," I said, trying again.

But the priest looked at his watch.

"Excuse me," he said. "It is almost time for dinner. Much pleasure, señor. With permission. Adiós."

He walked down the beach, holding the woolen scarf to his face. There went the medieval church, dark and portly, full of titles and riches, bound for the refectory. I thought of the priest at Mazamitla working with his villagers among the pine trees, making them seal a tree before they had quite exhausted it of turpentine and spoiled it, going round their little gardens and binding a graft neatly onto their apple trees. He was a youngish man, not more than thirty-five. I don't know if he had ever been in Rome, but he never mentioned an encyclical. He didn't ask for news of Europe. He asked if I thought Northern Spies would do in the cold uplands of Mazamitla.

"Elpidia, who lives over there," said Candelaria, with the accustomed vague gesture of an Ajijiquense giving a direction, "has a nice guajolote to sell."

In Castilian a turkey is called a pavo, and the world is commonly used in Mexico. But the Mexicans have too the Amerindian word guajolote, which fairly gobbles at you.

So I went to look at Elpidia's guajolote, and it turned out that she was the toothless owner of the handsome white turkey cock which I had seen when first looking for Venustiano. Elpidia asked me to come in and see the turkeys she had for sale.

In a corner of the veranda was sitting Elpidia's boy, Silvanito. He was about twelve. For years he had been helping in the fields, but only now was he learning to read and write. He had an old-fashioned copy-book and was practicing pothooks. He sat hunched up, with his sombrero on, and his tongue working agitatedly out of the corner of his mouth.

We went to look at the birds. Turkeys are hard to rear anywhere, but here, where poultry have no shelter, they are still harder. Elpidia had two turkeys besides the white cock, all that had survived the rains, when all Ajijic poultry acquire all manner of diseases. They weren't attractive birds. But perhaps it would be possible to fatten them up a little in time for Thanksgiving. She wanted eight pesos for one and nine for the other.

"Look, señor, it is much bigger, much taller."

It was taller, it had longer legs. But it didn't look any bigger. I was going to bargain, and then I remembered the room we had passed through to get to the yard where the birds were. The room had three beds in it, and only one of them had any covers. The other two were bare bamboo slats, and the sleeper had to wrap himself in his sarape. Otherwise the room contained nothing but one chair. Outside, at the back, above a brick stove, hung Elpidia's meager collection of household pots. So I bought one turkey, the taller, at the price she asked, and said I would send Cayetano for it later.

On the way back I looked at Silvanito's copybook.

"How are you getting on?"

Silvanito took a deep noisy breath, tilted his hat, pushed the book toward me, and said with pride, "Look, I've done ten furrows."

"Get up, Silvanito, get up and take off your hat, oh, what a boy," said his mother.

But I told him to go on with his work, I was just going anyway.

And Silvanito, who has never heard of lines that weren't made in a field, went back to do another furrow.

An old Indio, to whom I had given some liniment for his rheumatics, brought me two squirrels, shot on his land.

"But it's most good, very rich," said Candelaria. "I will cook it, and you will see how little tender it is, like frog."

There are quantities of gray squirrels in the country round. They are the enemies of the Indio cultivator, who is probably too poor to own a gun. Every patch of land between hill and lake is used, all the way along the shore there is no break in the cultivation. Most Indio families own a plot of ground, but it is often a long way from home, and the unguarded fields lie at the mercy of the marauding squirrels.

From the tenderest age, all Indios are accustomed to agricultural work, and very hard agricultural work it is, if only because of the immense labor involved in irrigating. Sometimes this is done in the most primitive way by bringing water from the lake, hundreds of journeys for a man with two buckets, or gasoline cans, swung from his shoulder yoke. Sometimes, a little way out in the lake, is built a platform, whence a trough leads inland, slanting downward, and peons pour can after can of lake water down the trough. But this is inconvenient, owing to the sharp seasonal changes in the lake level, and mostly there are wells, for usually you do not have to dig deep to find water. Then perhaps a platform is built at the wellhead, and the long wooden troughs gurgle with water all day long as peons haul the heavy cans. A more usual method is to have a high post beside the well, and, bound to it, a crossbeam, to one end of which is tied a big rock, while the bucket, or can, swings from the other. Thus the weight of the rock helps raise the water. The somersault, as this cantilever is called, saves a lot of work. But already the Indio is discontented with it.

"What I want," said the old man of the squirrels, who looks centuries behind the machine age, "what I want is a small little motor."

I have often asked the Indios about the films when the ambulant cinema comes to the village for an evening. But their answers are vague. "It was all about horses, with many shots," they say. Or else, "It was nice, very nice, I'm not quite sure what happened, but the girls wore lovely dresses." Films spoken in Spanish naturally please them most, but they are uncertain about the plots of these too. Perhaps it doesn't really matter whether a film is about anything or not. Today I asked Cayetano about last night's film.

"It was beautiful," he said. "All the people were beautifully dressed and lived in beautiful houses. And do you know, señor, they had a cocktail shaker just like ours."

It is only a few weeks since Cayetano learned what a cocktail shaker was, or began to learn how to use one. But now, with that statement, he put a seal of approval on the film. I gathered the plot had been concerned with love affairs among the idle rich. For Cayetano, they were all right, because they had a cocktail shaker just like ours.

I asked Nieves what the film was called. She looked anxiously at Candelaria. They consulted, but neither knew. That evening they both wanted to go to the cinema again.

"Are they giving a different film?" I asked.

"Oh, no," said Nieves.

Today the turkey vanished. Candelaria came in while I was having breakfast and said, "The turkey has gone up the mountain. That Cayetano can't have shut the door of the hen run properly."

"But," I said, "Cayetano didn't do it last night. He had the afternoon off."

"Then it was that girl," hissed Candelaria. "She forgets things."

"But Candelaria," said Nieves, who was sweeping the patio outside the door, speaking clearly and without anger, "you said you would feed the chickens yourself, because of the white one that's sick."

Candelaria was dumbfounded for a moment. Then, unabashed, she said, "It flew. It flew over the wire. I always said Elpidia hadn't clipped its wings properly, and I always said Cayetano hadn't put the wire high enough, and that was what I always said to you, señor."

And having put us all in the wrong, she scampered back to the kitchen. Happily a diversion was almost immediately caused because someone was asking for me. Candelaria came back and told me there was a señora who wished to speak to me.

At the door was a woman in black with a veil of black chiffon on her head.

"It's Magdalena," said Candelaria. "You know, the daughter of my comadre, Germana. The baby of her sister died."

I hardly recognized Magdalena, whom I used to see in a very faded dress of patched lilac mirror satin.

"I was wondering, señor, whether you have any films in your camera?"

"Yes," I answered. "I have."

"Because, you see, last night my sister's little boy, Gabrielito, died—"

"I was sorry to hear it," I interrupted. "Please give your sister my condolences."

"Many thanks, señor," said Magdalena, smiling quite cheerfully. "If you have a film would you be kind enough to photograph him?"

As I did not at once reply, she went on: "He looks so pretty in his little coffin with flowers and candles."

I agreed to photograph Gabrielito, and, when I had fetched my camera, went with Magdalena to her sister's house. There were a number of mourners about, and Gabrielito's brothers and sisters were playing fairly quietly in the yard.

I was led into a room which was lit by one window in the far corner and by two candles. On a table lay a small white coffin, banked round with white roses and four unlit candles. The baby, in a white dress, was very small and wizened.

"But I don't think it will come out very well in here," I said. "There's practically no light at all. Isn't there another window?"

But there wasn't. At first, everybody seemed to think I was making some deliberate and unnecessary difficulty. But finally I managed to convince them that photography needs light. So the whole table was carried out into the yard for me to photograph it. The bearers crossed themselves as they picked the table up and as they set it down, and the mother, who had been quite silent, wept loudly throughout the photographing. I took three or four shots.

"When will it be ready?" asked the father. "Tomorrow?"

I explained that the negative would have to be developed and printed in Guadalajara and that that might take a couple of weeks altogether.

"And how much is it?" asked the father.

When I said it was nothing, he protested, and when I overruled his protests, thanked me profusely. It did take about two weeks for the prints to come. The morning after I had sent them round Magdalena's sister brought me a bunch of flowers and a basketful of lemons. They were poor people, but they had a lemon tree.

"Have you been drinking, Cayetano?"

"Oh, no, señor, nothing."

"Nothing all day?"

"Nothing nothing."

Pause.

"But there was a wedding."

"I see."

"Somebody brought some beer." Cayetano coughed. "Then somebody found a carton of beer."

He sat down abruptly on the edge of a chair.

"But if I could have four pesos, señor, or even three-fifty, then I wouldn't have to sell my pig. You see, it is only a little pig and if I keep it till the fiesta of Guadalupe I can get more for it. I could sell it for twenty pesos now but it would be better to keep it. But if I had four pesos or three-fifty I could go to Chapala and buy a new shirt and a new belt and I shouldn't have to sell my pig. Look at my belt, señor." And he whirled the loose end of his belt to show me how frayed it was. "So you see with four pesos I could go to Chapala, and with a new shirt and a new belt I should be able to go to the plaza for the fiesta, otherwise I would have to sell my pig. I can pay you back from my wages and anyway if I keep the pig maybe I'll get thirty pesos for him next month and it won't cost much more to feed him so I shall easily be able to pay you back and then we'd stay planks, we'd be all square."

Cayetano got up and sat down again quickly.

But I did not give him any money that night.

"Come and see me tomorrow morning, Cayetano," I said. "I'll think it over and we'll talk about it then."

And in the morning the attention of everyone was diverted, for the turkey had returned.

"Do you mean somebody found it?" I asked when Cayetano told me.

"No. It came back," he said.

And that appeared to be the fact. The turkey had just returned on its own. When Cayetano arrived, it was standing outside the hen run, and when he opened the door, it walked in. An imprudent bird to return in time for Thanksgiving.

Señor González de la Comarca wrote me saying business was bringing him down to the lake, and he would like to call on me. I answered, inviting him to lunch.

On the appointed day he came from Chapala by launch, not wishing to risk his automobile over the Ajijic road. Typically, he came in one of the largest launches, which are ordinarily used for big parties plus musicians. He had with him two mozos, who worked for him in Chapala. With Mexicans and Spaniards whom I do not know well, I am always prepared for extra guests. It is not unusual to bring them. But the chauffeur, if there is one, or the nurses, if there are children, will buckle to in the kitchen, helping wherever they are needed. Señor González de la Comarca had brought nobody. The mozos carried ashore some fruit and some fresh prawns which he had brought me. They also carried ashore a bottle. I could not help noticing the surprise that crossed the old gentleman's face for an instant when, inside the mirador, Cayetano offered him a Martini. I supposed the bottle contained refreshment in case there was none, and I rather think he expected that we would lunch off turkey mole, tortillas, and beans. But Candelaria had done better than that, and Cayetano, very scrubbed and in his white coat, remembered everything.

My guest complimented me on the way I had arranged things. I said that I had found the Indios very quick at learning.

"Oh, some of them are not stupid," he said. "But they are no good at all. It is a pity the Spaniards, when they came, didn't kill the lot. No good Indio but a dead Indio, you know."

I was glad that, following his lead, we were speaking French, for I have heard Mexicans of his persuasion talking like that in Spanish, and I should not have liked Cayetano's feelings to be hurt.

"Yes, you are pleased with them," he went on. "And I will tell you, that you can enjoy this country so long as you do not engage in business in it. Otherwise—" He shrugged, a Spanish shrug that had lived

108

in Paris. "The government is a government of bandits. All the Indios are treacherous. Do not trust them. They are all alike."

"Don't you think it's usually the mestizos who are untrustworthy?" I asked, rather to get him off the Indios than because I think there is any need for a halfbreed to be untrustworthy.

"One is as bad as the other," he said. "They say there are only ten per cent whites in Mexico, and of the remaining ninety per cent half are Indios and half are crossbred. So that makes just eighteen million things wrong with the country. Just eighteen million things." This remark is traditional among Mexican reactionaries, and not a few gringo reactionaries too, but he made it as if it were a new idea of his own. He chuckled delicately, and his fine hand caressed his wine glass. I use only the glass of Guadalajara which is rough and thick, and, being all hand-blown, does not come in even sizes or shapes. It is made in turquoise blue, royal blue, deep red-purple that is almost black, amber, and a washy green. Of these, the turquoise is far the loveliest and the most unusual, for there is little turquoise-blue glass made in the world. At the factory it is cheap, and my glasses cost thirty centavos each, the wine glasses forty. All the glass in the house, in bedrooms or dining room, is of this sort. They have told me at the factory that 80 per cent of what they make is exported. It is not much appreciated by Mexicans, who would usually sooner have a nice smooth machine-made glass imported from the United States, and much dearer. I have had Mexicans exclaim over one or two of the finer pieces I have, and quite unwilling to believe that they were local products. I wondered what my guest would think of it, made as it is by Indios, who are usually and very properly allowed an artist's license in choosing the forms they will make.

"I had much of this glass in Paris," he said, surprisingly. "It is beautiful, and you are right to use it. It was a great success there. Everybody was crazy about it—tout le monde s'en raffolait. Yes, there are beautiful things in Mexico."

And for the moment it seemed to me that he was a Mexican at heart and that perhaps it would be possible to unite and combine all the clashing classes in this heterogeneous country. But then he said:

"You should have known it in the old days. Before the revolutions, under Don Porfirio. Then the Indios got off the sidewalk for a white man. Do you know that big furniture shop in Guadalajara, on the corner of the square? That was our house. Long before the railroad, of course. The station spoiled all the neighborhood. We used to set out from there for a hacienda we had down toward Tepic. In seven carriages with six horses each. The journey took us some days, but we stopped on the way at the haciendas of various relatives. Then—"

He went on, but I am afraid my attention wandered. Life was very comfortable for the rich when nobody, not even the victims, questioned the rightness of putting three footmen to sleep in a cupboard under the stairs, and for us who can remember those days they have a nostalgic charm, but one has been wearied by the nostalgia of the dispossessed classes of half a dozen countries.

We were still sitting over coffee when Cayetano came and stood silently near us, in the way he does when he wants something, but doesn't want to interrupt.

"Well, Cayetano?"

"I wondered whether it would disturb you very much to tell me how much I have in the bank?"

"I think it is about twelve pesos, Cayetano. Why?"

"Because, you see, there's a man selling shoes, very good shoes, and I need some and I thought perhaps it would be good to buy some and they are seven pesos."

I told Cayetano to bring me a pair to look at, for huarache-wearing Indios do not know much about shoes, and are likely to judge them by brilliance.

He came back, surprisingly, with an unshowy pair that was, for the money, reasonably sound. So I approved his purchase and gave him the money.

When he had gone Señor González de la Comarca asked what Cayetano's bank was, so I explained the system that I had started in order to persuade him to save money, and which had been operating for only a month.

The old gentleman laughed. "Ah, you are a sentimental foreigner. You will see, it won't work. Or rather, it will begin to work, and then it won't work any more. He'll never have more than fifteen pesos in the bank, and that not often."

"Will you bet me that he'll not save up more than fifteen pesos at a time? I'll not urge him. In, say, six months from today?"

Señor Gonzáles de la Comarca accepted. He agreed, if in six months Cayetano had saved up fifteen pesos or more, to pay me twenty pesos and five more for Cayetano's bank. And on that he took his departure. We went down the huerta to the beach. His launchman wasn't in sight, and his mozos were asleep under a tree. He woke them, and sent them to find the launchman.

"You see," he said. "Lazy good-for-nothings, all of them."

But I really didn't see why they shouldn't have been having a nap.

Eliot and his wife came for Thanksgiving. Eliot is large and efficient and busy and he likes everything and everybody. Verna is very small and looks as though she were cut all in one piece. She is very smart in a mass-produced way and she is never in doubt about anything.

They have been in Mexico for about three months and have visited half a dozen places, and Eliot knows all about everything. He can reel off a lot of statistics, he knows what's wrong with everything and how it could be put right, and he can't understand a word of Spanish. He is in fact almost perfectly fitted to write a book on Mexico, and I daresay he will.

He is all for being a good neighbor, but if neighbors of mine talked and behaved in my house the way he and Verna do in Mexico, I'd throw them out.

"Isn't it crazy," said Verna. "Someone told me Mexicans are offended if Americans walk about Mexico City in slacks and sandals."

"They are, but Americans still do," I said. "After all, it's the Mexicans' city and they can fix the code of behavior. Did you walk about in slacks and sandals?"

"Sure she did," said Eliot.

"Don't think I don't like Mexico," said Verna, "I simply adore it."

"But Mexicans," went on Eliot, "have got to get a bit more up to date. Streamlined."

I was glad my other guests hadn't arrived, for I had invited to meet Eliot and Verna a young English-speaking Mexican couple, of whom the man is intelligent and educated and the woman smart and attractive and also, unlike most young Mexican women, uses her eyes to read with and can talk about something besides husband, child, and servant while having all three. They have a little house in Ajijic to which they come whenever they can. I thought Eliot might learn something about Mexico from Arturo and Xochitl, but it soon became apparent that he didn't want to hear about Mexico, he wanted to tell people about it. He did.

Verna didn't listen much. Her bright blue eyes snapped about the patio, not missing anything.

"Do they put on that shawl thing every time they go out even if it's only a few yards?" she asked.

The Indio woman hardly ever goes out without her shawl. It is her hat, her coat, her baby sling, her towel, and heaven knows what besides.

"Isn't that crazy!" said Verna.

"It's their custom," said Xochitl.

"Yes," Eliot was booming at Arturo. "Wonderful country, swell people, great possibilities, and everything so mismanaged. I wouldn't mind starting something down here myself if they'd clean up the labor conditions. They'll have to, of course. And they'll have to hurry. Naturally, we'll help every way we can to develop the country. After all, we live next door. Have to be friends."

"Perhaps it is that we don't understand each other very well," said Arturo, who has very polished manners and for whom this remark was tantamount to a snub.

Eliot sailed on.

"That's just it," he said. "You come to the States now. You come and stay with us. Delighted to have you—"

"Thank you very much. Very kind," said Xochitl and Arturo together.

"We'll show you everything. You'll see how we do things. Why, there are still some Mexicans who resent us having California and Texas. I always say, they'd only have to see them to know they'd never be the fine places they are if they'd stayed Mexican. Mind you, Americans have been all wrong about Latin America. But now that we've woken up to what the Americas mean, why, we're only too willing to help. In the modern way. No imperialism, just co-operation. And Mexico has an immense advantage in being the Latin American country nearest to the United States."

He beamed panamericanly.

"Yes," said Xochitl. "I've often thought that is a great advantage. The United States is compelled to defend Mexico whether it wants to or not."

There was a startled silence, broken by Arturo asking Eliot how he liked Ajijic and by Verna commenting brightly, as she watched Cayetano swishing the trapeador, "You do need a vacuum, don't you? I'd like to go all over Mexico with a vacuum cleaner, disinfectant, and a can of paint."

In answer to Arturo, Eliot had got Ajijic taped. He told us what it was like now and blueprinted what it could be made like, and just how the lives of the villagers would be altered. "Everything'd be different for them," he ended.

"And do you think we should like it?" asked Xochitl.

"You?" said Eliot, looking at her from the tip of her shoes to the tip of her hair. "I don't mean you. I mean these people here." He waved a lavish hand over Ajijic and its Indios.

Xochitl considered him for a moment. Then:

"We are all Mexicans," said the compatriot of Señor González de la Comarca.

I'm sure Eliot had no idea he had been at all tactless. When he was leaving he again invited Arturo and Xochitl to stay with him in the United States, and said, "You've a lovely country, a grand country. I wouldn't mind living here myself when it's modernized a bit. I feel at home here."

On November 21 begins the annual festival of Ajijic, the Saint Andrew. Andrew is the patron saint of the village, whose full name is San Andrés Ajijic. It lasts for nine days, ending on the greatest day of all, November 30, the day of Saint Andrew himself.

I first became aware of it a week before. On the day when Doña Porfiria made her weekly visit Nieves came to me, and said very shyly, "Señor—"

Then she relapsed into silence, her eyes on the floor.

"Well, Nieves, what do you want?"

At last she found courage.

"You see, señor, I'm getting a new dress for the Saint Andrew.

Wouldn't it be good if I paid Doña Porfiria four pesos now and then went on paying her a peso a week until I've paid for the stuff?"

I said I thought it would be good. Nieves turned on her best smile.

"Then, señor, perhaps you lend me the four pesos?"

That was the beginning. Two days later Cayetano wanted five pesos and permission to go to Chapala. Chui, who sells us milk, wanted three pesos, to be paid off in milk. All over the village this was going on, and anyone with an employee became a loan agency. The less provident endeavor in the last days before the fiesta to sell chickens, turkeys, all kinds of produce. Old and young alike are infected with the craze. One old woman went round the village trying to find a purchaser for a remarkable model T sewing machine. And all day there was a chatter of clients at the dressmakers'. They themselves had been talking for about six weeks of what a lot of work they had on hand for the fiesta, and about fifteen days before it they actually began to do the work, bent over their machines, stitching miles of brilliantly colored mirror satin. Then the secretary of the comisaría came round with a book in which he wrote the names of subscribers and the sums they had contributed for the fiesta. The money raised was to be spent for the music and the fireworks. Groups of girls undertook the decorations, cutting out miles of crepe paper for wreaths and garlands.

Before dawn on November 21 the first firecrackers went off, followed shortly by the band playing the mañanitas. The music went on until about eight, when it was too late to sleep again, and then stopped. But all day long, with short intervals, it played. And that went on for the whole week. Every morning firecrackers woke me before it was light. And very little work was done by anybody.

On the third day of the fiesta Cayetano came to ask me whether he might leave a little earlier.

"Because Primitivo has come, señor."

I had heard of his friend Primitivo because Cayetano had once asked me to write a letter to him in Guadalajara. They were old friends. Cayetano described him as "my twin," which means my buddy. When your first cousin is your cousin-brother, naturally your best friend is your twin.

"He's going to stay here. I knew he'd do like that at the finish and the end."

114

"Has he been away long?" I asked.

"Nearly a year, señor. He went away when he lost his land. It was the fault of that girl of his. He mortgaged his land, then he spent the money on her and when it was all gone she gave him squashes, she broke with him and he was very sad and went away."

"Where did he go?"

"To Guadalajara to become a mariachi. He was silly because he could sing very well and they offered him a job with the radio. They even offered to train him for a whole year and pay him all the time and they were going to write it down on paper and make it as the law says but he just said that he didn't like the city and now he's come back to Ajijic."

This seemed singularly improvident of Primitivo, for mariachis in Guadalajara can earn well, and a radio career was more than most village boys could hope for. The mariachis, who originated in Guadalajara and Chapala, are said to derive their curious name from the fact that the French, early foreign residents of the region, always had music for their weddings, so that the sound of guitars and songs suggested to everyone the French word mariage. Primitivo might have made a new life for himself, but the Indios, if they do not find a place or a job congenial, just move on somewhere else, and probably to a quite different kind of work.

"What's he going to do now?" I asked.

"He's going to work as a fisherman. I'm going to take him along now to see the señor owner of the seine net with whom he wants to work."

It seemed likely that the señor in question would be found up at the plaza, where, as every night this week, the band was playing and rockets were roaring, and no doubt it would be pleasant to discuss business in these surroundings. I gave Cayetano a peso.

"I expect you and Primitivo would like to have a drink together to celebrate his return."

A couple of days later I let Nieves leave early in order to attend the fiesta and gave her some money to spend. On her way she called in at the house, ostensibly to fetch something she had forgotten, but I think really to show off her dress of green mirror satin, shade of A in alt. Against the shrieking color her skin had the glow of cloudy amber.

She brought me a big bunch of flowers, among which was a superb lily. On a thick long stalk were four great flowers and a bud, creamy white with red veinings, of a sort I had never seen before. I asked her what it was called.

"Pues, it's a lily," she said.

"But those flowers that come floating down the lake, and that are really hyacinths, you call lily too," I answered.

"Maybe, pos," she said. "Ducks like to eat the lilies that comes down the lake. You should tell Cayetano to collect them for the ducklings. You see that obelisk?" She pointed to a deep rose hibiscus. "If you like it, I can bring you an elbow. They strike very easily."

The hibiscus is coming out now, the red single and the red double, and many shades of pink, pale and deep. I am collecting all the shades I can find, and the particular tint of the one that Nieves had brought I had not yet got. Of course, the grapevine has carried the news about, and often total strangers, a dirty small boy or a shiver of shy small girls, arrive with cuttings to sell. Not long after Nieves had left, an old woman, very bent and wrinkled, dragged slowly into the patio. She stopped at the mouth of the zaguán and peered around her. Motzín barked like a pack, she poked at him with her stick, and the more she poked the more he barked. I called him off and asked her what she wanted. She mumbled toothlessly so that I could not understand till she repeated what she was saying several times.

"You buy flowers?" she asked.

"Yes. Sometimes. Have you some to sell?"

"They told me you did. They told me you wanted obelisks. I haven't any obelisks." She stopped and swung her watery gaze round the patio. "So I bring this."

From beneath her faded wrapped shawl she produced a small tin that was so rusty that large parts of it had been corroded away entirely. In the tin was a small weary-looking begonia with a few white flowers. I must have looked disappointed, for she said, shaking her head sadly, "You don't want to buy it? But I haven't any obelisks. Pues, I would give it you very cheap."

The huaraches were almost dropping off her feet. Suddenly she saw the vase holding the flowers Nieves had brought, with the large flaunting lily.

116

"And do you like that lily? I know where there are some plants of that."

"Do you? Then if you can bring me that lily, I'll certainly buy it. And I'll give you fifty centavos for the begonia."

We made the deal and she thanked me profusely.

"And I'll bring the lily one day of these," she said, as she hobbled out of the zaguán. "I'm sorry I haven't any obelisks."

I was just going down to the beach when I heard the sound of an approaching launch. I changed my mind. It is all very well to be at the end of an agreeable boat trip for your friends, but sometimes acquaintances of friends had made me a sort of free roadhouse. People on vacation are often very inconsiderate to writers, who are popularly supposed to have endless free time. A few weeks before, a man I hardly knew arrived one midday by launch with friends and sent a message by Cayetano to say that eleven thirsty gringos were calling on me. I had no chance to say I was engaged because they all trailed into the patio behind Cayetano. There were eleven, and they were all thirsty. So before going down to the beach this time I sent Cayetano to reconnoiter. He returned in a few minutes.

"He is only one gringo, señor."

"Do we know him?"

"I don't think so. I have never seen him before." He paused, smiling broadly. "He doesn't have the face of being thirsty."

I hoped he wasn't coming to see me. He didn't. But later, when I went down to the beach, he was sitting under the eucalyptus trees. He said good morning in Spanish, and we exchanged a few remarks.

"My mozo thought you were American," I said.

The young man smiled. His clothes were American, but he himself was not. He had the densely black hair and eyes of Mexicans who have somewhere a strain of Indio blood.

"I am an American," he said. "All you United Statesers talk like that, as if you were the only Americans." He used the word Estadunidenses, which is as cumbrous in Spanish as its translation is in English.

"Sorry, I should have said North American."

"But I am a North American too. The United States, Canada, and

Mexico are North America. Then there is Central and South America."

"Sorry again. You haven't much reason down here to love the United States."

"I've nothing against them. Some places they're not nice to Mexicans, but they were all right to me." This time he spoke in English, and we went on in English.

"And which country do you prefer to live in?" I asked.

The young man thought.

"Well, my family is here. I am Mexican, and I like it here. But what chance have we? If there's an election, we—people like myself—don't bother to vote. It doesn't make any difference whether you vote or not. After all, we're really only four and not twenty millions who are capable of voting. No wonder everything's in a hopeless muddle. Look at me—I studied at Stanford and in Mexico City. And what d'you think I do? I breed dogs."

Of course in many countries dog breeding is recognized as a laudable profession for the highly educated and aristocratic. But in Mexico, where the educated middle class has only recently become aware of its capabilities, a university degree is expected to guarantee a career.

I asked what sort of dogs.

"Come and see," he said.

We went to the mole, and on the way he told me that his name was Raúl Bonilla. There in a launch, waggling and sleek, were five Dackel puppies with their mother. Two were tan and three black. They looked about three months old. Bonilla handled them very gently.

One, a tan bitch who seemed to have the longest tail and schnozzle of them all, detached herself from the others and began an attack on my trouser leg. Under the disapproving eye of Mamma I picked her up. She promptly dove into my shirt and wriggled round toward my back. A snout appeared out of the other side before the tail had followed into my shirt.

"I have kennels in Guadalajara," said Bonilla. "I sell these Dackels by the meter."

"How much a meter?" I asked, looking at the pup's tail.

"Sixty pesos."

"That's sixty centavos a centimeter," I said. "How much does this ᴏne measure?"

Bonilla didn't have a tape measure, so we carried her up to the house to find mine, and, before it was gnawed, she measured seventy-six centimeters from tail tip to schnozzle tip.

"She's grown a whole centimeter in ten days," said Bonilla. "Tell you what we'll do. We'll call it seventy-five, three-quarters of a meter."

Eventually Bonilla stayed to lunch and Motzín was introduced to all the Dackels, and between them they managed to destroy a number of young carrots before Cayetano schooed them away.

"Why is it," I asked Bonilla, "that so many Mexicans like yourself deplore the way your country's run but don't do anything about it? People like you never go into politics."

He shrugged, smiling a slow lazy smile that made his face boyish and sympathetic.

"Perhaps we don't like the people who do go into politics," he said.

I remembered once being told about a doctor that he was not a bad doctor but usually tight—"But then, you see, he has to drink a lot, he's in politics."

"Or perhaps we're just lazy. Perhaps we just want everything the easy way." He paused, and then added: "All the same, we like Mexico better than anywhere else."

When I came back from seeing him to his launch, Cayetano was staring at the new Dackel, and I heard him ask Candelaria what sort of animal it was.

"You know," said Candelaria, "one of those that come out of the water."

I imagine she meant a seal.

The day before Saint Andrew's day was a Sunday, so that made two holidays running. There was a great deal of bathing and hair washing in the lake in the morning, there were almost incessant Masses, and the church bell clanged like a streetcar. It was only a year old, and the village was very proud of it. This was the first Saint Andrew for which they had had the bell, and full use was made of it.

In the evening there was a battle of flowers in the plaza. All round the square were little booths, selling tacos and soft drinks and squashed bunches of flowers.

"Don't you want to buy my queens?" said old Refugio, holding up a bunch of white roses. "Or this little tortoise?"

Your procedure is to buy a few bunches, and then to join the circulating procession, boys clockwise, girls anticlockwise. You then present bunches of flowers to anyone who takes your fancy, girls giving to strange men as readily as men to strange girls. A round or two later, they should return the compliment. There is nothing against passing on flowers that have been given you. It would probably not matter giving flowers back to their original donor. In any case, they are so hand-pressed as to be nearly unrecognizable. All the time the band plays, and firecrackers split the air.

On Monday, Saint Andrew's Day, nobody did any work except the shopkeepers, the owners of cantinas, all those who had decided to sell instead of buy, and the employees of the post office, since federal offices don't recognize local fiestas. The band played all day long with vigor, but with a certain lack of co-ordination, due no doubt to prolonged exertion and tequila. The church bell rang madly. There were more services. The church itself, a long bare building, had been made gay with lengths of stuff, blue and yellow, much cut paper, and artificial flowers. In the evening it blazed with candles. The whole village was in the plaza, rockets roared, and in a corner the castle, a bamboo framework set with firecrackers, arranged so that one stage after another ignites, was being prepared.

At eleven the castle was lit. The big bamboo frame, this one seven stories high, was brought out. The maker and his assistants fussed around it, only too pleased to talk about their craft and this particular instance of it. The maker was a bit grand and condescending toward Ajijic.

"For rich villages," he said, "I have made much higher castles with twenty revestments."

At last the great moment came, and, as the band swung into a loud march, the lowest stage was set off. At each corner were Catherine wheels, and bunches of squibs everywhere. At intervals down each side were groups of rockets, which shot up into the air with a roar and a sizzle. As the last Catherine wheel spun slower and faded, the link firework set off the next story. So it went on, while the bell pealed, the band blared, fanfaring any particularly violent rocket, and people shouted and screeched. At last the topmost stage was reached, and there, at the summit, a larger, more elaborate Catherine wheel of white and red sprang to life and span and spluttered.

It was all very decorative, but of course this was a small castle with only seven revestments.

In Ajijic, the same thing happens one day with another. The day isn't important, and it wouldn't much matter if you forgot the year. I often confuse the days of the week.

"What day are we at?" I asked Cayetano. Candelaria always knows, but Cayetano is sometimes uncertain.

"A little moment," he said, and ran up the steps to the terrace on the roof. When he came down, he said, "Saturday, señor. I thought it was Saturday."

"And whatever did you find on the roof to tell you whether it was Saturday or not?"

"I looked for the boats. You see, every Saturday in the late afternoon, three boats with white sails put out from San Luis Soyatlán, and you always see them in the same place, more or less at this hour of the afternoon."

"And are they dependable? Do they always go on Saturday and never any other day?"

"Oh, always on Saturdays," said Cayetano. "You see, they go to the Sunday market in Chapala. So Saturday is a day one can always know."

I went up to the terrace myself, and there were the three sails holding out from San Luis. With the glasses I could see they were hull down. The sails were pearly in the late light, answering the pale flash of the sea birds that now in this month frequent the lake. There were gulls wheeling, their fierce beaks pointed straight ahead, and there were terns, their long slender bills angled lakeward, and the sunlight drawing an occasional red glint from their feet. No doubt it would be possible to establish the seasons when they visit us, and then one could place the date by saying, "It was the third day that the boats had put out from San Luis Soyotlán in the time of the sea birds."

Twice this month I have seen wedges of Ross geese flying down the lake from west to east. The first time I noticed them I was talking to

Merced, who was superintending the digging of the cesspool, while Don Bernabé attended to more delicate matters. A cesspool is called in Spanish the black well, or the black waters, suitably sinister terms. A cesspool is commonly roofed with brick vaulting, and it is advisable to have it somewhere where it is not much walked on. Brick vaulting is sound and strong, but many times it has happened that old vaulting has collapsed and precipitated the unwary into the filth below. So we were putting the black waters well out of the way of paths.

"You might be looking at birds like those and not notice that it was opening at your feet," said Merced.

The second time I saw the geese, I was down the beach, in the bay where the goldmills are. I pointed the birds out to an elderly fisherman, who sits every morning on a child-size chair mending his nets.

"Geese?" he said. "Are those ducks geese?"

With his homemade shuttle, he knotted a neat mesh.

"I had a goose once. We didn't like its eggs. I remember a señor, a foreigner, telling me that somewhere or other they nail geese's feet to the floor. Very rare." And he smiled to himself and shook his head, as if there were no end to the tall stories foreigners expected Indios like himself to swallow.

The sun had not shone that day, and when I got home there was no sign of lunch. Of the Indios who can read, many can read the time too, though they are unlikely to own a watch. But Candelaria can't. The sun is her clock, and she reads it very well. She pops out of the kitchen, glances at the shadows on the wall of the patio, and knows what time it is. She seems to be able to calculate according to the season, and serves meals punctually. If you asked her how she did it, she would certainly not know. But she can do it.

Today, however, far from being ready to dish up, she had just put on her shawl preparatory to going out. I told her it was already lunch time.

"Ay, help me God," she said. "And I was just going to see if the sugar had arrived from Guadalajara. Doña Arcelia was expecting it. I go and come."

She was soon back. The sugar had just arrived, late too. But then everything is late when the sun fails, and if you are all late together it is just the same as being punctual together.

DECEMBER

DECEMBER finds the poinsettias out everywhere, the Noche Buena, the flower of the Good Night. I cannot discover whether the custom of using poinsettias as the Christmas flower went from Mexico to the United States or vice versa. Nobody seems to know whether they were called here Noche Buena before Ambassador Poinsett took them home with him. But the Indios more often use the word catarina, so perhaps that is the more ancient name.

Here the bushes grow very tall, and the scarlet starfish shine high among sharp green banana leaves. But if you wish you can keep them trimmed down to three or four feet, neat, well-conducted border shrubs. There is another kind, pale lemon-yellow, the sort of yellow that white kid turns. The petals have the texture of kid too. The yellow does not strike as well as the red, whose cuttings flourish readily. As there is no poinsettia bush in the huerta, Nieves brings great armfuls two or three times a week. They come from her parents' garden, only it isn't really a garden, but a mud yard where their few animals are kept, a mud yard with a splendid poinsettia bush in the corner. They are awkward to arrange, for the flowers always look downward. You should hang them from the ceiling to see them properly. The stalks exude a white sticky milk, and they last better in water if you seal them with wax. You can only get the milk off your hands with gasoline. Wash as much as you like, until your hands look clean, and half an hour later there are dirty patches where dust has stuck to an invisible smear of the gummy milk. But in tall earthenware jars against the pale green walls of the patio, they look very beautiful.

I was telling Nieves where to put the jars when Cayetano came in and said, "Don't we want to buy a little deer?" He said it as if it were quite usual to buy deer.

There are wild deer in the hills, and not infrequently you can buy deer in the village. They are small, and this one, which had been brought by an old charcoal burner, stood about waist-high, shivering slightly and staring out of its big soft eyes.

I did not in the least want a deer. There was an Indio family a few doors off that had a pet deer. I had often seen it, going down with their cows to drink at the lake edge. Once when I had a chance of getting a pair of dik-diks in England I was discouraged by the fact that dogs, roused by the gamy smell, would have attacked the miniature deer. But in Ajijic dogs took no notice of deer. And now Motzín and the Dackel puppy snuffed round the fawn's feet and seemed rather pleased with it. The fawn pawed the ground, but without fear of the dogs.

"Ay, Most Holy Mary, what a pretty little animal," cried Candelaria, coming out of the kitchen with an egg beater in one hand and flour on her face. Then she scampered back.

"It could be in the corner of the huerta behind the wire," observed Cayetano, who was stroking the fawn's head. "Then it couldn't get at the vegetables."

Motzín jumped up at the fawn, wagging his stump of tail delightedly.

"And it's not high enough to reach the trees," said Cayetano, as if he were talking to himself.

I asked the charcoal burner where he had found the animal.

"I met it," he said, "in the hills."

Candelaria emerged again, this time with a saucepan in her hand. She caressed the fawn's head clumsily, as she caresses all animals, so that it winced and shied away.

She said, "Poor little thing," which is an endearment, not a condolence.

The fawn shied away toward me, gave me a startled glance, and laid its head on my sleeve.

"Look how affectionate it is," said Cayetano. "And when the man came trying to sell the little goat we didn't buy it."

I did not in the least want a deer.

"How much?" I asked.

The old man scratched his head and said hopefully, "Ten pesos? Or eight?"

"Five, five's quite enough," said Cayetano, taking out of the old man's hand the string by which he was leading the deer.

"Five," I said firmly, and gave the man the bill.

Cayetano, murmuring endearments, led the fawn away toward the huerta, with Motzín and the Dackel dancing round them both and barking ecstatically.

I did not in the least want to buy a little deer.

One way and another the beginning of the month was full of events among the livestock. The ducklings which had been given me had grown up. I had called them Gackerlbert and Gackerlinde, because the Bavarian Gackerl has always seemed to me the best onomatopoeic name for a duck, and because the drake was so very male and commanding and the duck so very female and submissive, in the best Teutonic tradition. They were from the same hatch, and they had mated, and there is plenty of incest in the ancient Burgundian sagas. Gackerlbert was persistently disagreeable to his mate; in fact, he was the most unpleasant-tempered drake I have ever known. He was always dirty, angry, and greedy. But Gackerlinde was relentlessly sweet and gentle. Often she would follow me about the garden, hoping I had a crumb in my pocket, but if I threw one it was always Gackerlbert who came, lumbering and hissing, and snatched the food. So I fed her from my hand, warding off meanwhile the outraged drake. He usually pecked her harshly afterward, and then she would make a little plangent noise, but she would not run away or defend herself.

Suddenly the ducks were missing for two days. Then Cayetano came to me with the remains of Gackerlbert. Not many remains, the mangled head and some feathers. They had been found several gardens off, and it was plain that a fox or coyote had eaten up Gackerlbert. But of Gackerlinde there was no trace. I thought she would have died submissively, and I wondered if Gackerlbert had tried to protect her, but I thought it far more likely that she would have tried to protect Gackerlbert.

"What do you think killed him?" I asked.

"Perhaps a skunk, or perhaps a fox, or perhaps a coyote," said Cayetano. "They all come down and steal the chickens from time in when."

"Or perhaps it was a tlacuache," put in Nieves.

"Whatever is a tlacuache?"

"It's an animal," she said. "Yes, I daresay it was a tlacuache, because Don Amílcar shot one last night."

"What does it look like?"

"Pues, it's bigger than a rat," said Nieves. "And it has white fur with black in it."

"No," said Cayetano, "it has black fur with white in it, and it's as big as a dog, and it has a tail that's long long."

"Without fur," said Nieves.

"No, with fur," said Cayetano.

"Pos, the one Don Amílcar shot last night has a bare tail," insisted Nieves.

"Some have tails with fur and some have tails without fur," conceded Cayetano.

Later on I found out by chance that they meant an opossum. I had been content for a tlacuache to be a mysterious bogey, for whenever a fowl or a fruit disappeared somebody was sure to say:

"It was the tlacuache that took it."

"I have worked it out," said Don Bernabé, "how many rails we shall need and of what lengthitudes."

He had in his hand an unevenly torn corner of light brown packing paper, on which his calculations and the results were shown. I could not easily disentangle one from the other.

"But what do we want rails for?"

"For the girders," he answered, his whole small wrinkled face corrugated with surprise. "For the girders, pues, to buy metal girders comes out much costlier than to buy old railroad rails."

And so it was. It is indeed a common practice to use old rails as girders. But how, in a country with so relatively small a railway system, there are so many rails on the open market is a mystery. However, I found out where to look for old rails in Guadalajara, and old rails we used.

The walls were rising now, and it was high time to start getting the girders. Don Bernabé and I checked measurements and made a list of the exact figures. I was standing, still talking to him, when a thin old voice behind me said, "Señor."

Sometimes the tread of soft huaraches is so silent that suddenly you look up and see an Indio beside you. I had heard nothing, but there was the old woman who had sold me the begonia and promised to look for the lily. She had a plant in her hand.

"I bring the lily," she said.

The plant had lily leaves, but no flower.

"You're sure this is the same one?"

"Yes, how not. Equal to the one you had in the vase. Very pretty."

So I bought it and took it back to the house. When it flowered it was a plain white lily, like a thousand others. But the weedy begonia, repotted, flourished exceedingly. There was enough of it to divide into a number of plants and within a few months it filled the whole wall box along the terrace parapet, a cascade of waxy white flowers.

Nieves said she would have to leave for a month. As usual with the Indios she had not told me ahead of time. She proposed to leave that very day.

"But what shall I do?" I asked.

"Of course, I wouldn't want to leave you planted," she said. "There's Chayito." Chayo is a diminutive of Rosario.

"And what is she like?"

"She's a cousin of mine. She's not my cousin-sister, but she's a good girl."

A good girl even if she were not Nieves' first cousin seemed promising.

"Could she come to see me?"

"She's here now."

For although the Indios will suddenly leave one they will almost always supply a successor. She seemed to take it for granted that that would be satisfactory. It took me some time to get her to explain why she wanted to go. She has a brother who has recently been received into the priesthood. The whole family has subscribed money for his education. Nieves has sent five pesos a month from her wages of twelve. And the brother is coming on a visit. It would not be dignified if his sister were employed in housework during his stay. Therefore Nieves is leaving. The grandmother of the new priest and of Nieves collects twigs on the beach and is a persistent beggar. I wonder whether the begging will cease for a month too. I told Nieves that I could not promise to keep her place open for her. I hope the cousin will be efficient. For Christmas will soon be here, and my friend Charles is coming. Charles is very exigent.

Nieves' cousin seemed shy or stupid, but willing, and I entertained hope. She started at once, learning from Nieves. She worked all morning and helped serve lunch. In the afternoon Nieves came to me and said she was sorry but her cousin had left.

"But why?"

"She said there were too many little things on the table, señor."

I considered the lunch table, bare of all but essentials. I suppose my stiff-necked insistence on clean knives and forks with each course was the real cause. Nieves' fine-boned tobacco-golden face wore a look of scorn for Chayo's unsophistication.

In the evening she appeared again. She had a girl with her. A girl with a round chubby expressionless face.

"This is Rafles," she said briefly.

The girl said nothing.

"She could work here," said Nieves.

The girl found her tongue, and she said she had worked in Guadalajara, and had only recently returned, and today she had learned that I needed a maid, she had heard from her friend Nieves.

"So you're a friend, not a cousin?"

"Oh, no, señor, we're not cousins. Of course, my aunt is comadre of Nieves' mother's sister."

But the genealogies of Ajijic are difficult enough without launching into the relationships of parents with their children's godparents.

"As she has worked in Guadalajara," said Nieves, "Rafles is used to tables with many things on them like ours."

Cayetano took Rafles in hand at once. This was the first time he had been able to instruct anyone in what he himself had only recently learned. In the dining room I heard him speaking in quite imperious tones.

"If you hand dishes from the right and not the left, it results badly.

And it gives the señor much laughter. If there are more people than saltcellars, then you have to throw a hand to a little glass and put salt in it. And you must always give yourself count of whether a guest lacks something. For when I am out, you must know for yourself."

The next day, Candelaria decided, was just the day for marmalade making. Most households, no doubt, do not embark on such extras on the first day of a new and untrained maid. But Candelaria doesn't think like that. She had had the oranges picked several days before, and she had purchased extra bitter ones, which we lacked. She could have made the marmalade before or afterward. But she seemed to delight in piling up obstacles and then making an enormous fuss surmounting them and then with a pleased tired smile viewing her achievement. So the new maid Rafaela, called Rafles, had barely learned how to make a bed when she was set to peeling, pipping, and juicing oranges. All day, her face quite blank, she sat in a corner of the patio working, and meals were served by Cayetano and Cayetano helped with washing the dishes. Candelaria enjoyed herself; everybody was doing somebody else's job.

"Go you, hurry you," she was calling to someone all morning, while she herself scampered all ways, falling over the dogs and crying: "Moursi! Moursi! Quit yourself, you pretty little thing!"

But eventually everything got done more or less on time, and nobody could deny that it was due to her efforts. So was the muddle, but that was another thing.

"See how well it all came out to me," she said, beaming.

The next day was the same, because Rafles spent the whole day squatted in a child's chair in front of a charcoal brazier on which a huge copper pot of marmalade was simmering. And the next day was not much better, because then Rafles was helping Candelaria hermetically close the screw-top jars full of marmalade, and when that was done some marmalade that was left had to be put into glasses and waxed over.

On Rafles' fourth day in the house she really began to learn her duties, and Candelaria, very proud of her work, had a pot of the new marmalade brought to the table at every meal with the cheese. Conserves of all sorts are rare and dear in Mexico, and a spoonful of jam may be served as dessert.

"I've never made this jam of orange before," said Candelaria. "So really I did it at the goodness of God." Which was derogatory to my recipe, but a pious thought. "Allah grant that you will like it."

Beyond the roofed terrace there is an open one, and when I went up I found it entirely covered with orange peelings.

"Whatever is that for?" I asked Candelaria.

It looked very untidy, but Candelaria usually has a reason for her untidiness. She lives in a state of deliberate but motivated disorder. She is ingenious, she finds uses for things, if she lacks something she finds a substitute for it. For instance, she does chicken in a sauce of ground almonds very nicely. But almonds have become so fantastically expensive that I don't buy them any more. Like all good Indios, Candelaria has a substitute. She uses peanuts. They don't taste quite as good, but they taste good. Now, too, there is no French vinaigre de vin blanc. That problem Candelaria solved too, making a very palatable vinegar out of Mexican white wine and Ajijic honey.

"To dry them," she said, looking with satisfaction at the orange-strewn terrace.

"Yes, but what for?"

"Pues, when they're dry, they burn very well. They're oily and they burn very well in a boiler. If you had the water arranged, and if you had a boiler, and if you had a tub, you could have a hot bath burning these in the boiler."

The fawn seems to live quite contentedly in the small wired enclosure in the corner of the huerta. Cayetano keeps its water bucket filled, and sometimes he takes it on a string down to the lake edge. It has become attached to him, and, as I annexed Cayetano's dog, he is annexing my fawn. This seems fair. At odd times during the day he goes down to talk to the fawn, leaning over the wire and murmuring endearments. Sometimes when he goes into the enclosure Motzín goes with him. Each time he snuffs the fawn it seems to be a new experience. He jumps up and down and gets very excited. The Dackel pup bites the fawn's legs, but has not yet received a serious kick.

The fawn loves peanuts, and peanuts grow everywhere in Ajijic.

You see them put out to dry all over the place. Often a whole side-walk in front of a house is covered with peanuts. Every evening Candelaria serves them hulled, skinned, and lightly fried in salt and butter. But I think I really buy peanuts for the fawn. All deer like peanuts. I remember when I was a child and was taken to any zoo, I never gave my peanuts to the monkeys. The monkeys had a surfeit. I kept all mine for the deer. They came running down their long narrow pens and nuzzled velvet-soft in my hand. So as soon as I acquired the fawn I remembered those other deer. The fawn had the taste, all right. He would always look for peanuts when I went down to his corral. He would even look for them in my pocket.

One night I was sitting on the beach in front of the huerta gate. It was an evening of thick soft calm. The lake was polished, blue-silver and yellow, and the sky was a distant pallor and the mountains were very dark and very close. There was hardly a breath on the air, just enough to stir the willow leaves lazily.

Cayetano brought my drink, and then began to gather up the eucalyptus leaves that, dry and yellow, lay all round. He made a mound of them, and asked me for a match. Then he lit the leaves deep down, in the center of the pile, and waited. Soon a wisp of pale blue smoke filtered out, and the faint breath on the air blew the wisp toward me, bearing a thin sharp spicy odor. Cayetano piled on more leaves, till the mound was quite big and nicely afire deep in its heart. The pale blue smoke wreathed toward me where I sat. Cayetano had calculated the wind drift well.

He fetched the fawn and led it down to the water. When it had drunk, they came up the shore again together. Just then, its heart consumed, the mound of eucalyptus leaves collapsed, and thin flames leaped up from it. The fawn paused, and pulled away from Cayetano toward the fire. It stood there to leeward, staring, the firelight glinting in its huge brown eyes. Then Cayetano threw more leaves on the blaze, the flames were smothered, and in the sudden smoke-spiced darkness I felt on my hand the snuffing muzzle of the fawn.

Charles arrived with smart luggage and his usual air of having just left Cannes. He said he had had very tough chicken on the plane. He looked coldly at the outskirts of Guadalajara. He asked why the lake called the Blue Water was blackish green. At lunch he said the soup was cold, that there weren't enough waiters, and that he'd had better coffee even in England. I felt discouraged as I thought of what Charles would say about Ajijic. But he is somebody I have known forever, in half a dozen countries, and as soon as he heard I was in Ajijic he invited himself for Christmas "because I've been in Fiji, but that only has three dots."

After lunch he accompanied me to see about some tiles. He was in raptures about the factory, which was disorderly, picturesque, and had an air of what Charles called cheerful negligence, which pleased him. He liked the workmen too, with their gay shirts and headkerchiefs.

I was ordering quantities of cheap tiles for the veranda, and a few more expensive pale green ones for indoors in the two rooms. Charles did not think much of the tiles. Unlike so many of his European friends, Charles is still rich, and I think that even if he lost all his money his mind would still run on in the furrow of riches. However, he was in good humor. He caught a flea, and he enjoyed complaining about the flea.

On the way down to Chapala he was in high spirits. The country-side pleased him, and reminded him sometimes of Algeria and some-times, surprisingly, of Scotland. Like the Prince Consort, Charles is always reminded of somewhere where he is not. He was contemp-tuously amused by the tiny schoolhouse outside Ixtlahuacán de los Membrillos, but subsequently diverted by trying to spot one of the quince trees for which the village is named.

There is a moment crossing the pass between Ixtlahuacán and Cha-pala when the lake suddenly flashes into view. I always wait for this moment. And the lake had put on a show too. It was all pale rosewood under a pale sky. Sometimes it takes on this curious tint. One has seen lakes at sunset and at dawn turn rose and salmon and carnation. But Chapala can put on this rosewood tone at high noon. Charles ap-proved, and it did not remind him of anywhere. As we ran down the pinkness faded, the water was almost the shade of pale milk chocolate, and when we reached its level it was silvery.

Charles liked the Indios.

"I do hope nobody ever makes them wash," he said.

In Chapala I found a boy to drive the car with the luggage on to

Ajijic, and took Charles by water. A little wind had come up, and we bounced down the lake. The sun was going down, and painting ravines of violet on the eastern slope of every fold of the encircling hills. When we reached Ajijic, there was Cayetano on the shore to meet us, having spied us from the roof. Those who arrive in Ajijic by launch can be heard for about twenty minutes and seen for at least ten before arrival.

"But why ever did you put him into that ridiculous white coat? He ought to have one of those shiny sham-silk shirts in a shrieking color—and he's got shoes too."

But just then Cayetano, who was all dressed up for our visitor's arrival, handed Charles out of the launch and kissed his hand. Charles was quite impressed too by the ardent welcome that all Mexican servants know so well how to give: "How have you been—how did the journey go with you—how good—how nice, come in, sit down—you're not too tired?" Charles became quiet and subdued and did not criticize anything, though I saw him sniff carefully at the Martini Cayetano brought him. After some minutes Charles began to feel better. A lizard climbed the screening of a window, puffed out its throat, and reminded him of an American-Roman princess. A late hummingbird consented to drink out of the sugarwater tube while he held it. Daylight went out in lilac and ravenswing. Charles had another Martini. I explained to him that one didn't eat dinner at night at this altitude. Happily nobody could have quarreled with the fish soufflé Candelaria had made for supper.

The next day Charles examined Ajijic. He was very amusing about the one-room houses with their bare earthen walls, and genuinely appreciative of many beautiful things. He noticed at once how any group of Indios, casually gathered at a street corner or in a shop door, falls into a balanced composition.

Bright remarks poured from his lips by scores. He had talked that way for years. It had been so entertaining in the tinseled twenties, it had been a diversion from worry in the threatened thirties. But now we were in the furious forties. And we were no longer in a blue Dalmatian evening, Cannes was a long way ago, and in an Indio village poverty and dirt are not really very funny.

Charles was very agreeable to everybody, but in the house his presence hung like a mist. Candelaria scampered more quietly and less often. Rafles never sang at all. Cayetano spoke in a hushed voice. Meals were unnervingly punctual. Once or twice I was punctual myself.

Yet Charles is not stupid or unkind or insensitive. He simply could not understand, for instance, that Venustiano, who sleeps in a bed mattressed with bamboo slats and covered by a sarape in the same room with his wife and two nieces, is a well-bred and gracious person, and that when he talks about the future of the Indio he is much more interested in the future of personal dignity than in the future of mechanical civilization. Charles should not really have come to Ajijic until it had become more of a place, with striped umbrellas on the beach and all the little boys saying O.K. When he had stayed with me in Andalucía he had not jarred like this, but there we were only fifty miles from Málaga, Paris itself was only just behind the Pyrenees. In Ajijic he was all wrong. Even his clothes were wrong. They were beach clothes, but beach clothes for Florida. Cayetano eyed them enviously, and never wore huaraches, but always his best shoes, even to fetch the drinking water from the plaza. Charles wore huaraches, but they were very new and shiny, with closed toes. I took Charles into Chapala, and there, with a café table to sit at, he looked less out of place. He talked away merrily, and so often had I listened to Charles talking at café tables that, shutting my eyes, I could easily believe that we were in any past European year, sitting at Florian's or the Pré Catelan as we had so often sat.

We went to visit some friends who had a house in Chapala. Their terrace overlooked the lake and gave onto a path that led to a little walled-in harbor for boats. The harbor was reed-grown and picturesque. We were sitting there when up the steps from the harbor and along the path came waddling a white duck. She came on slowly but undeviatingly, on and up the few steps to the terrace, where, my friends said, she had never been before. It was Gackerlinde, and I suppose she had recognized me, perhaps hearing my voice. I have no idea how acute the sense of hearing in ducks is. Charles made a great fuss of her until I told him she had ticks. Then he put her down in a hurry.

My friends, it appeared, had been out in Ajijic to a piece of land they own there, and in a corner they had come upon the remains of

Gackerlbert and, watching faithfully beside them, Gackerlinde, whole and untouched. They said she was very quiet and weak, as if she had not eaten but had been determined to commit a sort of suttee. They had made inquiries as to where she might belong, but nobody knew. So, rather than leave her there, they had brought her back with them and turned her loose in the little harbor. I fed Gackerlinde some crumbs, but I did not take her with me, for I had nothing so safe and luxurious as a private walled and reed-grown pond to offer her.

The next day some Mexican friends came down. Charles wasn't much interested in them, though they spoke English. When he asked them if they knew New York, they replied that they had never been anywhere, and that anaesthetized the conversation. All through lunch it didn't quite recover, though everybody made gallant efforts. My visitors had brought with them a friend, a woman who runs a kindergarten, or, as they say in Spanish, with splendid disregard for German grammar, a kinder. (The Spanish are very sensible about foreign words, and once they adopt them they grant them full nationality, spelling them in a Spanish way—nocaut for knockout—and conjugating verbs like cachar—to catch—according to Spanish rules.) The kindergarten is a very good one, as good as I have seen anywhere, and everything in it—the little swimming pool, the swings, the miniature furniture, the garden, even the model house and the buildings themselves—the children made or helped to make. It is not, as one might suppose, for children of the rich. It is situated in a poor part of Guadalajara, and it is for the poor barefoot children of the neighborhood. It is supported by federal funds, but it is really the creation and the lifework of the woman who runs it. It is unusual in Catholic Latin countries to meet unmarried women engaged in and devoted to public work. But there are some in Mexico now.

Afterward we were sitting on the beach under the eucalyptus trees. There were children of all ages everywhere, and each carrying a bucket, a tin can, a box, or some sort of container, which he filled with sand. There were some repairs being done to the church, and the contribution of the children, even the smallest, was to bring a little sand from the beach to mix with the cement. They were of all sorts, some very poor and ragged, some neatly dressed.

Charles enjoyed watching them. He was amused by the little girl of

135

twelve with a baby on her left hip and a big bucket in her right hand, and by a tiny very dirty boy wearing nothing but a pair of white cotton drawers whose waistband clung round him below a potbelly, and by a little barefoot girl who had nothing but her shawl to collect sand in.

The woman who ran the kindergarten viewed them bleakly.

"Poor little things," she said. "I talked to one of the schoolteachers, and asked her what method she used to teach reading and writing. She looked at me as if I'd frightened her, thought hard for a minute, and then said, 'I use all the methods mixed up together.' "

"Oh, look," cried Charles, "look at that infant there. He dropped his banana in the sand, then he wiped it off on his dog's back before eating it. Isn't that divine?"

The teacher looked at him wonderingly.

"Divine?" she said. "But that's what I'm spending my life trying to change."

There came one of those silences that follow the entry of sincerity with no clothes on.

"Yes, of course, it's frightful really," said Charles. "But you must admit the kids are happy this way."

"Happy?" said the teacher, and if she were not so distinguished I would say she snorted. "Yes, happy like oxen."

For Christmas Eve I had invited various people from the village. I did not ask any children, for I was planning to make a party for them on the Day of the Kings. But we had a Christmas tree. It came from up in the mountains over by Zitácuaro where there are a great many fir and pine forests and where the government has been taking afforestation seriously. It had been brought by a friend. In Guadalajara they sell Christmas trees from the States, and very dear and dry they are.

For the party we had ordered the band, and we asked the carpenter's son and his family, Venustiano and his nieces, the superior young men from the comisaría and the shop, the daughters of various prominent residents, and so on. It was practically the Ajijic social register.

Charles was very active with the tree and he thought of several very original ways of hanging up poinsettias and paper garlands.

"I once had a party in Provence for the village," said Charles. "And it went on for a day and a half."

The first guests arrived, the three dressmakers and Joaquín from the post office. They were very elegantly dressed, the boy in a dark suit with an old school tie or something very near it. Charles was overwhelmingly attentive. He had carefully learned a few phrases such as Felices Pascuas and Siéntese por favor and sprinkled them liberally.

More guests arrived, and the music. Cayetano disposed the musicians in a corner of the patio and hissed in my ear that perhaps a little preliminary drink would get them going. He took them a bottle of tequila.

When most of the guests had come, Charles distributed the small presents from the tree, and when we had finished with that and had another drink Charles started the dancing, leading off with plump Doña Arcelia of the shop.

Gradually things got gayer. I made Cayetano dance with Rafles, and at length I saw in a corner a girl and a boy dancing the jarabe tapatío, that best-known of Mexican dances, in which the girl dances round the brim of the man's hat when he throws it down. The audience clapped hands and most of the dancers stopped and watched.

"Ah, but we ought to ask Tiburcia and Avelino," said Doña Arcelia.

"Who is Avelino?"

"You must know him, pues. He lives over there, and he always wears a blue sash."

I did know Avelino. He was tall and thin and melancholy looking, not young.

"But you don't mean to say that he dances the jarabe?"

It was easy enough to believe of Tiburcia, with her roving eye and colorful past.

"Oh, yes, very well, unbetterable. He and Tiburcia dance it very well together."

"Well, let's send and ask them."

Cayetano went and in half an hour was back with the two of them. Avelino walked as if he were all made in one piece, without joints, as if he could never dance. He was in clean white pajamas, ironed into the proper small squares, with a blue stuff sash and huaraches. Tiburcia, plump and pleased, swayed her hips and swayed the big earrings she had unearthed somewhere. She wore a full-skirted dress of lilac

137

print. She looked much more gypsy-like than the real gypsies who had come to Ajijic. She might have been a gitana and danced in the caves of Albaicín, where it is not youth or beauty that is as important as knowing how to dance.

I said I had heard that she danced beautifully. Would she oblige us?

"Who knows if I can."

"What music would you like? Will you tell the band?"

"Who knows."

I caught Cayetano's eye. He brought two cuba libres, strongly laced. "They need gasoline," he said.

After the gasoline the band started the quick-darting music of the jarabe. The guests clapped their hands. And suddenly Tiburcia and Avelino swung into the dance. In the jarabe, as in the fandango, you never touch your partner, and it is a dance you can dance on a dime. Their bodies hardly moving, the woman with hands on hips, the man with an arm raised, they jogged on twinkling feet. Tiburcia held up her print skirts, showing ankles that were not shapely and old black sneakers. But that did not matter, for the pattern the sneakers wove was exact and graceful. She looked down at her feet, but her sharp black eyes glittered glances at the company, not a few at Charles. With precise daintiness she toed it round the brim of Avelino's sombrero when he threw it on the ground. The audience was enraptured, and indeed I have never seen the jarabe better performed.

"This is lovely," said Charles. "But how do you get them to stop?"

There seemed no reason why they should stop. The band played the same short repetitious air tirelessly, the pair jigged on, the on-lookers clapped. And they might perhaps be dancing yet had not a wreath of cut paper near the Christmas tree caught fire. There was immediate pandemonium, as everyone shouted. But the fire was easily put out, having scorched only a branch of the vine.

"It must have come undone and fallen into the flame of a candle," said the mother of the dressmakers, whose things never come undone. But I had seen Charles putting his matches into his pocket just as we saw the flame.

"And now what about supper?" said Charles, who likes his food.

Tiburcia and Avelino went to the kitchen for refreshments. This was obviously expected and approved by the rest of the company.

Village caste systems are rigid in most parts of the world. And Mexico is not an egalitarian country. It may become one, when education has leveled the present sharp discrepancies. For centuries its upper class had close relations with France and Spain, and was as far removed from the bourgeoisie as any European aristocracy. There are many of this class left, and they are not by any means all ruined. Illiteracy and absence of higher education created further class barriers. And there is a color barrier too. Nobody looks down on the Indio as much as the white Mexican or the Mexican with a portion of white blood. Among the Indios themselves there are innumerable distinctions. An Indio of Ajijic is further removed from a Tarahumara, walking the plateaux of Chihuahua attired in a G string, or from a Cora wandering the west coast in feathers, than he is from Lázaro Cárdenas, the ex-president, who is also an Indio. Of the first citizens of Ajijic some are quite white and some are not at all white. Here it is position, not race, that counts.

In the dining room there was a buffet of everything cold that Candelaria could make or get out of a can. Everyone was very shy. And now Charles was at his best, charming everybody with his attentions, seeing that everybody ate and drank. And when all had been refreshed it was almost time for midnight Mass. Charles went, escorted by the whole party and with Cayetano to see he didn't miss the way home.

He came in to see me afterward.

"Too marvelous," he said. "All that lovely Catholic theater, and the rows and rows of coppery faces. But it was simply frightful, that woman who brought in some eggs this morning was just by me, you know, the one who wanted three centavos more for a turkey's egg."

I knew her. It was she who kept her chickens on the strip of land sold me by Rosario. She was very poor and had several children and she made a little money buying eggs and reselling them at some minute profit.

"Well, she was right by me, and she had an infant in her arms, a perfectly disgusting infant. Its eyes were running and it was slobbering and blubbering all over her pink satin. She ought to have left it at home."

"But she hasn't anybody to leave it with."

"Anyway it was quite revolting. I shan't go to the church again. I think I shall just look at the Indians from the roof or across the street. That way they're lovely."

Charles shuddered.

The next day Refugio, the woman in question, came to say that her youngest child had died during the night and she had no money for his coffin.

Charles was leaving, because he had promised to spend New Year's Eve in Taxco. He would have enjoyed himself much more with the guests I was expecting for New Year's Eve than with anybody else he had met here, but he would enjoy himself even more in Taxco. There, in that lovely place largely ruined by all the people who used to live at the Dôme and the Ritz bar, he would be less out of place than in Ajijic. I thought that the next time Charles came to Mexico I would meet him in the capital.

Candelaria, whose hand was wet, gave him her wrist to shake and became quite girlish over Charles's fantastically large tip. He is one of those people who tip largely in dollars, and even more largely in minor currencies, never realizing that it is discourteous to the inhabitants of any country perpetually to be showing that you are much richer than they are.

We drove into Guadalajara in the afternoon, for Charles was taking the night train for Mexico City. Charles talked animatedly, but I could see that he was glad to be leaving. If Refugio's baby hadn't died, his visit would have made one continuous story. Even the filthy slobbering infant would have been a joke. But it had died. And people like Charles do not belong where there is tragedy or death. They have their place. They belong to societies of riches and ease, with time to think, and these are the societies, not those whose total energies have been devoted to keeping alive, which have made civilization. The Charleses are the audience, uncreative but often the first to recognize and appreciate creation. Charles looked much more fitting in the lounge of the hotel in Guadalajara.

When I got home Cayetano said all in one breath, "Here is five pesos, which the señor gave me, for the bank, and Motzín's other ear has come up."

This had been a worry to the whole household. It would have been dreadful to have a dog with one ear permanently pendant and one erect. And suddenly I saw a resemblance. I went and fetched one of the clay figures I had bought in June, an animal figure, with four squat legs, a wide flat body, and a face with a pointed nose and two big pointed ears. Motzín frontface and the idol or incense burner frontface had a striking similarity.

The Chihuahua dog is noticeable for its wide ears. It is the smallest dog in the world and weighs about a pound. That is to say, the smallest variety does. But there are several varieties. There are hairless Chihuahueños, minute revolting ratlike creatures. There are hairy Chihuahueños, rather larger. And they say there are still wild Chihuahueños, that hunt in packs, and that will even attack small deer. Motzín is not pure Chihuahueño. There was miscegenation in his family. But that wide pointed earspread suggests that the Chihuahueño is an ancient and well-known Mexican dog. And, of course, also, that Motzín, far from being an originless mongrel, has really an aristocratic Mexican ancestry.

"I always knew," said Candelaria, "that he wasn't just any current dog."

I heard Cayetano running across the patio. Cayetano seldom runs. He knocked loudly on the door and rushed in, holding the dog's drinking bowl out in front of him.

"Look, señor, look! Motzín left his bowl outside in the huerta last night and look, the water woke up jelled."

He used the word that means jell or set, applicable to anything from a sweetmeat to someone's character. It had almost certainly never frozen in Ajijic during his lifetime, and he probably connected the word frozen with ice creams, which are called frozens. He was very excited. There was a thin coating of ice over the water, and Cayetano, taking great care not to touch the ice with his fingers, picked up my comb from the dressing table and prodded the ice gingerly.

"Do I go and put it in the icebox," he said, "to help the other ice?"

Having invited the village for Christmas I was having a mixed set of friends for New Year's Eve. Since in Mexico it is quite normal to eat at nine or ten in the evening one is spared the problem of filling the pause between dinner and midnight. I fixed on nine as the hour of invitation, fairly sure that nobody would arrive before half past and then we should probably eat at half past ten.

Candelaria started working herself up to the necessary degree of excitement at least two days before. At intervals she would come scampering in, saying, "Look, señor, at these nice little cabbages of Brussels. And how did you say the purée of chestnuts was made?"

Having had a surfeit of turkey, we were going to eat venison, and with old memories of Germany, I had decided it should be roasted and served with cranberries and sour-cream sauce. The cranberries I had found in Guadalajara, imported from the United States and costing more than a dollar a pound. Candelaria had listened distrustfully as I talked about the sauce.

"Sour cream?" she said, doubtfully. "Sour cream? Oh, yes. I'll make the struggle. We'll see how it comes out."

But when she nods her head ominously like that, whatever it is usually comes out very well.

"And the little cabbages of Brussels round the purée of chestnuts? I've never done that. But we'll see."

She was a little hurt when I wouldn't let her stew the oysters from Guaymas into a soup, but brightened when I said she could make some ice cream. She had been fretting to do this for a long time, proud of her ability to do it.

Then there was the mull for midnight. I was using the red wine of Santos Tomás in Lower California, tolerable as a rough table wine, but much better mulled. I was using an old recipe for Hamburger Glühwein, and Candelaria, as she had never made it before, was at once non-co-operative, if not obstructive. Yes, there had been some cinnamon once—of course, one needed it for the various hot punches she knew how to make—surely it was in one of those drawers over there. And the cloves? Pues, she had seen them about somewhere, sometime. Lemons were very very scarce, and I wanted such a lot of them. As for marjoram, there was probably some growing down the huerta, some-place, she would go and look at once, although it was dark, for of course tomorrow she would be far too busy preparing and basting the venison to go and look for herbs. And what could she boil so much water in, let alone put the whole brew into? She couldn't think. It would give her much pain to cause me a deception.

Meanwhile Cayetano was swelling with excitement, and I had seen him go out with his white coat, doubtless for his mother to wash in time for the feast. He had already decided that the cocktail shaker would be inadequate and had evolved an elaborate plan for mixing the cocktails and storing them in a big jug. And Rafles had taken every one of the napkins and table mats to be washed, so that I had lunch off the bare table.

Then, as Cayetano was talking about the cocktails, I saw how very dark he was and decided that he should be our first-footer. I started to explain. I made the mistake of being too thorough, and had to open with a long account of where and what Scotland was. But eventually he grasped the idea.

"I go out before twelve, and come back—the year that enters?" he said, grinning with pleasure.

I explained to him his whole part, but it was plain that there would be need for rehearsals yet. Anything done with the hands Cayetano can learn in a twinkling, but other things come hard to him.

In the morning of the last day of the year itself Rafles arrived with armfuls of poinsettias and a sister, both unexpected. The poinsettias were stored in water until later, and the sister was set to washing the patio. The sister was Rafles' own idea and involved me in no extra expense, except that of giving her something to eat. Rafles herself has become much more efficient than I ever thought she would, but I have yet to see any expression cross her round face. In the evening, said Rafles, her mother and her older sister would be along to help wash the dishes. In Mexico, you often find that you are feeding several of a servant's family. But when you have a party the family comes along and works like mad just for the hell of it. The dishwashing is a very real problem, since it is unusual to have sufficient dishes or cutlery for a whole meal, and dishwashing therefore goes on incessantly. They do it with soap and cold water and powdered pumice applied with a twist of rope for scouring, using as a dishrag a bundle of maguey fiber, another product of the Mexican plant whose leaves can be eaten and from which they make string and tequila.

Cayetano had been up with the dawn, squeezing liters of orange and lemon juice for the mull, and hanging Chinese lanterns on the vine. And Candelaria, by now beaming with satisfaction, had her joint nearly ready for roasting by breakfast time. At every minute through the morning, somebody seemed to be arriving with something. Half the village, no doubt, knew by now who was coming and what we were going to eat. Things sent from Guadalajara by bus are usually dumped in the shop and left till sent for. But today the boy came down to the house toting a sack of oysters, and having a good look at the growing decorations in the patio. There seemed to be an idea that there were no limits to the eggs that we would need, and at times there were three or four children in the entrance, each with an egg or two to sell. A fisherman, a friend of Cayetano, from whom I often got fish, sent a present of a catfish. Cayetano suggested that his twin, Primitivo, would be pleased to come and help him wait.

"I think he can be useful to us, señor. It sees itself since at once that we need another besides me. And I can show him what to do, because of course when he was in the city he worked as a waiter too but then they do things there less finely than we do. At the finish and the end, he could run back and forth to the kitchen. Here he is now to see you."

At once Primitivo came round the corner, grinning, hat in hand. His shirt was very clean. I said he could come, and then went down the huerta to do a little work away from the hubbub of the patio.

Later Cayetano said to me, "I told Primitivo to come in this afternoon, he can open the oysters, there are such a lot of them."

"And what ought I to pay him?"

"Nothing, señor, nothing," said Cayetano. "He'll enjoy the party. Of course if you like to give him fifty centavos—"

Then he added: "I thought we could let him wear my other white coat. The less good."

Lunch was sketchy and very late. Afterward I put Rafles' sister to waxing the stalks of the poinsettias and tying them up in big sheaves, to hang on nails on the walls of the patio. They would last the evening. Primitivo arrived and disappeared into the huerta with dishes, the sack of oysters, and an opener. From the dining room came sounds of frenzied cleaning and furniture moving. We had to team up almost all the tables in the house to make a U big enough for us all to sit round. Sizzles of basting came from the kitchen, and altogether too much smell. By six Cayetano had readied the table in the patio where he was going to serve cocktails, and set the big table in the dining room. He had been very ingenious with tablecloths that didn't really match. He asked leave to go home, wash, and change. Then he would come and help Candelaria churn the ice cream.

"I want to make the cocktails at the last hour so that they won't throw themselves to lose," he said.

"Very well," I said. "And then I'll tell you exactly what you have to do tonight."

Then suddenly there was a lull. Primitivo and the oysters had vanished. Cayetano had gone. Rafles was nowhere to be seen. And in the kitchen Candelaria sat on a hard chair in a minor doze. The patio was still full of the litter of preparation—poinsettia leaves, excelsior, paper. The furniture, with the exception of the cocktail table, was in disorder. But that is also typical of Mexico. Suddenly, after frenetic work, everything is dropped, and long before preparations are complete. But don't worry. Just when you are in despair, everybody reappears, clean and prettied up, and in a twinkling the final arrangements are made. By eight everything had been given a final dust and sweep and polish, and not a chair was out of place. The kitchen was brimming with female relatives of the servants, and suddenly Primitivo appeared, smiling and self-conscious in Cayetano's second-best white coat.

I put him to help Candelaria with the ice cream, and took Cayetano to the other side of the patio to teach him what he must do at midnight. By the kitchen door Rafles was explaining to her impressed relatives what finger bowls were and why, as she polished them diligently. She sent a junior sister down the huerta to pick sprigs of orange blossom to float in the bowls.

"The señor says there are countries where azahar is very rare," I heard her saying. Spanish has that special musical word, azahar, that derives from Arabic, for orange blossom. "But of course, even there, it is always done to put flowers in finger bowls."

She was really being disagreeably superior and didactic. But it was her own idea to stud a great bunch of purple grapes with other sprigs of azahar.

When I had looked four times at the venison, once each at the sour-cream sauce, the ice cream, and the little cabbages of Brussels, it was still not nine o'clock. Candelaria, all her affairs well in hand, was standing at the door of the kitchen, wearing the smile of the satisfied laborer, and talking. She was not listening at all, and the company seemed to be taking the very sensible line of continuing its own conversations and letting her continue hers.

Cayetano had made the cocktails and put them in a big jug, but at intervals he poured back a shakerful and agitated it briskly. Primitivo was standing, fingering his jacket, and obviously ready to dash forward with filled glasses at the first hum of an automobile engine. There was a sudden flurry when Cayetano discovered that the olives had not been speared with toothpicks. I think he himself had forgotten it, but he put the blame on Primitivo in very audible tones:

"Very stupid of him," said Cayetano to me. "And he knows it. Look, now he's in the oven." Primitivo turned scarlet in the face and with trembling fingers repaired the omission.

At nine-thirty Cayetano brought me a cocktail and insisted on my taking it.

"No more than to see that I have made it right," he said.

I must say that this was not an orthodox cocktail. It was made of equal thirds of orange juice, an orange wine that they make out at Atotonilco, and Mexican brandy. It is one of those drinks that taste no stronger than lemonade and really have a kick like a mule.

At a quarter to ten he tried to make me have another.

"It's really making much cold, señor," he said.

But I dislike being too far ahead of my guests, and I refused. And just then the first car was heard.

Everyone jumped up and said, "There they come," and Candelaria crossed the patio and told me again, "There they come."

Entertaining guests to sit-down meals in Mexico is attended with difficulties of communication, for I know no country where more languages are constantly spoken or where one more often needs to use whatever languages one can even stammer in. Tonight I was expecting English, Americans, Swedes, Germans, Spaniards, the young Mexicans with a week-end house in Ajijic, Arturo and Xochitl, a Frenchman, and a Dane. Almost everybody spoke at least two languages, but the seating of the table was not easy, because by separating people from the groups they had arrived with, as like as not you sat them with people with whom they would not be able to talk. This difficulty was already felt in the patio, as the guests arrived and were introduced. But at any rate they could circulate, and Cayetano and Primitivo did a good job of ice-breaking with cocktails. By the time we went into the dining room things were going quite well, and the seating had not turned out too badly, except for a monolingual Spaniard who was marooned between an American and a Swede who had about the first four lessons of Hugo Spanish, but she was a pretty Spaniard and they made out.

Dinner went off in perfect order and calm. This is very Mexican. Beforehand, there is terrific fuss. Everybody expresses grave doubts as to whether he will be able to perform his task satisfactorily. The cook wonders whether she will be able to cook that dish. Everyone talks as if the menu would be fried disaster followed by baked breakdown. But when the time comes everything has turned out all right, everything goes smoothly, and everybody has thought up a little extra detail of his own. By the end of dinner the party was going strong and a Swedish painter had a long talk in Swedish with Xochitl who only speaks English and Spanish. We had sat down toward half past ten, and finished with only about a quarter hour of the old year to go.

I went out to the kitchen to see about the mull. But Candelaria, who had been so discouraging about it, and so hard of hearing that she couldn't hear what I wanted for it, let alone how I wanted it, had apparently had a moment of revelation. She had made the mull, and she had made it right. Cayetano had the largest tray ready, and on it a very small lump of charcoal, a huge pile of salt, a roll of bread, and a silver peso, doubtless his own. In a corner of the kitchen, while those present giggled subduedly, he rehearsed in a whisper the speech he was to make when he came in with the New Year: "And then I give the tray to the very blond lady, the lady who was sitting next you. Yes, I know."

Everything was ready.

A few minutes before twelve I sent Cayetano out into the street and shut the door. And as twelve finished striking he knocked as loud as thunder. When I asked, "Who?" he replied, "The New Year," clearly, and he came in with a fine flourish. But when it came to making his speech of good wishes as he handed the tray with its symbols of warmth, hospitality, food, and wealth to Swedish Astrid, confusion

147

set in, and he stood tongue-tied. For a moment the black-haired, copper-skinned Indio and the golden-haired, honey-skinned Swede faced each other in silence, and in the silence that held and sundered them it seemed that the new year, even the terrible year that was dawning, held promise of tomorrows of which mankind would at last not need to be ashamed. Then Astrid took over the situation and the tray, she and Cayetano stopped being symbols, and in a twinkling all the people who had been in the kitchen were weaving among us carrying tall glasses of steaming mull. We went into the huerta and stood round a bonfire that Primitivo had built. And when one of the Germans jumped over it, this Teutonic custom had an immediate success with the Indios, who jumped over it half a dozen times each. For long after the party had broken up and my guests gone home, sounds of gaiety and odors of spice and hot wine were wafted from the kitchen.

I lay in the dark and remembered Astrid and Cayetano as they stood together at the gates of the year, the fair and the dark, the Indio and the Swede, children of two ancient races oceans and cultures apart, beautiful and extreme.

JANUARY

NEW YEAR'S DAY opened with the sound of Candelaria's most metallic tones crying:

"Señor! Señor! My little chicks! A skunk has taken four of them, and two of the fattest! Ay, the poor little things!"

"Or perhaps it was a tlacuache," said Rafles.

Candelaria rushed into my room, to show me two heads that the skunk had left. She told me at length and with excitement exactly how the skunk, or tlacuache, had entered, how it got through the chicken wire, and from which hen each chick had been hatched. In the course of the recital she put down the heads absent-mindedly on the dressing table. Without change of tone or speed she went on to discuss the day's menu. She proposed making rice with black beans, called Moors and Christians, with fried bananas on top, and kidneys en casserole. Suddenly she said:

"God of my life! The milk! I can hear it has gained over me!" and left in a scamper.

When Rafles brought my breakfast she shook her head, said, "Ay, what a Candelaria," picked up the chicken heads and took them away.

When I was up I looked at the chicken run. Some of the wire had been torn, but Cayetano had already mended it with some quite insubstantial string. I was down by the run when Rafles came to tell me that a gentleman with some furniture had arrived.

This turned out to be Don Estanislao, whom I had seen so agreeably drunk when I went to order my chairs. He had a train of burros with him, and on the burros six equipales. They were nicely made, and the leather was a beautiful fawn color, though, like most Mexican leather, badly flawed. But they stank like a tannery. All new equipales do. Some recommend leaving them in the sun and some recommend leaving them in the shade. I have no idea which method enables them to stink most and longest But once the stench is gone, they are among the most comfortable chairs in the world, take up very little space, and last forever. They had arrived only a month late, but then Don Estanislao was making me a present of a small round table of wood and leather, which looked exactly like a drum, and which had doubtless come out of what was left over from the equipales. I paid him the fifteen pesos remaining due to him, and we arranged the equipales, some in the sun and some in the shade.

"When next you visit my factory," said Don Estanislao, "you will see it much bettered. I have put in a new door."

All this activity upset Candelaria, and at intervals, as I passed through the patio, I heard friends who had dropped in for a chat or to sell an egg being told about the skunk, or about the equipales. And at lunch she was still so unnerved that she forgot to put the fried bananas on top of the Moors and Christians. Suddenly she rushed into the dining room, brushing past Rafles. She was carrying a small frying pan and saying over and over again, "Ay, what a silly I am!" Regardless of Rafles' hissing at her, "A spoon, Candelaria, a spoon!" she dumped the bananas on my plate with her fingers. On the way back to the kitchen she realized what she had done. She sat down at her table, buried her head in her arms, and cried throughout the rest of lunch, which Rafles had to dish up and serve.

Today there was great excitement among the well diggers. They were down eight meters when they found a big tree trunk. It was almost stone-hard and certainly centuries old. When they got it out, they all started shouting, "A spring! We've found a spring!"

Everybody temporarily left work on the house to go and peer down into the well, where one could see nothing at all.

But a spring it was, and very handy. There are many such in Ajijic, but the chief ones have been lost. Legend says that a pre-Conquest queen of Tonalá, by name Zihuapilli, used to come once a year to Ajijic in order to bathe in seven sacred springs, whence presumably Ajijic derives its name, The Place Where the Water Springs Forth. Nothing is known of the location of these old shrines. But if they existed at the time of the Conquest, one may be reasonably sure that the church is built on the site of one at least, and that the principal one, for such was the invariable practice of Christianity. Ajijic was certainly anciently settled, but it is poor in remains and legends. In general, in Mexico, the Azteca, who were imperialists, overlaid or obliterated cultures anterior to theirs. Their own provenance they explained picturesquely.

There was a place called Whiteness. It was far to the north. And from the seven caves of the place called Whiteness seven tribes set out toward the south. The leader of the last tribe was named Meci and his people called themselves Mecitín. All the seven tribes came from Aztlán, which is whiteness in the Nahuatl tongue, and all the seven tribes were called Azteca, the people of whiteness. They came down from Aztlán and wandered southward with many stops, deviations, and adventures. This migration was probably taking place in the second half of the eleventh and the first half of the twelfth centuries.

Nobody knows how far they came, and where to look for Aztlán. You may refer the place called Whiteness to a tradition of Asiatic migration to America, you may say that Aztlán is the whiteness of Siberian snows and Behring ice. Or you may say that Aztlán is own brother to Asgard and never existed at all anywhere. Nobody knows whether the Azteca took over an older legend and adapted it to themselves. Nobody knows by which of the many possible routes the Amerindians filtered southward. So it would be absurd to expect to know anything about a village called The Place Where the Water Springs.

But not far from the tree trunk, the diggers unearthed a stone idol about two feet high broken into three pieces. The idol's face is square and grim. I shall not take him away from his place. I shall mend him and let him guard the well.

Candelaria came and asked me to read a letter to her. Having given me the letter, she sat down and fixed on me an attentive and unwavering gaze. There was a long pause. The letter was written in pencil, and it was frequently misspelled. Most of the v's were b's, but then most of the b's were v's, to make up. Some words lacked an h at the beginning, others had one added on. Some words were split in two, the first half attached to the preceding, the second half to the subsequent word. It was not an easy task to make sense of the letter, and there were one or two passages that I never deciphered.

The letter was from Candelaria's mother, Remedios. It had been written by a niece who had been to school, and announced a visit. She was coming the following week.

I asked Candelaria about her, and learned that she had been born in Jiquilpan, where she still lived. Now Jiquilpan is the town where ex-President Lázaro Cárdenas was born, and he has done a great deal for it. It has a stadium and a hotel and almost all the houses are newly plastered and painted. Candelaria's mother did not like living there before all this was done, but now she is happy there.

I asked Candelaria why her mother didn't come to join her in Ajijic.

"So I said, señor," she answered, "several times I've said it. But she doesn't like villages, and she always says that she has some nice chickens which it would give her much pity to leave."

Candelaria would have enlarged on the theme, had not Cayetano just then hurried in and said, "Says a gentleman, if we don't want to sell him our slack?"

As I did not at once answer he repeated: "Says a gentleman, if we don't want to sell him our slack?"

"But whatever is it, Cayetano?"

"The charcoal slack, señor."

"And what does he want it for?"

"For making bricks," said Cayetano. "One can always sell slack, and we have much."

I said we might as well sell it and asked how it was measured.

"By donkeyload."

"Yes, but how much is a donkeyload?"

Cayetano thought for a minute. Then he said, "It varies, señor. It varies according to the size of the donkey."

I gave up, and told Cayetano to get what he could for the slack. He was away a long time, but when he returned his face was beaming. He laid some coins on the table.

"The gentleman didn't want to pay more than two pesos fifty," he said. I followed his glance, which was fixed on the money. Hurriedly I counted it. It was two pesos seventy-five. I congratulated Cayetano on his success, and he deprecated my congratulations and thanks. He gave a little nervous cough.

"Anything like that, señor, it would be good if you let me do for us, so that we aren't cheated."

In the morning arrived the big earthenware jars which I had ordered for the children's party. Dressed in gaudy paper they are filled with fruit, hung from a tree, and smacked at with a stick until they disgorge their contents.

"Elpidia knows very well how to make piñatas," Candelaria had said. So as soon as the jars arrived Candelaria set to work to make flour paste. Cayetano got out the many rolls of brightly colored crepe paper which I had brought from Guadalajara and Rafles went to fetch Elpidia. When she came she set to at once in a businesslike way, cutting up paper into elaborately fringed frills, soon acquiring a crowd of assistants, including her small boy Silvanito and various female relations of Rafles. Candelaria came with a pot full of paste. Then Elpidia put one of the jars on a table and surveyed it. She screwed up her eyes, retreated, put her head on one side, opened her toothless mouth and shut it again, advanced and fingered the jar's curving sides, and then announced, "I am going to make a carrot."

She smeared the whole jar with paste, then arranged row upon row of orange paper till it was entirely covered. Then she tied a cord below its rim and swung it from a rafter, while she added the long point of the carrot. Then at the top she put on long plumy green leaves. And the work of art was complete. Cayetano and Rafles filled the jar with an assortment of fruit, peanuts, and sugar cane, and the piñata was complete.

I suppose she saw me eyeing the jars, because she said, "Why don't you do one, señor? It's very easy."

I decided to make a pineapple, folding innumerable small squares of yellow paper into diamonds and sticking them in overlapping rows. It was much harder than it looked. In no time I was sticky from head to foot with flour paste, and was relieved when I was called away to talk to Don Bernabé about the roof of the coal shed and could turn over my pineapple to Rafles, who had decided not to sweep the patio but to make piñatas instead.

On the afternoon of January 5 a number of children had collected on the beach in front of the huerta gate, anticipating the party by a whole day. On the sixth, the Day of the Kings, by two o'clock they were gathering again, though the party was scheduled to start at five, which meant any time after six. However, there they sat with Indio patience, the tiny ones accompanied by their mothers, the elder on their own. They were all in their best clothes, the little girls mostly in mirror satin with ribbons in their hair and wearing earrings and any other bits of jewelry they owned. The poor, dirty and without fresh frocks, were rare, and somewhat self-conscious. All the boys had on clean shirts with clean blue trousers or overalls.

In the middle of the afternoon arrived the actors who were to perform the miracle play, the Pastores. The girls were all very much beribboned, carried tall staffs hung with paper streamers, and wore flat straw hats decorated with upstanding paper flowers. They were very bright and gaudy. The boys represented various personages and wore masks. A monk, a devil, and so on. By this time the audience had considerably swollen. We had calculated on a couple of hundred, but long before five Cayetano estimated that there were already more than two hundred there, and more were arriving all the time. And now, on the fringes of the crowd, had appeared quite a number of grownups.

Inside the huerta, in the covered mirador, Cayetano had collected the piñatas, as well as big baskets filled with fruit, candy, and cheap toys. When the schoolteachers arrived, he opened the door and brought out some chairs, which he arranged in a stiff row against the wall. A thrill went through the crowd. Something was happening. I greeted the teachers, two men and two women, and sat down with them. Nothing more occurred for some time. Then one of the teachers suggested that they should separate their charges into groups, boys and girls, big and small, so as to maintain some sort of order in the proceedings. They set about doing this. It took some time.

Then Cayetano came out and began hurling his rope at a suitable arm of a eucalyptus tree, to the annoyance of quantities of bees, who are now making eucalyptus-flower honey. Catcalls greeted one or two failures. Then the rope leaped an arm and settled cosily into a convenient crotch. By now the crowd was buzzing.

Suddenly, out of the huerta, came Cayetano and Rafles, each carrying a piñata. A shrill chorus from the children:

"Look! Look! Two of them, and there are more inside—at least four more—"

Two of the schoolteachers rose and took the stick from under Cayetano's arm, and Cayetano hitched onto the rope the piñata that was a carrot. Then he took the other end of the rope and hauled the piñata up into the air. One of the teachers blindfolded a small girl, spun her round, gave her the stick, and the fun began. The crowd formed a ring, and inside it the small girl charged hither and thither, guided and misguided by shouts from friends, whirling the big stick in all directions, while Cayetano, tugging and releasing the rope, made the piñata rise and fall and dance, always just out of reach of the swipes of the stick. After a minute or so the girl was retired and a small boy was blindfolded and given the stick. And so on, one after the other, amid a lot of noise and laughter. When the seventh child was hurtling about the ring, Cayetano let her hit the piñata. And the next blow caught it as it rose and smashed the earthenware jar. Oranges and bananas and lengths of sugar cane poured out and suddenly what had been a ring was a squirming mound of bodies as everyone scrambled for the fruit. In a moment a cloud of dust hung over the scrum. No doubt it would have been even worse if Cayetano hadn't watered the beach. The teachers extricated infants, cuffed the bigger boys, shouted, and generally added to the confusion. But when it was all over and the scrum dissolved, leaving not a scrap of fruit, not a shred of colored paper, miraculously no one had been hurt.

The same routine was followed with the remaining piñatas, nobody getting tired of scrambling or watching others scramble. Banana skins and sugar cane fiber accumulated on the sand. At last, the final piñata, the elaborate pineapple, fell into shreds, and Cayetano, sweating shinily (for it is work hauling heavy piñatas up and down, as I discovered when I took a turn at the rope), emerged from a smother of small boys.

Now the schoolteachers took over, once more separating male from female, and this time lining them up in two long crocodiles, stretching from the huerta door far along the beach. Inside the mirador stood the teachers, Candelaria, Rafles, Cayetano, and myself, prepared to hand out the presents.

In spite of the teachers' efforts, there was a lot of muddle, and to my certain knowledge one very small boy, with big eyes put in with a smutty finger, came by five times, each time tucking his loot inside his shirt and arriving on the next round more and more adipose. Others begged for extra things for an imaginary brother or sister who was ill and couldn't come, who had to stay at home and look after the house, or who was "just over there, don't you see, behind the tree, señor, he's hurt his leg and can't go well." We began lavishly, with three packets for each child, fruit, candy, and ribbons or dolls for the girls, fruit, candy, and tops, tin automobiles, or balloons for the boys. But the trays and baskets were emptying while the double line of children stretched far along the wall and we had to reduce. But at last it was over, everybody had had something, and Cayetano had run up the huerta to cut a few oranges and limes for a very small boy who had been found inside the mirador underneath the table, and who had been too frightened to compete in anything, was indeed too frightened even to talk.

Meanwhile, the Pastores, who could not risk their costumes in the piñata scramble, had been given previously reserved packages of fruit, and had received their toys. And now Cayetano rearranged the chairs along the wall. We sat down, somewhat exhausted ourselves, and after not more than twenty minutes the show began.

The Pastores stood in two lines, one behind the other, facing us from a distance of a few feet, with their backs resolutely turned to almost the whole audience, and proceeded to act straight at us. Chanting rhyming couplets, they performed a simple dance. Two steps forward, two steps back. The tall flowers on the girls' hats swayed, the paper streamers on the staffs waved. The tallest girl marshaled them into line and hissed and grimaced at them, in the interval smirking at us. She fancied herself. The boys banged their weapons on the nearest resonant substance, the two lines went on taking two steps forward and two back, and they went on reciting interminable verses in high monotones. As suddenly as they had started they stopped, all except the smallest girl, who was left speaking alone. One look from the tall girl who fancied herself reduced the child to scarlet silence. The star herself then took the stage. She came forward to within about two feet of us and began to recite alone. She had three gestures and she used them all. She was starting the story of the Nativity, and she was easier to understand than the chorus had been. She talked for quite a time. Meanwhile, the other actors whispered together, and one or two left the stage to chat with friends in the crowd. The smallest girl remained stock-still, gazing with rapture at nothing. The stalk of one of the tall paper roses on her hat had been bent and the flower hung down, tickling her forehead. She made one or two attempts to move it with the discreetest headshakes. In vain. She stood frozen in military stiffness, and a large tear gathered in the corner of her eye. But just when the situation became intolerable, the star finished her piece, whisked back into line, beckoned imperiously without looking behind her, and there they all were again, dancing two steps forward and two steps back in straight lines and chanting away. I saw the smallest girl, who at the moment was behind a boy wearing the mask and horns of Satan, break off the bent flower and throw it away.

That figure over, there ensued an immense and quite unintelligible conversation between the small boy dressed as a monk and another small boy of unguessable disguise but who spent most of the time on all fours and was no doubt an animal. Then there was another dance. And so it went on, lengthy dialogues alternating with short reels.

It was dusk now, and behind the Pastores, behind the squatting audience, the willows were dark lace against the topaz water. We had not noticed the sunset, and now it was fading. Cayetano came with a couple of hurricane lamps which he put on the wall, Candelaria and Rafles held flashlights, and someone brought some torches of oily kindling wood, which willing hands upheld. The darkness gathered, and still the interminable chanting, the endless two-back two-forward shuffle went on. I got a little chilly, and thought of a cocktail in a melancholy way. The teachers sat stiffly, with faces of stone. From a snatch of verse, it seemed to me we had got about as far as the flight into Egypt, and I had no idea how long the show would go on. It is the same with peasant spectacles the world over. They don't know when to start and they don't know when to stop. Beginning late, they go on forever. It was now after eight.

Then Cayetano whispered something to me, and I turned to look inside the huerta door. The mirador had been cleared of all the remains of the present giving, and instead there was a table set for supper, strewn with great poinsettias, and lit by red candles, grouped around the Wreath of the Magi, a cake in the form of a ring in which is hidden a small doll baby. On a table behind were glasses and bottles. I don't think the teachers were unwilling to come and drink, while outside the Nativity play droned on.

A lady called Lupe sent to ask if I would like to buy some plants for my garden. She had been at yesterday's party and had observed that I had no tuberoses and very few little Bethlehems. The Bethlehem is a small plant, really wild but much used in gardens, which grows bushy to a height of about a foot and has glossy foliage and single flowers, each shaped like a phlox blossom but larger. It comes in all the red, pinks, and whites you can imagine.

"And who is Lupe?" I asked.

"Oh," answered Rafles, "she lives in a very nice house just over there. You'd know it at once, it has steps made of brick. She is the sister of Bernardina, she of the little shop. She is rich, she often goes to the capital. She sells plants."

Later in the morning I went along the principal street and had no difficulty in recognizing Lupe's home. It had not only brick steps but a brick sidewalk.

She herself was middle-aged and buxom and aflash with gold teeth. She led me into a veranda where the light fell green through trailing ferns, and whence one could see not only the new-painted green furniture of the veranda itself but into a kitchen whose wall was hung with enough earthenware to furnish a large banquet and into a bedroom where a brass bedstead, draped in stiff pink muslin tied with mauve silk bows, stood dominant.

After a little conversation she led me round the garden. It was so full of flowers and flowering shrubs that paths had been reduced to trails. They meandered without plan and we ducked under curtains of jasmine, edged round bushes of poinsettia, and balanced our way along narrow stone ledges between stocks and hollyhocks. We met a very large and fierce duck. It was about the largest duck I have ever seen, and it glared and hissed.

"I am the only woman she doesn't attack," said Lupe. "And she would defend me. She's equal of useful to a dog."

The walls of the garden were lined with flowerpots, ollas, broken shards of earthenware pots, and old cans, and in these varied containers grew roses and carnations and violets. She had whole beds of tuberoses. I had intended to buy a plant or two, but I ended by making quite a considerable purchase, about twelve pesos' worth. Lupe promised to dig up the chosen plants in the cool of the evening and send them round to me.

"Even so, won't they feel the change a lot?" I asked. "Won't they get hot and dry up?"

"That yes no," she said. And when later a mozo brought them round they were perfectly fresh. But then each plant, with a generous blob of earth about its roots, was covered with damp grass and wrapped up in a folded green banana leaf, which was then tied with banana fiber. Nothing could be more practical, nothing simpler and cheaper. Wrappings? Why? You have them right there in the garden. When you unpack you just throw the wrappings away. There are plenty more. Baskets? String? Moss? Why?

The first I knew of the arrival of Candelaria's mother was hearing a strange thin voice in the kitchen saying, "Candelaria, can I get meat every day, every day without fail?"

Candelaria answered in one of her shorter spates, and I didn't listen. Then the mother's voice came again:

"But I must have meat every day. You know I must. Remember, Candelaria." Remedios' voice was very authoritative and she added: "That is what I don't like about living in the country. In the city, one has shops and cinemas, and meat every day."

Candelaria herself looked well on toward fifty, but probably was not far into the forties. However, I was interested to see this sophisticated mother, who was presumably at least sixty, old for an Indio.

Entering the kitchen I almost fell over a crutch. Beside the table, in Candelaria's chair, the chair that she never allowed Cayetano or Rafles to sit in, was a very small, very wrinkled, very bent old woman. Aslant across her nose, with neither lens in front of an eye, was lodged a pair of spectacles. But as one eye was quite white with cataract and the other seemed to be affected, no doubt that did not matter.

Candelaria prodded the old woman and hissed at her, "The señor, this is the señor."

The old woman heaved and hoisted herself to her feet uncertainly, and then extended a hand which, with the thin forearm, looked like a cornstalk. Candelaria stooped for the crutch and shored her mother up with it, and, after greetings, we talked for a few minutes, while old Remedios swayed and wavered to and fro, pushing at her glasses with her free hand, and assured me that she didn't like the quietness of country life, not for herself, but Candelaria was different, and she knew that Candelaria was very happy working for me.

At this point there emerged from under the table a skinny and apparently elderly turkey hen. A string was tied to its leg and the other end of the string was knotted round Remedios' wrist. They had traveled together.

"The turkey hen," cried Candelaria. "Give it to the señor, Mamma. Remedios has brought it as a present for you."

All along the shore the fishermen have been building little promontories of rock, about ten yards apart and jutting a few feet into the lake. Now the whole shore is divided into neat compartments. These are very handy for those who fish with the atarraya, the circular hand cast net, for throwing it into one compartment will not disturb the fish in the next. Behind the fishermen's promontories are built little piles of dry dung, about one pile to every five or six compartments. As dusk falls they set light to these piles. They do not flame, but sparkle and glow and send up pillars of gray smoke.

"Yes, señor," said an old fisherman in a shower of diminutives, "the little smoke and the little fire attract the little charal."

He sat on his haunches watching closely the water in his compartment. His trousers were rolled almost hip-high. His atarraya was in his hand, and to his back was strapped the tall basket with one flat side, like the French peasant's hotte, in which to put his catch. I could note no change, no ruffle in the surface, no shadow passing beneath the water. But suddenly the old man rose, and, crouching, went softly toward the compartment. So gently that not a ripple moved round his ankles, he entered the water, stopped after a few steps, stood poised, and launched his net. It fell with a plop in a shining circle, and he stooped to draw it in. In its center he had three or four score of the shining little fishes.

It grew dark. And all along the shore pinpoints of fire glowed, and in the thin darkness shadowy figures moved. There was no moon, and in the sky the Milky Way was a shining surf and the stars gleamed very white above the red stars ringing the shore.

I had to go to Guadalajara and got back after dark. Several lamps were burning in the patio and in their light were gathered the servants, their relatives, and their friends. The group parted and I saw in its midst Cayetano. He was lying in a steamer chair and he seemed to be unconscious. One of his legs was stretched over a kitchen chair. The trouser leg was rolled up and his knee was dark with blood. None of the many people present was doing anything, but they were talking a lot. They all spoke to me at once and Cayetano opened one eye a little and made a movement with his shoulders that sketched graphically a desire to rise and the conviction that no one would let him.

It appeared that Cayetano had slipped and fallen and landed with his knee on a piece of broken glass, right here in the patio. This took a little time to disentangle from the cries of "I saw it happen, señor, ay, God of my life" and "Poor boy, how it bled" and "He has the face of being very bad."

When I had washed the wound, it was obvious that it wasn't very serious. The cut was about three inches long, slanting down from the kneecap, but though it looked deep the boy could flex his knee readily. No serious damage had been done. Maybe it would have been better for a few stitches, but there was nobody to stitch it. I doused it in alcohol, padded it with gauze, and bandaged it. I told Cayetano that he would be well quite soon, whereupon he sat up with no effort at all and stopped behaving as if he were unconscious. He had a little fever, and I decided to take him home to bed. Eight or ten of the audience assisted him into the car. It was quite plain that Cayetano enjoyed driving home through the village with the car door open and his leg, stiff as a post, sticking out of it.

Cayetano recovered quickly. In three days he was back at work. In a week he was forgetting to keep up his interesting limp. But the day after the accident, by midday, I heard that gossip said that Cayetano had been wounded with a knife by a jealous woman in Chapala. After that, any rich item of village gossip was labeled "a case of Cayetano's knee."

Candelaria is most upset, because her mother wants to leave already. Old Remedios says she cannot stand the quietness of village life. Peering out of her near-blind eyes, with her glasses rakishly askew on her forehead, she told me that there was nothing to look at. In Jiquilpan, she said, there was always something going on. It is true that the Mexico City–Guadalajara highway goes through Jiquilpan, and maybe Remedios can still distinguish something as large as an automobile. She also told me that she has a very nice house in Jiquilpan, far nicer than Candelaria's here. I think she considers it a lot nicer than mine too. She said that it contained a fine room, which has the adobe walls plastered halfway up inside, all except one whence much plaster has fallen. The house also has a big yard, where she has seventeen chickens and two turkeys. And, above all, it has outside the front door a bench built of bricks. I think this is what Remedios really likes. Probably she spends half the day there. Even if Ajijic were full of things to look at, there is outside my door no such bench. So Remedios is going, and she is very scornful of Candelaria's fears for her on the journey. She came to Guadalajara with relatives, and with friends on to Ajijic. But she is returning to Jiquilpan alone. She says she is going next Saturday.

The whole day long Candelaria's metallic monotone, which anyway always sounds as if she were scolding, has been resounding in the kitchen as she tried to dissuade Remedios. Not the coffee grinder, not the most sizzling frying could drown it, though it seemed to me that Candelaria managed to put a resentful note even into the frying. Like most deaf people, Candelaria bangs about. But today has been a high point, even for her. She is a good cook, and she is honest. But at times I wish the kitchen were a hundred yards away.

As if I had not had enough of Candelaria and Remedios, the next day brought a new flurry. It was very early in the morning and I was lying in bed sniffing the coffee that was roasting for breakfast, when I heard a great commotion. An excited voice started to talk in the kitchen, another broke in, and a third made the conversation quite unintelligible. Then Candelaria screamed. There was a crash as the coffee grinder fell to the floor, and I emerged from my room to see Candelaria scampering out of the house, with her shawl in her hand. Something is really urgent if an Indio woman doesn't wrap up her head before going out. Several people explained what had happened.

"It's Remedios, señor. She's fallen in the well."

This indeed seemed serious. I went round to the little house where Candelaria slept. There was a well there that was no longer used for water but as a rubbish dump. It was still ten or twelve feet deep and had a little water in the bottom.

When I arrived there was a crowd round the well, and Candelaria was lamenting loudly and calling on a number of saints. Cayetano had fixed a rope to the old crossbeam and was just disappearing down the well. We waited, straining to hear the muffled sounds from below. Then Cayetano shouted to haul up the rope. It was hauled, and up came, neatly knotted into the rope, Remedios' crutch. This was something of an anticlimax, and Candelaria wept loudly. Down went the rope again. After another long pause Cayetano shouted. This time the rope came up slowly, heavily.

"God of my life! Little mother! Little mother!" screamed Candelaria as over the edge of the wall appeared Remedios' face, her spectacles unbroken but hanging from one ear with a lens on her chin.

Slowly she came to the surface, was pulled in, unknotted, and helped to her feet. She shook off her helpers and reached for her crutch, which was given her. Candelaria, still weeping wildly, fell upon her in an embrace which almost knocked her down. Remedios was unresponsive. As soon as she could she said, "Why do you upset yourself so, little daughter? I want my breakfast. And I want steak."

It appeared that she had been down the well for half an hour before anyone heard her cries. She had steak.

The night was cold with that nonstimulant heat of the tropics. I had a fever and couldn't sleep. Suddenly I saw something moving at the top of the high door. In the shadow, it was a tendril of creeper in the wind, a ribbon of seaweed on the swing of the tide, but in the beam of the flashlight it turned out to be a snake. A couple of feet of it were weaving about into the room, its flat head darting and its body rippling. I am not used to snakes, and I have a horror of them, the sort of horror some people have of cats. I wished then that I had let Cayetano sleep outside the door as he had wanted to. It was far too late to call him now, and my stick was in the other room. I took the Flit gun and Flitted the snake. Afterward I learned that this was a most unorthodox procedure. Anyway, it worked. The snake retreated, vanished, and did not reappear. In the morning it was seen at the top of the door of another room, and was killed by Cayetano. It was a coral snake, poisonous and very beautiful.

My chill kept me in bed. Everyone was very attentive, but it is when you are ill among ignorant people that you think longingly of telephones and urban conveniences. There used to be many people who thought it bold, if not rash, to live in Ajijic. I have known people in Guadalajara who were afraid to go to Chapala, and people who lived in Chapala who would have been afraid to live in Ajijic. This is all changing now with the bettering of communications. But such fears were always rubbish. By and large the Indio will treat you as you treat him. I live here with doors unlocked, protected by easily scalable walls. I have no firearms, for invariably, in the Old as well as the New World, I have found one is much safer unarmed than armed among primitive people. I knew a man who, in the wilder regions of Mexico, did carry a gun. But whenever he rode into a strange village he handed his gun ostentatiously to his mozo, who rode behind him. Here I have not even a large dog, only my big-eared Motzín and my Dackel pup. Fears of robbery and violence don't haunt my fevers. But as the thermometer registers 104 degrees, one has wild imaginings of really serious illness exposed to village treatment. That night Cayetano insisted on sleeping outside my door on a mat, and he asked to have Motzín and the Dackel sleep with him.

"Because I sleep very well, señor, but then if you called the dogs would hear and they would wake me."

The next morning my temperature was down, and I was able to enjoy it when Candelaria, hearing that I still had a bad headache, came with some leaves of a bush called gigante, which is said to be poisonous to animals (and indeed in the driest season, when cattle search the shore for any blade of green, I have never seen a gigante bush touched), and bound them to my forehead, saying that they were of the most best for headaches.

"For a fever," said Rafles, her round eyes staring blankly out of her round face, "I heard say that twelve little crabs stewed in water are very good."

"Pues, when I was so ill with my kidneys," said Aurora, rather hoping, I thought, that I was ill with my kidneys, "I took grasshoppers' legs and got well very quickly."

A couple of days later I was lying in a long chair on the beach in the shadow of the willows and watching the fishermen hauling the big seine net. Their long slow motions do not give the impression of hard work, though hard work it is, but are very soothing to watch. They had some mojarra in the net today, small fish, bony, but with a good flavor, and not caught very often. I bought them for lunch. There was a catfish too, and when I refused to buy it, saying I didn't like its soggy flesh, the fisherman said, "But if you cut it into little beefsteaks and grill them or bake them, you have a flesh as firm as you could wish."

So after that I had to buy the catfish too.

Before lunch I went round to my land. Don Bernabé was not there, nor was Merced, and there wasn't a full complement of workmen. One of them looked quite startled to see me. Presumably the grapevine had failed to report that I was no longer in bed. Practically no work had been done.

Just then Don Bernabé arrived, courtly as ever, and with many hat wavings complimented me at length on my return to health.

"And see, señor, how well the works of construction have progressed."

The tank indeed had been put on the roof of the garage, but it had not been connected to anything. And I knew as well as he did that plastering in the kitchen had been nearly done a week before. He then showed me a narrow trench, destined to be part of the drainage, which he said had been particularly difficult to dig owing to the quantity of stones in the soil. When that was done he gave a number of brisk orders to his workmen, and everyone began to move about quickly. He himself then turned to me.

"Dispense me, señor, that I do not continue our sympathetic and so enjoyable conversation, but the works of construction take precedenci-ency of everything."

Then he put down his hat, took off his sarape, and went up a lad-der with speed and agility.

Candelaria had cooked the mojarra, and had grilled steaks of cat-fish according to the fisherman's recommendation, and had made small dull squashes interesting by stuffing them with cream cheese and capers. I slept all afternoon, but was awakened because Candelaria had found some coffee.

"It's very dear," she said. "It's one-twenty a kilo, and last year it was only a peso, but it's very good, look, and you can have twenty kilos."

She held out a coffee bean and herself bit and munched another. I relied on her judgment, and said we would buy the twenty kilos.

Cayetano, who had been there during the conversation, said, when Candelaria had gone, "It isn't dear, señor. This year some people are selling at one-forty. Sometimes Candelaria is too economical." And he tapped his left elbow with his right hand. "She has the hard elbow, she is a little mean."

And I felt that this was a reproach to me, for not having let him arrange the transaction, as he recommended after his masterly han-dling of the sale of charcoal slack.

Remedios had decided to take the bus that runs along the lake shore to Jocótepec, and there to change and catch the Mexico City bus for Jiquilpan. Nothing could alter her decision, and at last the day came for her departure. By now Candelaria, who had been weep-ing daily, was smiling again. Having failed to induce her mother to stay, she seemed to have decided to make her a heroine of boldness. She was expatiating on the risks and dangers of the road, on Remedios' blindness, age, and general infirmity, and on her will of iron, to all and sundry.

I went with the rest of the household to see Remedios off. On the edge of the sidewalk outside the shop at which the bus stops was an astonishing assortment of baggage. I counted thirteen pieces. Two of them were ollas and one an enamel saucepan, and all three of these were stuffed with goods, covered with cloths, and meshed in string. There was a string bag full of fruit whose provenance I did not inquire. There were baskets of various sizes, one cardboard grip, and an attaché case. And there was a very small pig.

At last the bus arrived. With surprising efficiency Remedios and her bundles, including the pig, which shared her lap with the attaché case, were stowed inside. And then there ensued a very long wait, while other cargo was unloaded and the drivers had chats with friends and a lemonade apiece.

Among other things unloaded from the bus was a big brown globe of a parcel. It was lapped and wrapped in about twenty yards of string, in the Mexican way, for here string is mostly soft and fragile. Under the string was brown paper. The man who should have caught it missed it, and it fell heavily and rolled down the road. When it was retrieved it was found to be addressed to me. It had come from a glass factory in Guadalajara.

"How nice," said Candelaria, into whose charge I gave it, "we are wanting that glass. Oh, no, it'll be quite all right, done up in its little straw."

All this time Remedios sat in her place and every now and then Candelaria went to the window and bobbed up and down like a chicken after grain, straining to hear her mother's voice. Every now and again Remedios seemed to look at me and I smiled and waved.

"The señor!" screamed Candelaria. "The señor is waving to you."

Then Remedios, who had of course not seen me at all, smiled in what she imagined to be my direction and nodded her head. This happened about every five minutes.

By now all the passengers were aboard, and the drivers too climbed in. But the bus did not start, though everyone was waving. One of the drivers had forgotten something. He got down and disappeared up a side street. There was an anticlimactical pause. Pointless conversations were begun, Candelaria bobbed again, I waved, Candelaria shouted at Remedios, and Remedios waved vaguely. And then, without warning, quite suddenly, the bus roared into motion with a terrific jerk and bounced away up the street. The driver had returned and climbed in on the other side where nobody had seen him. Candelaria was left crying shrilly, "May it go well with you, little mother! Don't forget the little pig's little dinner! Allah grant that you arrive well! May it go very well with you!"

Then a great cloud of dust obscured the departing bus, and Candelaria flung her apron over her head and sobbed her way back to the kitchen.

After a little while she came to me, with a turquoise-blue goblet in her hand and in her hair a good deal of the dried grass that they had used for packing.

"Look, señor, just as I told you, not one thing broken. I've washed everything and put it all away."

There was a little paper tab with a trademark gummed to the bottom of the goblet.

"Couldn't you get that off?" I asked.

"It cost me much work not to wash those off," said Candelaria.

Coming back along the beach as the evening wind was blowing I came across Venustiano. He had with him a boy and a young man. There was a petate spread on the ground, and beside it two tall baskets, one full of coffee. From the full one the boy was filling a flat basket which he handed to the youth, who raised it high above his head and poured the coffee slowly out, so that it fell onto the petate. As it fell, windpower husked it. Previously the coffee, after picking and grading, had been dried, and the husks fell away in shreds and powder. It is the evening wind, the Colimano, which is best for this.

The coffee crop is now being harvested. It has not been harmed by that unheard-of occurrence, the slight frost of last month. It is not an easy job, for the berries have to be picked one by one. If they are stripped by running the hand down a branch the small shoots for next year's flowering are stripped too and the bush spoiled. The berries do not all ripen at once, and it may be necessary to make three or four separate pickings at intervals.

When the basketful of coffee had all passed through the wind, they began again, returning it to the first basket. I stood watching, for the scene was attractive, with its rhythmic movements and the pale brown stream of beans and the whites and pale pinks of the men's clothes against the green-silver lake and the silver-green willows. Mexico is full of functional beauties.

I asked Venustiano whether the scene were too commonplace for him to see that it was beautiful as well.

"It takes a long time, of course," he said, "to husk the beans like this. But it's true, it's a beautiful evening, and we can enjoy it."

After supper I went out and walked along the beach again. It was dark with many shades of black, so that between the murk of sky and lake the mountains detached themselves in heavier shadow. Down the beach the fishermen's fires shone with tomato-red glitters, small and quiet and friendly. In the stillness one felt a positive peace. And it was almost a homecoming when, round the point by the palm trees, I came suddenly upon a brighter fire, a man's fire of sticks and con-stalks, and beside it a shack built of bamboo uprights thatched with banana leaves. When the fisher family moves on, the shack will be left, but the heats and the rains will demolish it and clear it all neatly away, and next year another will be built. It is the easiest way of living, especially if a few ollas and petates are all your household gear. The family was round the fire. A young couple, their handsome fine-boned Indio faces flaring amber in the firelight. A little girl of six or so, demure and adult-looking in her shawl, and in her lap, asleep, a baby, who was, one felt somehow sure, a man-child. Perhaps the man was not fishing tonight, or fishing later, or perhaps he had a partner who was at work somewhere with the net. But I could easily believe that the family was there for me to enjoy, sitting still and rapt and serene, all in tiger colors, even the leaf walls leaping tawny. The fire was so small in the night of the huge lake that its crackles seemed timid and defiant, whistling in the dark. Except for the furtive swishing of cast nets, and, distantly, filtered through the thick mango trees, a faint singing back in the village, with a guitar splashing sometimes above the high strained voices, there was no other sound. Sneaker-soled and silent I had come, and I stood in shadow, beyond the fire's most daring snatch at darkness, and watched the family, that was any family and all families, that was youth and quiet and intimacy and had nothing at all to do with crazy slogans and huge drunken numbers. No man could watch a million families thus.

At last the little girl, folding her shawl neatly round herself and the baby, lay down to sleep. And then the man, tilting his wide pale hat forward over his face, leaned backward, stretched, yawned, and was still. The flames faltered as if they would like to lie down as well, and the young woman's face turned from amber to ivory. With the least possible movement she put some more sticks on the fire.

FEBRUARY

THE month opened with a snap of the January chill still on the air, but there were no more clouds and the sky was smooth porcelain of eggshell blue. The hummers haunt the blossom of the male papaya tree, small yellow flowers that grow in clusters. All the orange trees are in bloom, so that waves of perfume fill the huerta and in the still air rise, startling as light and thick as color, to the terrace. Many trees have flower and fruit at the same time, making a mock of human ambitions. One tiny orange tree, not more than eight or ten inches high, has one white flower—which must of course be cut. The orange trees wear their flowers in a certain disarray, but the tangerine trees wear them very neatly, they are debutantes' bouquets. They are young girls in caprice, too, because for one season or maybe two a tangerine will blaze with fruit, and the next flower fruitlessly. The rich foliage of citrus trees somehow suggests running water, and they are never so beautiful as when the irrigation trenches are agurgle. But it is difficult to get the mozo who comes to help Cayetano to believe that, much as it needs irrigation, a tree should never be touched directly by water, but that the trunk should be earthed up and the water allowed to flow outside this bank and within a wider banked circle. Damp will cause the tree to gum.

"Thank you very much for the paint of Bordeaux," said Venustiano. "I think it has stopped my trees gumming. It is good not to let water run around an orange tree when it is in flower, unless it has always been much watered, or it will drop all its blossom. And my father always said, 'Never try to make a burro carry more than he knows he can, and never prune an orange tree.'"

On the first of the month Don Bernabé told me that his compadre in San Antonio would send the tiles from the church roof immediately. It was so long since the day we had passed through and Don Bernabé had talked to his compadre that I had forgotten all about these particular tiles. But Mexican memories are very capricious, and as often as not work in the end. The tiles were a little dear, but I did not want to go back on the understanding now.

It is fairly practical to make your roof of tiles, laid on impermeable paper, with bound bamboos under that. But I did not like bamboos as a ceiling, because however tightly they are bound there are gaps and interstices in which insects and scorpions can conceal themselves. But then, if you are making this sort of roof, you can give your room a ceiling made of stretched cheesecloth, painted. This looks like an ordinary ceiling, and it doesn't sway or billow. You may hear little feet pattering on it—a spider will sound like a rat and a rat like a race horse—but whatever is up there stays there and can't fall down on you. In the two main rooms I was putting brick vaulting and in the others painted cheesecloth.

Hardly had the tiles been promised than they arrived. And hardly had they arrived than there came too a quantity of piping that I had ordered three months before. We actually had everything, the workmen were all on the job, the weather was fine, and brick seemed to be sticking to brick with remarkable speed. I felt well, nobody in the house had a tantrum, and Cayetano found somewhere some extraordinarily late avocados.

"It seems we're in luck at present," I said.

"It's certain that everything goes well now," said Cayetano. "Except for those tiles that are worth nothing. But then, there's no ill that doesn't make for some good."

After all, he had not been consulted about the purchase of the tiles.

I lost Motzín. He disappeared one morning and there was still no sign of him by the next afternoon. Cayetano had been out since dawn hunting for him and making inquiries round the village. Suddenly Candelaria came rushing into the patio.

"Ay, señor, he's not lost. Says Don Amílcar he saw him in the hills, with many other dogs."

She had been gossiping—she called it buying a few centavos of little peppercorns—at the shop when Don Amílcar had come in from the hills and said that Motzín was with half the other dogs of the village outside a cave where they had run to earth a bitch in heat. The cave apparently wasn't far up the hillside, and I decided to walk up with Cayetano, a decision which I very soon regretted. All the year round, the hottest hours in Ajijic are between three and six, and the Colimano doesn't blow till evening. On the shadeless path the sunning lizards scattered before me. It was so hot that even they seemed to resent being forced to exert themselves. They went as little way as possible and stopped, flanks athrob. I found a shady spot under a thorn tree and told Cayetano I would wait for him there.

"Now I come," he said, and walked off up the hill.

You will hear that all over Mexico. Someone will say, "Now I come," and then walk out of the room. He means he will be right back, and he may be back in five minutes or five hours. I watched Cayetano till he was out of sight, and there I sat, looking down onto the belt of vegetation between mountain and lake, a band of all the greens there are. They were harvesting peanuts and men and women in some fields were cutting chili. It grows readily all round Ajijic and is an easily marketable crop. The low green bushes stand in lines too along the shore where, as the lake receded, the Indios have reclaimed fields. The commonest sort of chili is called Comapán, and bears round red berries that turn black. I have a little chili growing in a pot which has the engaging habit of bearing simultaneously berries of mauve, white, purple, pale yellow, orange, and scarlet, all in different stages of ripeness. It is very decorative. The hottest kind of chili I have had here is the one called chili of the tree, which grows on a tall bush in the huerta. Whenever I have Mexican guests, Cayetano says, "And I will put a little plate of chili of the tree."

It got hotter and I got tired of waiting. A very small grasshopper, who had been keeping me company, stretching his bright red hind legs at short intervals, got tired of waiting too, and with one or two athletic red flashes was deep in cool-looking long grass under low bushes, where I would have liked to follow him. A big zopilote circled over the next valley, in long planing swoops above something that was dying. The heat thickened till it was a syrup about my face. I heard the clip-clop of a heavily laden burro coming toward me downhill. A man was walking beside it, and when they drew near I saw it was Venustiano.

"What have you got there?" I asked.

"Manure of ants," he said. The Indios swear by this ant manure. They say it does not attract the lixticuil, a sort of cockchafer that breeds freely in animal manure, and they will pay three times as much for it as, for example, for goat manure, which is both stronger and better.

"Where do you get it from?"

"Here in the hills. All the old nests are up here. There's one I know that must be all of fifty years old."

"Really? Where?"

Venustiano's wrinkles set into firm lines, a screen before his thoughts.

"Ah, there are many nests. My father, before he died, told me where the best ones were. I have no son, but before I die, I shall tell my nephew Chui where they are." And he smiled the smile of a man with property to bequeath.

"Are the nests bigger than the ones I have down there?"

"Yes, how not, much bigger. You see, the queens make their nests about five inches deep, and then they descend from there, new tunnels are being made all the time. I have known nests deep of from three to five meters. Oh, yes, they're much very big."

Venustiano went on his way. A squirrel came, looked at me as if he thought me very impertinent, and chattered away. A thoughtful spider, after consideration, spun a thread from its web to my shoe. When at last Cayetano appeared, the sun was going down and a thick shadow was groping up the valley beside me. Cayetano was carrying Motzín in his arms.

"Poor little thing," he said. "He was very far from the mouth of the cave. All the other dogs were much bigger, and they wouldn't let him very near."

And when I looked at Motzín, I saw what a hangdog expression really is.

I thought it was inconsiderate of Cayetano to be whistling, as we went home, the song whose words are:

He who has a true love,
Let him tend it,
Let him tend it. . . .

Cayetano was cutting oranges to sell to an Indio woman from the village who sometimes buys for her brother-in-law's stall in the market at Chapala. Cayetano was on a homemade ladder, consisting in two rough uprights, with crooked rungs at very wide intervals. The woman was collecting the oranges as they came down, catching them in her shawl. She laid them in a heap beside the tree.

"Now," she called to Cayetano, and Cayetano went on throwing down oranges, because she meant, not that the number was complete, but that completion of it was being approached.

The woman began to count the oranges into a big basket. She gathered them up in groups of five. Putting the first five into the basket, she said, "One." When she reached ten in her counting, that meant she had fifty oranges. Then she started again, counting up to ten once more and putting groups of five into the basket. The second fifty made a hundred. They say that Indios still count in fives because of pre-Conquest tradition, because at one time they couldn't count further than the fingers of one hand would take them. In any case, you still see oranges, lemons, and even peanuts arranged everywhere in little pyramids of five, four at the base and one on top, and the little piles arranged in neat quincunxes.

There were a few oranges over the hundred.

"Those we give you," said Cayetano, coming down the ladder, "in case there are any broken ones."

When she came to pay me for the various lots of oranges she had bought, she owed me fourteen pesos. She gave me four pesos in silver and two postal orders for five pesos each. They had been sent to her from Guadalajara and she had duly signed them, and this was a perfectly reasonable way of paying. But a difficulty arose. The orders were payable at the Ajijic post office, but when I sent Cayetano with them he brought back the compliments of Joaquín, the spectacled and superior young man who runs the office, but regrets that there wasn't enough money to pay them. If I wished, he would send them to Chapala, and the money would be forwarded in a day or two. I sent

Cayetano again to tell Joaquín to do that, since I wasn't myself going to Chapala for the present. He took several letters for the post, and money for the stamps. When he came back he gave me the change and accounted carefully for the centavos spent.

"And Joaquín charged two centavos, señor, for the envelope."

"What envelope?"

"The envelope he used to put the postal orders in to send them to Chapala."

It is no good making a fuss in Mexico when a government office hasn't ten whole pesos with which to pay orders drafted on it or when it then charges you for rectifying its own inefficiency. It is after all something to have a post office. But the system, or lack of it, in the Ajijic post office does not operate only against you. The same afternoon I had to send a telegram. I had only a twenty-peso bill, which could could not be changed anywhere.

"Joaquín says never mind. We can pay tomorrow," said Cayetano, who associates himself with me in all enterprises.

"But has he sent the telegram?"

"That yes yes."

You can't get a postal order cashed, but you can send telegrams on the cuff.

I finally had to give up buying my milk from Chui. Sometime after her week end in the hills the capricious cow had disappeared again, and was only found five days later, grazing her way peacefully along the shore of the lake toward Jocótepec. But Chui was very concerned and took a lot of trouble to see that I got milk from somebody else, and he did not ask to have my order again when and if the cow returned. But perhaps he hoped for it, for at the full moon he sent me round a cutting of the rust-colored bougainvillea which I had admired growing on the wall of his house.

I met him in the street quite early one morning, and took the opportunity to thank him again and to remind him about some sunflower seeds he had promised me.

"I have not forgotten the little seeds of the turnsuns, señor. Last

176

week, no more, I put them out to dry themselves and the chickens ate them all. But I will find you others, I know a place where they grow equal of big."

He paused, and pulled his sarape nose-high across his face.

"It makes much cold in these days, señor. I am going to the shop for my calmer. With permission."

A calmer consists in many noggins of very cheap tequila, taken straight between cups of black coffee. It would be hard to imagine a less calming concoction. The Indios will take it when there is a cold spell. It ought to be warm by now, but this morning the Mexicano blew with the sharp breath of a wind that has passed over snow. That an Indio of Ajijic would not recognize, for most of them have never seen snow. But Chui doesn't need the sniff of snow to know that it is weather for a calmer.

Indios seem usually to stay quite sober or to get very very drunk indeed. Merced, Don Bernabé's son, does not ordinarily drink. That is to say, he doesn't get drunk. Abstainers are not commonly met with in Mexico. But the day before yesterday Merced went to a party, yesterday he was not at work, and today he was not at work either. I saw his wife and asked her about it.

"He only drinks from time in when, if somebody starts him," she said. "Then, in exchange, he drinks a barbarity."

I could hear him snoring in the next room.

"I see. And does it last long?"

"No," she said, "not long. Perhaps fifteen days."

Now Merced has taken charge of the brick vaulting, which he is good at, and we are just at a stage of building when we need to have the roofs of three rooms done. There was a time when we were waiting for bricks, and another time when we were waiting for rails, and another time we were waiting for lime. Now we have them all, and Merced is useless. But there is nothing to be done about it.

I did not say anything to Don Bernabé about Merced's little lapse, but he himself referred to it, indirectly and with his customary stateliness. I found him up a ladder and had congratulated him on his agility.

"Even," he said, "even without any help from my son, I would be

177

able, though I am not young, to directate the whole construction of the house myself."

So I left it at that.

As it happened I could not go to see the progress of the house so often for the next few days, because Françoise came to stay. She is a Belgian and she collects all manner of antiquities. She has been everywhere and she has always managed to get the object nobody else can get. She has a Khmer head, which it is strictly forbidden to take out of Cambodia, and she has a very plain bowl which shouldn't have come out of Cyprus. It is forbidden to export antiquities from Mexico. They say there are many standing organizations that will take charge of slipping them across the frontier, and certainly large numbers do leave the country. Françoise was naturally hot after Mexican antiquities.

We went out one day, idol hunting. We went down the lake, through San Juan Cosalá, and on to Jocótepec, where we left word that we were after idols and would be back in the afternoon. Then we went along a stretch of the Mexico City highway as far as the turn that leads to Autlán, down toward the Pacific.

A little way down the road, on a knoll to the right, stands a small circular roof supported by pillars. What it is doing out there in the country is as unguessable as the origin of Teotihuacán itself. Opposite it the ground looks the same as the surrounding countryside. But take the little path that winds down to a plank bridge over a stream, and already you have changed climate. From there, go on up the stream a little way to the first of its falls, the first of its rock basins. You can go much farther, in a narrow ravine, between walls dripping with damp and moss, to two higher basins, of which the first one is a deep turquois blue, and above the highest basin to a plateau at the top of the hill. If you try to follow the stream yet farther, your way will be barred by undergrowth. And it is said that the water springs from some subterranean source. Anyway, it is warm, or rather tepid, very pleasant to bathe in although the pools are in shadow. For on each side of the ravine, at the top, grow tall trees whose boughs interlace from side to side. And in the trees hang orchids. You are down in the tierra caliente.

We did not bathe, but had a picnic lunch in a grove of mango trees in the bottom, where one can buy beer, Coca-Cola, and lemonade, kept by the Indio purveyors in a simple refrigerator. They have a circular stone wall, the height and diameter of a table, closed by a wooden lid. Inside the thick stone walls the bottles are laid on damp earth, and very nice and cool they keep.

Afterward we came up to the temperate region of the road and drove on, sharply downhill, to the town of Santa Ana, which is prosperous and well painted and has a neatly uniformed garrison and a sugar industry. Beyond Santa Ana the road runs across a flat plain between canebrakes. Ahead is the marshy lake of Santa Ana and beyond that a line of straight hills. There was no other traffic. We drove on between the sharp green sugar cane, toward a distance that was blue and humid, and all around were white herons. Some were leg-deep in the channels between the canes, and some were flapping lazily about. Françoise found the scene Chinese. The herons that were on the roadway had great contempt for the car. Only at the last moment would they move, and then slowly and only a few yards. From the roadside they watched us with indifferent eyes as we went by.

When we got back to Jocótepec, the boy we had spoken to in the morning jumped onto the running board as we ran into town.

"There are many little monkeys," he said, for that is what the Indio calls pre-Conquest idols. "Mounds of them, many very nice ones."

In the plaza were half a dozen people, men and women, awaiting us. What they had brought was not worth much. There were strings and strings of the little pots that are found at San Juan, and plenty of animal incense burners, but very few larger objects, and most of these had been broken and badly mended. Françoise bought a score of carved stones that had been necklace beads and one or two small gods, and left me a fertility goddess, swollen in pregnancy and with a long-nosed face of exquisite serenity.

When we had done with the buying and the bargaining we went into a bar for a drink. It was a dusty day. We got talking to a man who was propping up the bar. He had a dark Indio face, and a smile that flashed dazzling with the fine teeth of the Indio interspersed with gold teeth. Françoise, who hadn't much Spanish, was at first gracious in French. It didn't seem to matter. The man told me he was the municipal president of Jocótepec. He firmly ordered us another beer each and whispered to a small boy. We continued to converse. He had, I think, never come across a Belgian. The French, yes, he knew them. But Belgians, no. Actually Françoise was more Parisian than anything else. He was fascinated when I told him that we weren't related, weren't fiancés, and that Françoise had the habit of traveling all over the world alone.

Françoise likes Mexico. She is never insensible to its beauty, and she likes its inhabitants. Her curiosity has led her into odd corners, and she has a dozen tales of the charm and kindness of the Indios. It was easy for her to tell the president these things in her broken lilting Spanish and easy for him to be charmed by them. Just as naturally, she could ask him why he didn't have the sidewalk outside the café mended. She has the practical sense of the Gaul, and she would not have mentioned any of the vast lacks that are evident in Mexico. But a few paving stones, or some pebbles pressed into mud, that any little place can manage. The president was not at all offended, he said that he had thought of it himself.

Suddenly there filed into the bar half a dozen men carrying musical instruments. They doffed their hats politely, and settled down at the end of the room.

"And which song would you like to hear first?" asked the president.

Françoise, flashing with Gallic tact, asked for "Jalisco nunca pierde." We had it. The noise was deafening. Under the low ceiling it rolled and reverberated. All the while the president maintained agreeable conversation. Objects, as we were, of such signal municipal attention, we were plainly unable to leave at once. And we stood there for at least an hour, our heads swimming with the echoed brass while our beer glasses magically filled themselves again and again. Finally we called a halt. We were not allowed to pay for anything, except such drinks as I had ordered.

Outside, quite a crowd had gathered for the free concert, and we reached the car, escorted by the president with his hat in his hand, helping Françoise carefully over the broken sidewalk, through a lane of hat-doffing Indios. Goodness knows who they thought we were. At last, exchanging interminable thanks and courtesies, we set off.

"I have a dreadful headache," said Françoise.

But after a little while she recovered and said, "It was charming, really charming. What a country, where the mayor of quite a big village entertains two total strangers like that. Oui, la vie est belle."

This month we have to strip the vine. It had shed most of its old leaves by the end of November, and new shoots were appearing everywhere. Now it is leafy and pretty again, and there are a number of sprays thick with tiny fruit. But it must all be taken away. Here, where flowers of many kinds, such as roses and geraniums, flower all the year round if you let them, the vine too tries to give two crops a year. But it can't do it. And by stripping it completely in February, it will be able to make a good crop of grapes for July and August, As a roof for the patio this gives it an advantage. In the winter months, when sunshine is welcome, the boughs are bare or thinly leafed, and in the hot months of May and June they give a thick green shelter and bathe the patio in a green watery light. With roses, which don't do well here, the only thing to do is to prevent them making bud for several months so that they may rest. But they are unsatisfactory. Perfume they lack, and after a little time the finest sorts tend to produce flowers that are cabbagy. It is usually best to concentrate on the flowers suited to the locality, and there are so many that bloom here in profusion and for many months on end that you can have color in your garden all the year round.

With vegetables it is very different. In Ajijic you can buy tomatoes, carrots, onions, squash, cabbages, potatoes usually, and chard and lettuce sometimes. That is all. In Guadalajara the market is crammed with all sorts of vegetables, but in Ajijic you usually cannot get the common turnip or beet, let alone eggplant, peas, cauliflower, or leeks. Since I live largely on vegetables, I wanted to have as many as possible in my garden, and I could not see why anything should fail to grow in Ajijic, given the proper care.

I went round to see Venustiano and ask him about it. He was sitting on his veranda, reading a pamphlet of André Gide on Russia.

"Here," he said, when I had explained what I wanted to know, "here everything will give."

His shirt was not quite clean, and the chair he sat on was broken. But he sat very straight, and as he spoke he tossed his head as if he were the lord of the manor of Ajijic, boasting of his lands.

"That was what I thought," I said. "I imagine that if you prepare your ground and sow and water properly, nature will do the rest."

The fact is that the Indios do not know other vegetables, and stick to the things they know, the things that have a certain market and preferably those that give a quick crop.

Venustiano rose to his feet. He picked up his folded sarape and flung it across his shoulders. The day was not at all cold, but the gesture was quite regal.

"Here," he said, "here there lacks nothing but the impulse of man. Come, and I will show you what I have in my garden. It is enormous of big, it is the biggest squash I have ever seen."

So we went and looked at the eternal squash, which had benefited by the impulse of man.

When I got back Cayetano was watering the lettuces. He had never learned how to blanch a lettuce. I explained to him, and said, "Run and get some string and we'll tie up a few to show you how."

"Yes, señor," he said, and, turning round, pulled off a leaf from the banana tree and tore it into long shreds. It was probably better than Mexican string anyway. I had set out to give a lesson, and I had been taught one too.

"You see, Cayetano," I said, "all that it needs is the impulse of man." It went down very well.

The stripping of the vine is convenient for the hummers which come down into the patio to the sugarwater tubes sheltered from any wind, and for the swallows which are nesting in the bamboo roof of the veranda and the zaguán. Now they can fly out between the naked branches, avoiding perfectly the wire on which the vine is trained. There are four families of swallows. One of them has chosen a very favorable position. Six inches or so from the mud nest stuck to a beam is a broken bamboo, which hangs down and then turns horizontal, making a nice perch for the male swallow. Every year they come here, and they like the rafters of the zaguán. There are two nests there, and all day long the zaguán flashes with black and yellow-fawn as the birds dart in and out. Here, as elsewhere, swallows bring luck to a house and nobody would turn them out any more than I would.

I was talking to Cayetano about mulching the vine when Candelaria joined us. Over her shoulders she was wearing a checked duster knotted on the breast.

"What the vine needs," she said, "is the manure of bats. Ah, look, señor, the little swallows, the poor little things. We must put down paper of periodicals in the zaguán underneath. But manure of little bats is what the vine needs."

The plaza used to be surrounded by jacaranda trees. Years ago public enterprise planted all the village plazas along the lake with jacarandas. It is an elegant tree, with lacy acacia foliage, and in the spring it blazes with violet-blue flowers that turn sapphire in the horizontal light of evening. All the time the jacaranda is in bloom flowers fall, not yet faded, and in April the plaza would be roofed and carpeted in color. Quite suddenly the comisario had all the trees cut down.

The public reason was that flowers would not grow under them. I know no reason to believe that that is true, and flowers in any case have not been planted. I think that in fact it was all due to a desire for progress and improvement, and, means being lacking to advance or improve anything, the desire could at any rate find outlet by changing something. In place of the trees it was intended, I heard, to install a public library, surrounded by benches on which the library's patrons might take their literature, their ease, and their fresh air. I went up to the plaza and saw one bench, a very rough affair of untrimmed wood. A few days later the secretary of the comisaría came to call on me.

He explained that they were trying to collect a library.

"I know you have such mounds of books," he said, looking at my shelves. "Of course, only any you don't want."

"There aren't many I don't want," I answered. "But actually that doesn't make much difference, because I've got very few books in Spanish."

"Oh," he said, and I felt that he wouldn't at all mind having a few volumes in French and English, just for the look of the thing.

"And I've hardly any Spanish magazines either."

He considered. "But you have some with pictures?"

After all, many people in Ajijic cannot read, so that pictures are better than print. I found some old copies of *Life*.

Some time afterward, being up in the plaza, I saw the library. It was a sort of booth made of packing cases, and it contained a few worn paper-bound feuilletons and a quantity of twenty- and thirty-year-old Mexican magazines. A man had laid out little five-strong piles of peanuts for sale on one of the benches, and on the other was sitting a very small boy in blue overalls, clutching a string that led to a big pig that was fast asleep.

I am worried about Aurora. She has now had a new series of disasters. Her nephew, who used sometimes to help her a little, has had an accident with his truck. It seems not to have been his fault, but until the affair is settled the truck is impounded. It is a curious idea, to arrest the vehicle concerned in an accident, but in Mexico it happens. The idea is, I suppose, that if the owner is adjudged liable for damages the vehicle is there as surety for them. But the result is that Aurora's nephew has no means of livelihood. He earned his living driving the truck. It was not his truck and now he has no job. In addition, her elder daughter has malaria and cannot go to her work, which is housework, and her elder boy has what sounds like typhoid or paratyphoid.

One cannot do otherwise than help her, but at the same time there is no doubt that she is a nuisance in the house. She is a trouble shooter, and gets the other servants quarreling. She is a sneak, and is forever coming to me, shuffling quietly into the room, and saying in a small voice, "Señor, I am so preoccupied, maybe I shan't be able to work here any more—"

And then, in an insinuating way, she manages to say something disagreeable about Candelaria or Cayetano or Rafles, or suggest that one of them is trying to get her fired, or that behind my back one of them has done something he shouldn't do. All this with that thin martyred smile on the face the color of potato peel. Then she says, "What do we do pues?" and shuffles away in inconclusive regret.

There is really nothing to be done about it all. It is best to be Mexican and let it slide. For in Mexico nothing ever lasts but nothing is ever finished. One does not decide these situations, one lets them run on. As often as not an apparently final crisis dissolves into air, as when Pedro came back from Tampico breathing rage against his family, never to be mentioned again. The pig that Cayetano didn't want to sell in order to buy clothes for Saint Andrew I never heard any more of. And the threatened crisis arising from the affair of Nieves' father with Tiburcia never materialized. Today Aurora is trying to tell me that Candelaria hates her and is doing everything possible to frame her in some unpleasant way so that she will lose her job. Next week the two of them will be gloves again and as like as not will be complaining jointly of Cayetano. And that will not last either.

"I am not interested in the conversation in the kitchen, Aurora. I'll come along and see your boy later in the day."

"Of course you're not interested, señor," she said, patting my shoulder. "How should you be? You are so very good to us all, I'm sure there oughtn't to be any disgusts, nor much less. There oughtn't to be. Allah grant that there won't be. What can I do pues but work and earn my beans—" She blew her nose loudly on her shawl.

I positively hated Aurora as she trailed out of the room.

Later I saw that both her children were really ill. I gave the girl ata-brine and the boy entero-vioformo. I have never seen a room so wretched. The two beds were almost without covers. There was one backless chair, and no other furniture at all. And above the floor there was a sort of shimmer in the air, inches deep. It was a shimmer of many fleas, hopping. I was glad the washing never went to Aurora's house and that the ironing was all done in a shed down the huerta. I suppose I shall have to let Aurora off work for a while to look after her children, and I suppose I shall have to go on paying her wages because that is all she has, and I suppose I shall have to take her back when the children are well.

I sat on the beach and thought what a nuisance it all was. Aurora and her troubles, Merced and his drunkenness. Everyone who lives in Mexico thinks occasionally that the muddle is more than the merriment. I think it was Harold Nicolson who observed that mankind has got to choose how much regimentation it will put up with to escape how much disorder, and how much disorder it will put up with to escape how much regimentation. You certainly can't have it both ways. Perfect order is nobody's liberty. The ideal of anarchy is perfect liberty for everybody, which is splendid so long as everybody knows how to behave and behaves. Here there is a good deal of disorder, but there is an enormous amount of personal liberty. In the village in Andalucía where I lived there was a young man who said he was a communist. One day he asked me where Russia was. "Is it bigger than Spain?" he asked. "Is it farther than Madrid?" So then I asked if it were true that he was a communist. "Certainly," he answered, "I am a libertarian communist." I inquired what libertarian communism might be. "It means," he explained patiently, "that everyone does just what he wants to." That is no-rule, that is anarchy. Mexico is a democracy. But in outlying regions perhaps it is nearer to an anarchy, in the proper and best sense of the word. An agreeable anarchy. Perhaps all the Indios don't know how to behave themselves in a way that would fit them for a true anarchy. But when a village such as Ajijic can exist with no police and no garrison, that is not bad. There have been one or two murders. I expect there are proportionately more in New York. I haven't heard of any other crimes in Ajijic. And Ajijic ought to be average Mexico. The sophisticated cities are not Mexico, nor are the savage tribes. Ajijic has much of the unspoiled Indio character yet, but it is advancing. It is nowhere in particular on the road of progress. It is allwhere, anywhen. But it gets along nicely without police or crime, an agreeable anarchy.

There had been a rough wind, but it had dropped, and the sun set in the palest tones, as if mildness were the final sum of all things. The vast east was all fainting china blues and the west was glazed in ivory. In the immensities of the wide view, Aurora and her whimsies seemed trivial things. I walked along to the building and saw that they were working late. And Merced was there. He greeted me as if he had not been absent from work, as if nothing had happened. Everything was so normal that but for his bloodshot eyes I could almost believe that nothing had.

When I got home Candelaria came scampering into my room, followed by Rafles.

"Imagine, señor, what's happened. I prepared everything for the fish, the cream and the herbs, and the potatoes are ready to go on top to do the fish with all its smells, and what d'you think? This girl says there is no fish, that she doesn't meet not one." She grimaced, plainly indicating that she was convinced there was really plenty of fish if Rafles had looked properly.

Rafles showed me the empty plate she was carrying as if to say she really had been trying.

"I went until very far along the beach, señor," she said. "I couldn't find a whitefish anywhere, only catfish."

"Why don't you send to Cayetano's friend, Primitivo?" I asked.

"He's a fisherman, he ought to know where to get some if there are any."

"Oh, no, señor," said Rafles. "He doesn't fish any more. He got rheumatism, being in the water so much."

"Then what's he doing now?"

"He's a haircutter, señor."

So Candelaria put a cauliflower in all the smells she had prepared for the whitefish, and we had that instead.

The fine woodwork for the house was being made in Guadalajara, but I had ordered from Robustiano, who is a carpenter and who lives in the village, certain windows with wooden shutters which I wanted for the garage and the sheds. These were not to be glazed and did not need to be very well made.

It was one Saturday afternoon when I went up to his house, taking sketches and measurements of the window frames and shutters I wanted. In the veranda of Robustiano's house several young men were waiting, and one was perched on a tall chair amid the planks, sawdust, shavings, and tools of Robustiano's work. For Robustiano is also a haircutter, and it was as his assistant that Primitivo, apparently without previous training, was working. It is not quite a pudding-basin cut they give, but very nearly. But Robustiano has a pair of clippers and achieves a very straight line across the back of the neck, in the Mexican manner, for in Mexico it is impossible to get your hair cut to a point on the spine.

He agreed to make what I wanted, and he said he thought he might get the things done in three weeks.

"Will you leave me something to buy the wood with?" he asked. "You want them of pine, don't you?"

I left him ten pesos, and again was assured that the work, which was easy, would be done by the middle of March.

Not that I built on that. No doubt Robustiano knew that those who think of time in strict divisions are much better pleased if you say to them that you will do some work by the end of the month or the week that enters or in the evening than if you just say quite soon. And the result is just the same anyway.

We had been waiting for more than two weeks for a load of lime which had been promised for within eight days. I had gone to sleep when, about one o'clock, a very noisy truck blustered down the road and stopped at the door. It was the lime. Nothing could have been more inconvenient, though Cayetano at once woke up and came out, and between them the truck driver, his mate, and Cayetano had to do all the unloading. They were a long time about it. But this is not really unusual in Mexico. You wait for weeks for something you have ordered, and then it arrives suddenly in the middle of the night or on a Sunday.

So now we had the lime and Merced was back at work. We were all set to get on quickly with the building. But the very next day one of the workmen came to the house quite early to say that Don Bernabé's wife had died, so that he and Merced were not working. I sent condolences and some flowers. The next day Merced was at work. He had a black arm band on his blue denim coat, a token which is definitely classy in Ajijic. I repeated my condolences and asked about his father.

"He hopes to return to the works of construction shortly, señor," said Merced, who sometimes catches his father's grand phrases.

But it was two weeks before Don Bernabé was back at the works of construction. A day or two after his wife's funeral one of his grandsons and two other lads were carrying him down the street, one at his head and two at his feet. His arms were waving and he was muttering and he was quite quite drunk. They had laid his big sombrero on his stomach. "Take me to the building," he muttered, "I am charged with the responrespibility—" Even in this grotesque and ridiculous position Don Bernabé retained an air of dignity.

It is, however, a fact that neither Merced nor his father is a drinker. It just so happened that within a month special circumstances had made drunks of both of them. I was lucky that they weren't both out of action at once.

"Poor thing," said Refugio, who was standing near me, having just offered me a small egg at double price. "Poor thing, he should have drunk the water of forgetting."

"And what is that?" I asked.

"Puesen, you wash the feet of the dead, and then you drink the water, and then you recover quickly from your sadness. Still don't you want to buy an egg?"

I was still fighting to save the plants on my new land from ants. I had had the fruit trees bound with pochote, and fitted their bases with rings of earthenware which were then filled with water. But it was impossible to do either of these things with every succulent young cutting that I planted. The land swarmed with ants. There is a certain amount of luck attached to ant fighting. Maybe you will drive them away—probably into your neighbor's huerta—after one treatment. But once, after I had destroyed all the nests over an area of about an acre, a few weeks later I counted ninety-eight new queens making nests.

Cayetano brought me a queen he had found on the new land. She was nearly as big as a bee.

"I think there's a new nest, señor, over by the well."

So after supper I went round with Cayetano to see.

I had tried several methods of destroying ants. At first I bought a compound called cianuro, which you crush into a powder and put into the mouth of the nest. But this only destroyed the workers that went in and out of that particular entrance, for while ants have only one exit through which they throw their refuse, there may be many different entrances to a nest. Later I tried cyanogas, a powdered calcium carbide, pumping it into the nest. This I found expensive, inefficient, and dangerous. It still did not appear to reach far enough down to destroy the center of an old nest, and I was once myself poisoned. I now use a fifty-fifty mixture of white arsenic and flowers of sulphur, vaporized by a charcoal fire and connected to an air pump by a rubber tube. This I have found efficient, cheap, and perfectly safe for the operator.

We arrived and played our flashlights down the walls of the well. I found where the ants were dumping their refuse. They like a clear drop, such as into a well, which fouls almost at once.

"D'you think you can reach to get the end of the tube in there, Cayetano?"

"What do you say, señor?" said Cayetano, who was playing with the adjustable focus of his flash. "Yes, how not."

The spot was not far down the well, but, even had it been at water level, I believe Cayetano would have reached it. He tied a rope to his

189

leg, attaching the other end securely to the trunk of a papaya tree. Although his legs never actually left the ground, while he was at work three-quarters of him seemed to be dangling down the well. I worked the pump, and we kept at it for about twenty minutes. In the beam of the flashlight I could see thick yellow smoke curling up out of the ground here and there.

"Let's see how many little smokes we can count," said Cayetano.

We counted eighteen in all, and some were fifteen or twenty yards away, two of them over in the next huerta.

"How many ants do you think we have killed this evening, señor?"

"I don't know, Cayetano, but many more than you have centavos in your bank."

"That yes yes," said Cayetano. And then he added after a moment: "And how is the bank?"

I met the cakeman. He comes once a week and walks all over the village, a big flat tray swaying and slanting on his head, calling his wares. There is a cloth over the cakes. The cloth effectively prevents any fly that has reached the cakes from leaving them again. Behind always trails Aurora's little girl Trini, picking her nose and hoping. One day, after all, a cake is bound to fall.

Today I bought Trini a cake. She was dumfounded at having to choose. She looked for a long time at the cakes with white icing on, and for a long time at the cakes with sickly green icing on, and for a long time at the cakes with only a blob of very bright pink icing on. Finally she chose the green. Even if it were less gay it certainly had more sugar than the pink.

She wandered along beside me, sucking the cake, and sticky sugar merged with snot all over her face. It was then that we met the priest. He had not been here long, and no tales of luxurious living had reached me, such as were told of his predecessor. It seemed he was of a sterner sort. I expected him to be pained by Trini's grubby state. But, though he at once fixed her with a steely eye, his thoughts were not of washing.

"Do you ever go to the cinema, little girl?" he asked.

"Yes, Señor Cura," said Trini. Aurora was always very particular about forms of address.

"Don't you know that I have forbidden all children under fifteen to go to the cine?"

This really had caused very little effect in the village. The priest could not enforce it. He spoke so sternly that some tears added themselves to the goo on Trini's face.

"The señor gave us centavos for the cine," she said.

The priest did not take up the matter with me, and I told him about Trini, and how Aurora was very poor and had been abandoned by her husband. He listened and then turned to Trini again.

"Does your mother teach you your prayers?"

"Yes, Señor Cura."

"Does any of your mother's family live with you?"

"No, Señor Cura."

"And your mother hasn't given you a new father?"

Trini stared at the sternly shaking head of the priest.

"I don't think so, Señor Cura, " she said, tearfully.

Yet the priest was not unsympathetic. We walked a little way together, and from his conversation it was plain that he took his duties conscientiously. But for him morals came before hygiene. I asked him if anybody knew what the infant mortality rate was in Ajijic.

"I don't know," he said, "but you have no idea how many couples there are who haven't been married, not even civilly, let alone by the church."

About now there comes into flower a tree which bears, on leafless ash-gray branches, big pale pink tassels. The flowers are just big pompons of baby pink, and they fall and scatter over the ground like huge rosy thistledowns. The children play with them, bombarding each other till the pink fronds are torn out and float lazily away on the warm air. I have heard the tree called the Indio's Beard. And that is a nice quip, not only because nothing could look sillier on a coppery Indio face than a fringe of what somebody French called rose indispensable, but because Indios don't have beards. That is, pure Indios don't. Those with more or less white blood may have more or less beard, and no doubt the universal distrust of the halfcast is responsible for a Mexican proverb which bids you beware of the bearded Indio.

But the purer the Indio blood, the less beard the lucky man has.

Razors and blades are not among his cares. So perhaps that is why Rafles came to me with a few blades which I had intended her to throw away and asked if she might have them.

"I know," she said, "how they can be made into little knives."

She thought for a little, staring at the blades, and went on: "In my house we have a hen that has nine chicks. When one is big enough, I will bring it for you."

I told her there was no need to bring me anything, and forgot all about it. But on the last day of the month she came to the house with a nicely grown spring chicken and insisted on my accepting it. It is the first time I have traded used razor blades. But Mexico is full of surprises, and it was the same day that I couldn't find my nail clippers. At last I found that Candelaria had them in the kitchen.

"Yes, how not," she said, "I took them when I went out to cut the string beans. I saw you used the big little scissors"—she pointed to the garden secators—"to cut big things with, so I thought the little little scissors were to cut little things with."

"You don't know how to treat Mexican servants," said Venustiano, who had called in to return a borrowed wheelbarrow. "You're too easy-going with them. Mexican servants need a good scolding once a week."

"But I don't like scolding. And on the whole I think they give me good service."

"But see how careless they are with things like those scissors. At least you should hang that big calendar of yours in the kitchen."

It is a religious calendar. Each day bears a short account of the saint whose day it is, and above the day sheets shines a great brilliantly colored picture of Our Lady of Guadalupe.

"What good would that do?"

Venustiano's wrinkles deepened so that it was impossible to see whether there was a twinkle in his eye or not.

"You don't understand," he said patiently. "With that calendar before them, the servants will be more careful of your property. And they will not steal, for they will be always reminded that the eye of the Most Holy Virgin is on them."

MARCH

THERE is a cart standing in the lake, and it will stand there for some time. Now that March is here, everything is drying, even the wood of oxcarts, of which there are many in use. They have high sides of untrimmed uprights. Some have spoked wheels, but a good many have solid wheels, great discs of wood, and look like the sort of vehicle in which the sluggard Merovingian kings proceeded about their nominal domains. It is usual practice in the dry season to take these carts down to the lake and stand them in the water, wheels and floor covered. They are left there for a week or two to have a good soak.

But, since this is Mexico, where everything is used and often for an improbable purpose, the cart is not idle. A big sailing canoa has come in, and has tied up to the heavy cart, which has therefore become a temporary quay. It is also a diving board for small boys, and occasionally, by having a dress draped over its side, a dressing room for lady bathers. And some fishermen from the other side of the lake, patronizing Ajijic because the shoals are at present running here, tied to it a big barrel-like float made of bamboo in which they preserve their catch alive till wanted. This is the only time I have ever seen such a thing in Ajijic, and it was practical and cheap to make.

The owner of the oxcart is not perturbed by the uses to which his property is put, which, indeed, do it no harm. So when Candelaria told me that the canoa had brought potatoes and did I want to buy any and if so could she take down the kitchen scales to weigh them in, I was not at all surprised when the scales remained there all day long, under the willow trees, weighing the purchases of the whole village.

They were returned in the evening, quite undamaged, and the potatoes we bought were good and cheap.

One of the best houses here belongs to the dressmakers, who are among the wealthy of the village. Their brother owns some cows. Their mother, a vast kindly-looking woman the color of adobe, tends the garden behind the house, and it is always ablaze with flowers. They have what amounts to a dressmaking monopoly in the village. They themselves number three sisters. Or at least, I think so. But there are always so many cousins and nieces helping them that I have never been quite sure which were the sisters. There are also usually several women friends. It is a sort of club. The one room gives onto the street by a big window at convenient elbow-height from the sidewalk, so that passers-by who are going to talk for a mere twenty minutes or so talk through the window. There are several beds in the room, three sewing machines, a wardrobe with a long mirror (this is a recent acquisition; when I first knew them there was no mirror), several huge tinted photographs of mother and father, and various touches of pure luxury such as useless brackets with vases on them. They cut and sew remarkably well. Not only can they copy, which all Indios can do with ease, but they can make from a picture or a sketch. They had made my shirts for me before I asked them to make trousers. They demurred at first. But given a model, they turned out an excellent job, and since then have made all my trousers for Ajijic.

The eldest sister is the chief. She is a kindly-looking middle-aged spinster. When you ask how much something is, she says, "Posen, the making is seventy-five centavos. Then the buttons. I think they were four centavos each, weren't they?"

"No," says another sister, through a mouthful of pins. "Three."

"Ah, three, and there are one, two, three, four buttons. And the little buttons?"

"They were two centavos," says the third sister, without ceasing to whir her machine. "I got those."

"That's four for the wrist buttons. Seventy-five and twelve and four. You add it up, then you'll be satisfied it's correct."

The bill always ends in an odd number of centavos. And they never have any change.

Venustiano really calls in for a chat, but he always thinks up a pretext. This time he asked for the loan of a trowel. The Indios don't usually have trowels, which are called spoons.

"We must learn," he said. "Only so shall we be able to progress. So it would please me to try a spoon."

I told Cayetano to fetch it and while he was away Venustiano sat down.

"Do you remember Rosario," he asked, "my cousin-sister Rosa, whose land you bought? The one who went off to Mexico?"

I said I remembered her.

"Pues, she's back in Guadalajara. No money, the man waited till it was nearly all spent and ran away with the rest. So she's back. No land, no money, no work. And she's embarrassed, six months gone already. Isn't that a nice mix-up?" Venustiano's wrinkles wove a web of contemptuous pity.

He paused when Cayetano came back with the trowel. So to tell me about Rosario had certainly been the real object of his visit.

"But what is she doing in Guadalajara?" I asked, when Cayetano had gone. "How is she living?"

"Oh, she's with her sister-in-law. She was married, you know, ten years ago or more, but her husband abandoned her. Pues, now she's with his sister, who lives in Guadalajara. She'll be looked after all right."

Among the vast-familied poor there is endless charity.

Venustiano rose to go.

"Of all the people you paid money to when you bought your land," he said, "César, Lorenza, and I are the only ones who still have it."

Just as he went out there was a great chattering from the hen run and we looked to see what was going on.

The gray turkey hen which Remedios brought has made herself lady in first authority of the chicken run. She organizes everybody and marshals the birds about. She stands, commandingly tall, among the hens at feeding time, pecking viciously at greedy ones who are getting more than their share. And she leads the procession into the coops at night.

She is also very vigilant. As we came round the corner to the run, we saw all the hens hustling their chicks into shelter. The turkey hen herself, crying frenziedly, got under a banana tree. And then a shadow passed over the run and a sparrow hawk skimmed very low, so low that I could see the gray and reddish brown of its feathers. The sharp-eyed old turkey hen had spotted the raider in good time. But, just as the hawk reached the farthest side of the run, he swooped, and a small fluffy chick, which had imprudently lingered just out of shelter to investigate a putative grain of corn, was snatched away from home and family.

There was considerable fluttering while this was happening, but no hen emerged, not even the bereaved mother. After a few minutes the old turkey hen herself came out, craned her long skinny throat with its cerise wattles, looked round very carefully, and clucked the all clear.

"A pity she didn't have the money instead of Rosario," said Venustiano.

In Mexico, in all the diplomaed professions, you must, after finishing your examinations and before being eligible for your degree, do six months' social service. The engineers are sent to prospect for new roads, the doctors are sent to small towns that are doctorless, and so on. It was hoped that the doctors, finding an open field, would stay on and that thus medical facilities would become distributed over the country. But this has rarely happened. Usually, city-bred doctors have been discontented in small places, and have not found there sufficient remuneration to tempt them to stay. The result is that, though there are regions without doctors, the cities are very overdoctored.

Ajijic has no doctor. The nearest is in Chapala. Friends of mine have a daughter who was the first woman to study medicine in the University of Guadalajara. Long before she was fully qualified, her arrival in the village brought a collection of the sick to her parents' house. And she came down at the time when the so-called planet was doing its malefic work.

"You see," said the old woman, "it's all due to the planet, but as you are here, señorita, I should thank it much if you would look at my Magdalena." She had said good evening to us both, to me as to an old friend. Where had I seen her before?

"I hope you've been very well," she said. "I haven't seen you since you were kind enough to photograph my little grandson who died."

Then I remembered she had been among the family of the dead child. And Magdalena, I recalled, had been there too at her nephew's coffinside.

"Very well," said Beatriz. "I'll come later."

It so happened that recently a certain number of women had died in childbirth and at the same time the village had heard of the approach of a comet, the difference between a comet and a planet being negligible. It was said that all pregnant women were under the malign influence of the planet. At almost any hour of the day you could see two or three of them praying in the church and old Germana was worried about her daughter, Magdalena, who was near her time.

In the evening I accompanied Beatriz to see Magdalena. The front door was open and in the beam of the flashlight we could see that the whole wall above the stove was covered with quantities of earthenware cups and jars, hung on nails in elaborate triangular and zigzag patterns. There were enough for two families. It must have been Germana's one extravagance, the one touch of the decorative superfluous which she could afford. We went through the dark passage to the veranda, falling over various animals and chickens and colliding with a burro. At first we could find nobody; then, preceded by two dogs, a woman appeared in the doorway of the only room, wearing a crumpled dress of white mirror satin.

"Are you Magdalena?" asked Beatriz.

"Yes, señorita, at your orders."

We entered the room which was lit by one candle stuck into a bottle and furnished with a bedstead mattressed with cross-slats of bamboo and inadequately covered with a straw mat. There was a table in the room too and one small chair. Then Magdalena's mother arrived. She took charge at once, giving her daughter brisk orders. Do this—do that—do the other—lie down on the bed. When Magdalena had lain down the old woman covered her fully clothed body with an old sarape and herself stood at the bed head holding the bottle with the candle in it, while I, at the foot of the bed, turned my flashlight on the proceedings. Beatriz was expected to make her examination by groping under the sarape. And somehow she did. However, she firmly told Magdalena that her child would be born the next day and that she would herself return the next morning unless they sent for her before. She gave them some instructions about cleaning the room and told Magdalena to stay where she was. During all this the patient had said nothing, but now she was heard to murmur something about the planet. Beatriz did not have to venture into astrology because at that moment, shifting my weight from one foot to the other, I kicked something hard under the bed, and with much soprano grunting four small pigs which had been asleep there shot out of the room. Germana put down the candle and disappeared after them, returning shortly with all four in her arms. Beatriz told her that they could not come back—had she not just explained that the room must be kept clean?

"But where do I put them, poor little things?" said Germana, looking round the narrow veranda already occupied by the chickens, dogs, and the burro.

"I don't know," said Beatriz. "But here, no."

And then we left them.

At ten, at eleven, and at one a neighbor of Germana's came for Beatriz, but each time she inquired about Magdalena's symptoms and refused to go. She went early the next morning and, at about eight o'clock, Magdalena with very little trouble gave birth to a perfectly normal child. The malign influence of the planet had been averted.

Beatriz told me when she returned that the four small pigs under the bed had been joined by their mother.

I had known Gudrun in Munich. Whenever I was there I spent an evening in her apartment, which looked over the Isar. There would always be chairfuls of students, Germans and Slavs, and an immense amount of earnest talk, and eventually everybody would have supper in his lap off pumpernickel and sausage and pickles and creamy cakes and beer and schnaps. After supper everybody would sing German folksongs. In the days of the Weimar Republic, Gudrun had been a social democrat and an ardent feminist. She had lectured and written, and people had listened to and read it all. She is very highly educated and immensely capable. In 1933 Gudrun left Germany, and she had been leaving one place or another ever since. I don't know how she got to Mexico, but she was here, and suddenly she wrote proposing a short visit with me. She had neither money nor inclination for air or Pullman travel, so she came by second-class bus from Mexico City all the way to Tuxcueca, and there caught a small motor ship (known in spite of its motor as a steamer), which plies across the lake to Chapala. She is the kind of person who finds out that sort of way to travel in a strange region with no difficulty at all. The first I knew of her arrival was when Cayetano brought down a small battered grip addressed in care of me, which the bus had left at Doña Arcelia's corner shop.

"They say the señorita is coming on foot," said Cayetano, obviously amazed.

"She is a señora," I told him. Gudrun was married at some period in her life, but it didn't stick. Whereas in France every woman is Madame until you know she is Mademoiselle, in the Spains every women is Señorita unless you know she is Señora.

An hour or so later Gudrun arrived, her flat hair plastered to her head with sweat, her face red and sunburned, covered with dust and perfectly happy.

"My whole journey cost me thirty-three pesos," she said, the moment we met, "including a night at Morelia and the return bus ticket. What a lot of servants you have."

Gudrun thoroughly enjoyed herself in Ajijic, about which she considered I knew nothing useful, not the accurate figures of population, birth, death, infant mortality, or incidence of tuberculosis and syphilis, or even how many schools there were and how many children in each.

The first day she went to see the priest, from whom she extracted some statistics of a sort, but she didn't think much of him. She tried the comisario. I found her sitting in the comisaría on a chair hewn out of a tree trunk. The comisario was looking so uneasy that I lured Gudrun away. Then she began talking to everybody she met. She went into houses whose owners I had nodded to for months but had never visited, and told the inmates how they could improve this or that detail of their installations, at no cost or practically none. She talked to all the women about women's rights, and they all agreed with her, and said, "Yes, yes, how not, señorita," but it is doubtful whether they understood what she was talking about. She said that their lives were "beautifully uninhibited" and she found out in no time that Tiburcia the wisewoman made her love potions of menstrual blood. I should have said that she is multilingual, and one of those people who absorb languages out of the air. She was now earning her living working in an office in Mexico City and writing some sort of Mexican notes for an American paper. She was still thinking and writing about the future of man and the rights of women, but what she wrote was no longer being published.

She did not get on so well in the house. Candelaria, like all good cooks, doesn't like people, especially women, in her kitchen. She will let me mix my salad, but only with a condescending smile, as she would let a child play with a little bit of waste dough and pretend it is making cakes. But Gudrun has to see how everything works and she usually finds a way of making it work better. Unfortunately she is almost always right. I was glad she hadn't been here for the birth. Her recommendations, all of them sensible, would have been intolerable. In no time at all, she decided that Candelaria could get along with two instead of three of the shallow circles of charcoal alight, and that the ice would keep longer if the icebox were in a different place. She said so, and nobody liked it at all. But tact is not a common German characteristic, even among social democrats.

She did better on her second evening. It was still and the air was warm and we sat on the beach outside the huerta and Cayetano made little fires of eucalyptus leaves. The lake was black oil and the stars were so thick as to seem a golden gauze. Gudrun got sentimental. She remembered back to Germany, her Germany, and she began to sing. She had a slight mezzo, and, as she was of course once a Wandervogel, a tremendous repertory of songs.

Cayetano stopped searching for eucalyptus leaves and listened, and gradually I became aware of several little groups under the trees. Gudrun was singing sentimental songs—"Ein Sträusschen am Hute" and "Nun leb' wohl, du kleine Gasse"—and the listeners liked them. I felt they wouldn't have liked the monotonous march time of the merrier Volkslieder. Finally she realized that she had an audience, and began, rather shyly, to sing "Tener un amor secreto." She sang it well enough, and several voices joined in. And when we went up to the house there was a little scattered applause.

It was two weeks since I had been to see Robustiano about my windows and shutters that were to be done in three weeks all told, but now he came and said he was sorry, he had a lot of haircutting to do and he had to plow his field, and there would be a little delay. Being here, he asked whether I had any packing cases or wooden crates to sell, since he knew that I had many things sent from Guadalajara and he could always find a use for wood.

I asked Cayetano to look out what we had, and finally Robustiano bought five packing cases, and paid one peso fifty cash for them.

"They'd cost him a lot more than that anywhere else," said Gudrun. "You're pauperizing him. You never did have any sense of real social values."

Gudrun had only a few days' vacation—vacations in Mexico are ridiculously short—and she soon had to go. She visited several houses where she had been before, to remind Indios of suggestions she had made or to see if they had carried them out. She repeated all her remarks on feminism, even addressing some to Candelaria, who, childless and independent (though with, I believe, a romance behind her somewhere), has all the rights she wants and who became almost completely deaf. And she asked Cayetano if he understood what he did when he voted..

"Yes, pues, señora," said Cayetano. As far as I know he has never voted. If he has I am sure he didn't understand it.

Rafles had her malaria coming on and was shivering, so Gudrun, seeing her thin cotton frock, gave her a tweed skirt. I know that it was one of two that Gudrun had.

She left me quite exhausted. I do not know if the world will be saved by people like Gudrun, but certainly they work very hard. I thought of my three recent visitors, Charles and Françoise and Gudrun. Both Charles and Gudrun had been out of place in Ajijic. Gudrun had not made any real impression on the villagers. You cannot rush Indios as Gudrun would like, and tries, to rush them. If anything, they probably preferred Charles' more spangled manner, though I had seen that it struck them as false. Of the three it was Françoise, who didn't over-tip, noticed everything that was beautiful, and, if there was small practical help to be given, gave it without more ado, whom the Indios had liked the best. And she was the one whom afterward they inquired about.

Rafles sent a cousin to say she had malaria, the chills, and couldn't come to work.

"But I come in her place," her cousin said, and giggled. She was a girl of about fourteen and looked extremely stupid, not just bashful-stupid like so many of the young village girls, but blatant-stupid, and pleased to be. I sent her to Candelaria.

About eleven o'clock the girl came down to the mirador, where I was working, with an egg that had arrived in Candelaria's absence. She gave a series of high-pitched squeaks and started to play with the Dackel, which promptly bit her shawl. She struck it on the head and, when I told her to leave it alone, danced up and down squeaking at it—or maybe at me.

"If you throw my shawl to lose," she squeaked, "I shall make you into a shawl."

The Dackel sprang again. The girl dropped the egg into the pup's basket, and in two swift swallows it was gone.

"She ate it with all and shell!" Squeak, giggle.

I gave her the money for the egg, and she squeaked and giggled her way up the path of the huerta, with the puppy dancing after her. I fetched the pup back, and held it by the scruff, looking into big brown eyes.

"And if you go playing with people when you're told not to," I said, "you know what'll happen to you. You'll be made into a shawl, a scarf, a tippet."

So the fool maid gave Tippet her name.

Early in the month came Carnival, and the village gave itself up to the excitements of The Bulls. This is not a bullfight but a jaripeo, that is roping with a little bareback riding thrown in. On the first day there go round the village in procession everyone who has a horse and a batch of bored steers and cows. Then, in a big enclosure, surrounded by walls and probably with a rickety grandstand on one side, the show begins, the band of course obliging with almost incessant music. I went up one afternoon, but only once, because the dust raised is terrific.

On arrival, you find all your old friends of the village acting as officials. There is the comisario on horseback, directing everything. Joaquín from the post office is taking the gate. The boy from the cantina takes you in charge, leads you up over several soapboxes onto a narrow and tremulous plankway, turns out a few children, waits while Doña Lupe who sells flowers and often goes to the capital, Doña Florencia who has a private income, Doña Arcelia who owns the corner shop, and a number of young girls in rainbow mirror satin move up with every appearance of pleasure, and when you are seated, accepts a cigaret and goes back to his icebin full of cokes and beer and lemonade.

I had purposely arrived late, about five, but still it was half an hour before anything happened. Then, from an inner enclosure, a reluctant steer was driven out by yells, kicks, and bangs with a stick. The village sparks, with many shouts, began riding about madly and whirling lassoes, and in a few minutes banks of dust obscured the proceedings. But it was evident that the steer only wanted to go one way, and that was home. He prudently allowed himself to be roped very quickly, and lay still and unresisting. A rope was knotted round his middle, and after considerable urging he got to his feet. Javier, the elegant youth, sprang onto his back, but the steer remained quite still. At last, kicked and shouted at, he moved, but quite slowly, and toward the exit. It took a great deal more incitement to persuade him to charge halfway round the ring, bucking. Then he stood still again, as if he had realized what was expected of him, but had now accomplished it. But at last he obliged again, and, amid hoots and catcalls from the crowd, Javier rolled in the dust. The steer made straight for the barrier and this time was allowed to depart.

This, with variations, was the show. Now and again a steer with a little more spirit bucked quite viciously, while the music swelled to strains of martial loudness, and all around, on every wall, perched in every tree, the crowd leaned forward and howled. Once or twice small boys fell headlong into the ring in their excitement, but nobody was hurt. It went on till sundown.

I was at home on the roof terrace when there was a great flurry in the patio.

"Oh, Most Holy Mary," cried Candelaria and was silent.

I heard confused cries, Cayetano being efficient, Rafles being plangent. But by the time I got to the parapet and looked down all was over. On the return procession a couple of bulls had come into the patio, that was all.

Every day for five or six days the same show is staged, and the same audience is content to watch the same young men trying to evoke ferocity from the same bored steers. And thereafter, on the beach, the little boys of the village have little jaripeos of their own. Any stray calf or burro, peacefully cropping the sparse grass, may suddenly find himself lassoed, roped, mounted, and generally teased into the game. Sometimes a donkey provides the best sport of all.

But on Ash Wednesday, Carnival is over and Lent has begun. Everybody wears a cross of ash smeared on his forehead, and it is not done to remove this by washing or rubbing. Candelaria's cross lasted into the third day. And I thought Don Bernabé still wore traces of his when he came on the Friday to see me.

"We cannot finish the drainage," he said. "We lack an elbow, a joint for the piping."

I don't know who had made this mistake, whether Don Bernabé had counted wrong, or whether the man who supplied the joints had delivered too few.

"Then what shall we do?" I asked. "It takes a long time to get another."

Don Bernabé considered, scratching his bristly white hair.

"Pues, there's that gentleman who's building in San Antonio, perhaps he'd have one that he's not occupying."

"That's possible. Why not send and ask him?"

Pause.

"You wouldn't like to do it? I mean, he's a foreigner, perhaps—"

But I didn't want to waste the morning going to San Antonio.

"Oh, no, you can send one of the men. It's only two kilometers. Has no one in the village been doing any building who might have some pipes?"

Don Bernabé considered.

"Pues, there's Lupe, she of the fierce duck. She just built a little tank."

"Perhaps she'd have an elbow."

Just then Merced strolled up and joined in the conversation.

"But who knows if it would be the right size," he said.

One of the workmen chipped in, saying, "They make them all the same size."

"Oh, no, they don't," said Merced, and some minutes were consumed in this theoretical discussion.

"Anyway, if it's too big, we can easily arrange that with cement," said Merced, carefully abolishing the objection he himself had raised.

"You know," said Don Bernabé thoughtfully, "what we want is one just like the one I have stored in my house."

I looked at him, dazed. But so it was. He had one in his house, and it was the right size, and he wasn't using it. But he had not mentioned it before.

Merced was sent for the elbow and Don Bernabé and I went round to the land to look at the work.

It is fascinating to watch the men making the brick vaulting. Having the four walls, and having placed the girders, they seem to build out into space, mortaring one brick to another. There seems to be no reason why the bricks should stay there, but they do. One gets the same impression when they build brick stairways. They appear to build a step, then stand on it and build the next one. But when they have got the sill and the two sides of a window built they fill it with bricks in order to give it support while they are setting the bricks at the top. I know nothing about building or any form of engineering, and I let them do things in the way they are accustomed to. No doubt it will all stand up. The house I am living in has stood already for seventy years, and it was certainly built in the same way.

"Where is the plumb line?" Don Bernabé was asking angrily.

Several of the peons were so concentrated on their work that they did not hear. One or two others answered.

"Who knows."

"I don't know."

"What plumb line?"

Just then Merced arrived with the elbow and Don Bernabé rounded on him.

"Now the plumb line's lost," he shouted, the white bristles dancing on his chin.

"Oh, no. It's not lost, nor much less," said Merced. "It's just that we left it there, and now it's stuck in the cement under the bath."

"In these days," said Rafles, "I need to go to church to make my exercises. I need to go three times a day, for five days. In the morning early and in the morning and in the late afternoon."

"Yes," said Aurora. "All the girls, all the unmarried girls, every year make the exercises."

There was a pause. Rafles' face was as blank as fresh paper. Over Aurora's spread a sacrificial smile.

"So how do we arrange the work of this girl?" she said. "I told her that I could do it for her. It's true, I don't know how to do those things well, but what can we do pues?"

"And when exactly do you have to go to church?" I asked Rafles.

"At half past seven in the morning and in the afternoon and at mid-day at eleven," she answered.

"I have bought three ducklings," said Candelaria, as though it were the most obvious thing to do.

"Why?" I asked.

"Pues, duck is good to eat, and duckling is good to eat, and then they were very cheap. A señora told me she would sell them."

When Candelaria refers mysteriously to a señora who has eggs, or papayas, or whatever it is to sell, she is always in fact referring to a relative or friend, perhaps Tiburcia, the wisewoman, who no doubt gives her a rake-off. There the ducks were, and it seemed best to leave it at that. Perhaps in any case they would clean out the pond down the huerta, which was getting very weedy.

But in the evening Candelaria was in a great state.

"Where can I put the ducks to sleep?" she said.

I didn't know.

"Ay, God of my life, God of my life," she went away muttering.

I heard a lot of routing about going on in an abandoned room next the garage, a room with an earth floor, bare adobe walls, and a leaky tiled roof, a room devoted to all manner of junk. After a long time Candelaria appeared in the patio, dragging a piece of furniture. It looked as if it had once been a dresser.

"Look, señor, what I have found. It's the dresser of Doña Carmen, the mother of Don Carlos who rents you the house. I remember it when I was a little girl. It must have been there in that room for forty years."

"But it doesn't look much use now. What d'you want it for?"

She looked at me pityingly.

"For the ducks, of course," she said.

She and Cayetano dragged it to the hen run and she dusted out its cupboard, from which one door was gone and where the other hung precariously. Then she herded the drake and the two ducks up from the pond, and bedded them down in the dresser cupboard. They took to it very happily.

"Now, you see, we don't need to buy anything special," she said. "I told you the ducks were cheap."

Cayetano was standing unnecessarily rearranging things on top of a bookcase, in a way he does when he has something to say.

"Well, Cayetano?"

He coughed. "Have you seen Don Bernabé, señor?"

"No. Why?"

"Then he didn't tell you that now the new roof is going on he needs another mason?"

"No. He hasn't told me."

Silence.

"Because I was thinking that perhaps, if we do need another mason, Primitivo would do."

"Primitivo? But I thought he was a haircutter now."

"Oh, no. Not any more. He didn't earn very well, and he didn't like it."

"He doesn't stick to anything long, does he? And does he know how to do mason's work? If he does I don't see why he shouldn't have the job."

Cayetano looked at me wonderingly. Every Indio knows how to lay bricks, just as he knows how to milk a cow and manage a seine net and row and ride and plow and reap and dig.

"Oh, yes, we worked together with Don Bernabé, repairing the house of Bernardina, she of the shop."

"So you know a mason's work too, Cayetano?"

"Yes, pues. But Primitivo doesn't know how to make a Martini."

It is not very satisfactory to work mornings in the patio. I thought I would try it because the wind on the terrace shivered and shook the paper in my typewriter. In a Mexican household everything happens in the morning. There is a crescendo of activity climaxed by the midday meal, after which the working day is more or less over. A patio is the hub of that activity.

A small girl brought some eggs and then had to come back a few minutes later because she had forgotten whether it was four or five she had sold us.

"Anyway they were all very small," said Candelaria.

Then Aurora arrived with the washing. I heard her querulous voice wailing at Candelaria.

"I haven't slept all night. First I woke with my back hurting, and then the water was so beaten I couldn't wash yesterday for all the earth in it, and then—" She trailed off into varicose and rheumatic woes with which Candelaria sympathized in a metallic monotone.

Cayetano was working in the patio, dividing some cannas. He has a system. He works in the shade when the sun is too hot and in the sun when the shade is too cool. Just then the sun went in altogether and he decided to visit the kitchen and say good morning to Aurora. I heard them all three joking together and then a few minutes later the sun emerged again and Cayetano resumed work—in the shade.

Aurora, who doesn't at the moment like Cayetano, said to Candelaria, "Allah grant that he isn't going to finish badly, that young man. He's vicious."

Candelaria smelled a piece of gossip. "How d'you mean?" she said, and gave a terrific belch.

Apart from the pat-pat of tortilla making there is another sound very typical of Mexico, and that is the belch. From your kitchen come suddenly quite stupendous belches. It is said that tortilla eating makes for good belching. Anyway, it doesn't seem to count as a social error, and among the Indios I have never heard it excused. Perhaps anciently the pre-Conquest Indios belched like this. Perhaps the acceptance of belching as a natural act derives through Spain from the Arabs, who are discourteous if they do not break wind to signify the excellence of a repast. Certainly no Indio need fear to fail in courtesy at an Arab feast. Often I have heard a song interrupted for the emission of a belch, and the song picked up again immediately after.

"How d'you mean?" repeated Candelaria after the belch.

"Vicious," said Aurora again, with a belch of her own, a little belch as if to show she hadn't eaten as well as Candelaria. "He's always up at the shop, drinking lemonade and playing the ten-center. Only yesterday he paid for seven songs on the ten-center."

There was comparative silence for a time, while Candelaria went over the washing, complained about the way the towels had been ironed, and said that the señor thought too much soap was being used (which he didn't). Then there was a loud cry of amazement.

"But what thing is that, Candelaria?" asked Aurora.

"A vegetable, pues."

"A vegetable? But you couldn't eat it. What—"

The excitement brought Rafles from the other side of the patio and Cayetano stopped work again to go and see what it was all about. The artichoke, for that was all it was, was taken out of the boiling water, examined, prodded, and put back, while Candelaria explained in a superior way how it was eaten, leaf by leaf.

"And afterward, when that little bit has been eaten, don't the leaves serve for anything?" asked Aurora.

Candelaria and Rafles laughed at her, and she left, shaking her head as if she knew no good would come of it. She probably thought I was vicious.

But just as I began to get irritated with patio life, the wind suddenly dropped, and I was able to return to the terrace. On the way up I noticed a little girl, whose knock Candelaria hadn't heard, standing outside the kitchen door. It was Trini, Aurora's child. I asked her what she wanted.

"Don't you have any little flowers of jasmine that you could sell me for five centavos?"

I told her I was sorry but I hadn't.

She still stood there. Finally she said, "Posen, señor, don't you want to let me ask Candelaria to show me the rare thing Mamma says she had in a pot and which she says you are going to eat pues?"

The man who sends the ice from Chapala comes once a month to collect his money. He sends the account on a small piece of paper: 30 days of ice, 12 pesos, and heads it The Gringo of Ajijic. There are almost always some days when no ice has come. Sometimes it hasn't arrived in Chapala from Guadalajara and there isn't any to send, sometimes the bus drivers forget to leave it and it goes on to Jocótepec, sometimes one of the ambulant vendors of ice cream cones steals it when it is left at the corner, sometimes a friend of the bus driver takes it on the way and pays for it. No matter. The bill is always for so many days of ice, the full number of days in the month. I then deduct the days when for one of the above reasons there has been no ice, and there is an argument. Or rather, a discussion, for it is not acrimonious.

Today I heard Candelaria at the door talking to the iceman, from whose account I had deducted only one day.

"That was the day when you were here last time," she said. "The señor paid you including that day and you said the ice was here in the village, but when the girl went up for it there wasn't any."

"But there was. I saw it."

"Yes, it had been there. One of the ice-cream vendors took it, and left the money for it at the shop, and that is the day the señor has deducted."

"But that was last month."

"Exactly. The day last month when the señor paid for ice and didn't get any he has deducted from this month."

"But this month it arrived every day."

"Yes. This month it arrived every day."

"Then the bill is twelve pesos forty for thirty-one days, and not twelve pesos as he has given me."

"But he has deducted the day when there wasn't any ice."

"But that was last month," said the iceman, and he sounded genuinely puzzled. So the conversation, having gone full circle, began again. I went away from the patio and left them to it.

Afterward Candelaria said, "The poor man puesen, he didn't want to understand anything."

I talked on the beach to a visitor. He was wearing a khaki shirt, whipcord breeches, knee-high laced-up boots, sun helmet, a cartridge belt, and a large revolver.

"Are you going up into the hills?" I asked. For high boots, at any rate, are advisable up there, where there are plenty of rattlers and maybe a tarantula or two.

"Oh, no, señor. I just came down for the day from Guadalajara."

I wondered about the explorer's outfit, and I saw him eyeing my beach slacks and sandals.

"And do you go around dressed like that?" he asked.

I said that I did. I felt apologetic. I said there was no need to dress up in Ajijic.

"But isn't it dangerous?" he asked.

"No. How dangerous?"

He shrugged. "Snakes? Scorpions? In the country there is danger everywhere." He crushed a harmless very small beetle with one of his enormous boots. "And no gun?"

"No. I haven't got a gun."

"You live here and you haven't got a gun?"

He shook his head at me. He was not disposed to dismiss the dangers of Ajijic.

"Look at that man there," he said. "Now he has the look of a bandit."

I looked. Behind his cows Venustiano was coming down the beach. I said good-by to my casual acquaintance and hoped he would arrive home safely.

I went up a block from the beach to stop by at Rafles' house. She had gone home, and had been away a long time, and Candelaria wanted her help with chutney making. The green mangoes make excellent chutney, and are delicious in curry.

I was received by Rafles' mother, a small, nut-brown woman with a twinkle in her eye. There was a big bare yard, the earth dry and scratched under the big mango tree. A donkey, an assortment of skinny hens, and a very small boy wearing nothing but a patched navel-length shirt were doing nothing in the yard. Rafles' mother invited me onto her tiny veranda, one end of which was the kitchen, and produced a low chair for me to sit on. I could see into the one room. There were two beds, another chair, several gaudy calendars, a little bracket with a figure of Our Lady of Guadalupe, and a small white marble cross of the sort that children's graves are adorned with.

I gave my message, and then I asked about the cross.

"Ay, señor, it was for the little one that died on me," said the woman. She stopped as though the explanation were complete.

"Did he die recently?"

"Oh, no, four years ago."

"But why do you have the cross here instead of on the baby's grave?"

The woman sighed. "Pues, you see, it was like this. First, I hadn't the money the buy a cross with. I had to save it up. Then I had to wait a long time for it to come, from Guadalajara. More than eight months it took, my brother in Guadalajara ordered it. And then, when it did come, nobody could remember where the little one's grave was."

She sighed again, and I found myself wondering what Gudrun would have thought, and said, about it. But then the woman's face brightened. She smoothed her brown hands over her thighs.

"But he's a little angel now," she said.

APRIL

BY APRIL everything is already very dry. The hummers are glad of the easy living afforded by sugar-water in glass tubes. A scuttering hen puts up a dust column. On books and furniture settle incredible layers of powdery white. But now the lake begins to get warm, and the laden air takes on new rich half-tones at sunset. The lilacs, the ever present lilacs of the Mexican landscape, deepen into velvet violets, brassy purples, pitched in the related keys of voluptuousness and anger. One day there was a haze behind the mountains to the southwest, beyond the corner of the lake. It seemed at first merely a little haze, but it straddled the mountains, insensibly it blotted them out. They blurred, they melted into mere phantasms of mountains, and then, in no time, they were gone, and in their place a dun-colored curtain hung from sky to water. The worst of the storm went toward Jocótepec, but slowly the curtain was drawn across toward us, growing wider and growing nearer, preceded by a narrow race of water, wind-lashed and yellowish. The wind struck. The air was gritty with dust. It rattled on the banana leaves. It clattered on an iron roof. It tinkled at the screening. It pattered like a million shod ants on the roof. Light, and its child color, went. There was only sound —the giant moan of the wind splintered by the dust's pygmy tom-toms.

Going out, I wrapped a scarf round my face. I met Cayetano choking and dust-layered.

"Why don't you cover your mouth and nostrils with your sarape," I asked, "the way you always do in the early morning?"

Cayetano looked at me through tears of coughing. "But that's dif-

213

ferent, señor. That's because the morning air, and the evening air, are most dangerous. That is why we Mexicans always cover our mouths and noses at those hours. The morning and evening airs are very strong airs. It is like if one rides on top of a bus and gets the air inside one, too much for it to be able to get out. Then it stays there, it may stay there for days, and it makes you sick. In the morning and the evening the strong air may get inside you. But this is just dust."

There were three women with Candelaria. One of them I recognized as her comadre, Germana. She and Candelaria and another elderly woman were all talking at once. The fourth was a girl. She stood silent and with her head a little bowed, but somehow there was no submission in her attitude. She was beautiful. Ordinarily in Ajijic the girls are not beautiful. They walk badly and have lumpy ankles. But this girl had fine bones and a light poise, and her skin was like pale rosewood.

Candelaria, seeing me, gasped. "Ay, señor! What hour will it be?"

"After two, Candelaria."

"Don't say so, don't say so. In just a little moment lunch will be ready. Cayetano! Cayetano! Have you set the table yet?"

"Yes," said Cayetano, shortly. "An hour ago."

But Candelaria had become deaf.

After lunch I asked her about the girl.

"You see, pues, Paz wants to get married," said Candelaria, settling her arms across her chest for a good gossip. "She wants to marry that Primitivo. A nice boy. But her parents won't let her marry him, nor much less, they've forbidden her to see him, because they've been quarreled with the boy's parents for years. At one time Paz was Chui's girl friend and her parents liked that, but they had a disgust and she gave him squashes."

"I see. The girl's pretty."

"Isn't she?" beamed Candelaria, as if she were responsible for the girl's prettiness. "And now she is in love in love, and if she can marry Primitivo she will be in the glory."

I did not remember having seen the girl Paz before, but that evening I saw her again. She was sitting under a willow tree on the shore, looking out over the lake, and the sunset flushed her rosewood cheeks with copper. She looked sad, but she did not look forlorn.

"Yes, she's very pretty," said Arturo, when I pointed Paz out to him and Xochitl, who were down for a week end. "But wait a year or two. By the time she's twenty she'll be just like the rest, quite shapeless and with four children."

"Or five," said Xochitl. "There might be twins. And then she may be left with them. Among the Indios, the man seldom has any sense of responsibility for his children. The mother's often left with the whole burden, even economic. Of course they have more liberty than the women of people like ourselves."

It has often been said that a culture may be judged by the position of its women. In that sense, Mexico has a long way to go. Women of course have a better position than they used to have, and, though they have not got the vote, legally they stand well. Professions such as diplomacy, law, and medicine are open to them. But practice lags far behind the law. In the home, a woman is still hedged by fantastic restrictions. She may not go out alone with a man who is not a member of the family. The old-fashioned will not permit a pair already married civilly to go out alone together before the religious wedding. Engaged couples, if they are left alone, are left in a room with the door open onto a more public room. Husbands do not allow their wives to have a job. Husbands should be obeyed, and a wife who wishes to rule her house must do so indirectly. A wife, I was once told, should never ask her husband where he has been, in order "not to oblige him to lie to her."

"Do you wonder," said Xochitl, "that most Mexican women end up in piety, scandalmongering, or some sort of neurasthenia, usually crazy jealousy of the husband—probably with reason?"

Some friends of theirs came down that afternoon, bringing their two small girls, who played on the beach with Arturo and Xochitl's little boy of five.

"I must take care of my little hens," joked the father of the girls, "with your little cock loose among them."

"And how can you expect," said Xochitl afterward, "that Mexican men will ever have any respect for women when they hear that sort of thing said all their lives?"

Suddenly this morning toothless Elpidia of the turkeys came running into the patio. She went straight to the kitchen and then emerged with Candelaria, who brought her to me. She had been too shy to come directly herself.

"Elpidia's boy little Silvanito has been bitten by a scorpion," said Candelaria. "She wants to know what to do."

Elpidia stood panting, with her mouth open and quite a blank expression on her cocoa-colored face.

"Did it just happen?" I asked.

She nodded.

I found the ammonia, put some in a small bottle, and told her to give it to him, two or three drops in a glass of hot water every half hour.

"Can you measure drops?"

She shook her head.

So I took out a dropper.

"How much?" she said.

"Two or three drops, like this," I repeated, showing her.

"Yes, how much?" she said again.

We went on like that for some time.

Then Candelaria appeared again.

"She means, how much does she owe you," she explained.

I told her nothing, but to be sure to return the dropper, and let us know how the boy was.

In the late afternoon she came in to say that Silvanito was quite all right. She had brought back what was left of the ammonia, but she had forgotten the dropper.

But it is not only with scorpion stings and cuts and such that one is expected to cope when one lives in an Indio village.

"I wonder," said Rafles to me that same evening, "if you know what I could do about my hair? It does keep coming out so."

This was moving from medicine toward the beauty parlor, but after discovering that she had a very dry scalp I gave her a mixture of equal parts of bay rum and castor oil and told her to rub it well into the skin.

"Thank you," she said. "I asked you because you know such a lot of things."

But the truth is that however little one knows about the commonest household remedies, still it is more than the Indio knows.

Attacked by illness, the Indios are at once stoical and panic-stricken. They are prone to think that the mildest malady will end in death. I often hear of somebody who is very gravely ill, who is at the point of agonizing, and a few days after he is up and about as usual. But they are stoical about pain and suffering. Such was the old man who died early this morning. He had died of cancer, and he had refused to submit to an operation which would at least have prolonged his life.

"No," he had said. "God might have taken my life when I was young, before I had lived and had a family. He might have taken it when I would leave widow and children without support. But he did not. Now my son is grown, my daughters have their little business. I cannot say I have not prospered. If now God calls me, I am ready."

So he had died.

As I had known him and his family I went up in the evening to offer my condolences, and found the death watch begun.

There were lamps burning on the veranda, and one or two torches of ocote, the oily kindling wood. And the veranda itself was full of people, mostly women, on their knees, praying aloud. I picked my way through them without their taking any notice of me.

Inside, the room was dominated by the coffin. It seemed enormous, and was surrounded by banked flowers, all the common flowers of Ajijic gardens, but in profusion. Under the trestles on which it rested stood a corkless bottle, labeled aguardiente, and half full of pale yellow liquid, and a tin can with some sprigs in it. The liquid was vinegar and the sprigs were herbs. This was hygiene.

All round the room were ranged chairs, on which the family and the mourners were seated. The mother and the daughters were all in black with black shawls on their heads. When I came in the mother was chatting in a low voice to a friend who sat beside her, the youngest daughter was praying softly to herself, the middle daughter was laughing quite brightly with some girl friends, and the eldest daughter was crying noisily. As I entered, the eldest daughter jumped up, turning off her tears as if with a tap, and welcomed me smiling. She led me to her mother, and the widow shook hands with me mournfully and tears trickled suitably onto her brown cheeks. Then I was accommodated with a chair. At intervals one or another of the family came to speak to me, and I heard three or four detailed accounts of the last hours of the deceased, accounts in which pious hopes mingled with the most shocking medical details, both expressed in the most matter-of-fact way.

"Ay, what shall I do without him?" said the widow suddenly, on the heels of a conversation about her garden, which is always very well kept. She shed some tears.

"You must remember," said little shriveled Doña Florencia, who has an independent income and indicated her superior social standing by wearing a shawl of black lace, "that now you have in Heaven the best possible advocate."

"Ah, yes, indeed," said the eldest daughter, dabbing at her eyes with her shawl. "Now he is surely in the glory, ten days he was never complaining but urinating nothing but blood, blessed be God."

Outside from the veranda came the flickering light of the torches and the long muffled rhythmic muttering of the prayers. And inside, conversation, tears, and a little laughter flickered round the company, who were going to stay all night. I was not going to do that. I had made various excuses of early departures on business, and so on. And indeed, I think it was not expected of me, who am not Catholic. For the watch is kept since the Catholic Church holds that the soul does not leave the body for some hours after death. I stayed for about an hour, most of the time doing nothing but looking before me or staring at the coffin, and then, with many condolences, I took my leave. At intervals during the night coffee, or some stronger drink, would be served. Those within the room would go outside, where a smoke is permissible. Those outside would come in to pay their respects to the deceased, to murmur a prayer, and cross themselves above his coffin. And the company would only disperse in time to wash and have a meal before meeting again for the funeral. The watch takes place on the night immediately following death, and the burial must take place, as in all tropical countries, within twenty-four hours of death.

When I came out of the crowded house into the spacious night I saw, low southward above the mountains, the Southern Cross. It was recumbent, tilted like the cross that lay on the breast of the dead man I had just left.

Don Bernabé has been making some of the balustrades. The Mexicans are very ingenious at making openwork balustrades and parapets of bricks of various sizes. I am having the low wall at the edge of the terrace done that way, and the parapet round the flat roof. Sometimes they are made with horizontal gaps, sometimes big adobes are slanted to make zigzags, sometimes they are built of curved tiles, so that the wall is tunneled like a honeycomb. All the manners are decorative, and produce an effect of lightness.

"We are all content," said Don Bernabé, "that our mode pleases you. Now come and see how, as a small surprise, I have comprehended an idea of yours, and collocated it. The little bath of birds."

I had bought an old stone font, and the notion of using it as a bird-bath had made Don Bernabé look his most solemn and judicial. The idea of affording birds such modern comfort was no doubt new to him, but he seemed to have grasped it. We went to the chosen place, below the terrace. There stood the font, nicely paved around. It was half full of earth and in the center rose a gawky geranium plant with two puny red blossoms.

"There you have it already," said Don Bernabé, "with all and flowers."

The Indio is very ingenious, but about something outside his experience he is often very stupid. Often, a man put to weed has grubbed up a gladiolus, a rosemary—after all, he did not know the flower, weeds come in all sorts of shapes. And a peon has, I fear, lost me the passion fruit, which was in leaf and even had a few first flowers, small white blossoms bearing the same stigmata as the garden passion flower. Merced had sent a man round to do some minor repairs to the wall of the garage. It is in that corner that the trunk of the passion-fruit vine stands. The idiot, wielding a mattock to break away the crumbled part of the wall he was going to mend, managed to strike the trunk, and to strike it such a blow that he cut it almost through. I doubt if it can recover. It will be difficult to replace, and I hope my landlord was not too attached to it. I have called the Indio who did the damage an idiot. And this is quite unfair. It was my fault. I should have warned him or overseen his work. Even though the vine was in leaf and flower, it was probably just any old climber to him, and a climber with an insignificant flower at that.

Almost at once there happened something as easy to resent and as necessary to forgive.

I had been in Guadalajara for the day, but I got back while it was still light, so I went round to the land. The first thing that I noticed was that the garage had window frames and shutters in it.

"Oh, yes," said Don Bernabé, "that Robustiano was here today and adjustanated them."

I went into the garage to look at them. The frames were of the right measurements, they fitted, the shutters opened and closed. But they were all made of the cheapest possible wood, not the best pine as I had asked. In fact they were made of packing-case wood, and across the inside of the shutters you could still read the trade names of the firms that had put out the crates. One shutter had JAB and below it CAR and another had ON and underneath ICIA. Jabón Caricia. That was a trade name I knew well enough. My grocer in Guadalajara often packed things in cases made for Caress Soap. Then I remembered how Robustiano had come and bought packing cases from me.

I went up to his house. His wife opened the door, gave me one look and disappeared into a back room where I heard whispering. She was too disturbed even to ask me in, and that is quite disturbed for a Mexican, who will always ask you to come in and sit down. I went in.

After a minute Robustiano emerged. He looked rather shamefaced.

"You've made my shutters of soapbox wood, and you had ten pesos to buy wood, and you bought the soapboxes of me for one-fifty," I said.

Robustiano said nothing.

"Well, there they are, and they're done, and I suppose if they're painted they won't look too terrible and they'll last a little time anyway. But what about my ten pesos, or at any rate eight-fifty? Your work isn't worth that."

Robustiano thought for a little.

"You see, señor, the reason I did it was this. Just when I had to sow my tomatoes, you came and ordered the windows and left me ten pesos, and as I had no money I bought the tomato seed. You know, I grow a lot of tomatoes and I don't know what we'd do without the money the crop brings in. I was wondering what would happen to us when you came and left the ten pesos. And then of course I hadn't anything to buy wood with. Total that I remembered you often had wooden boxes, and I bought them from you. And that was how it all was, you see."

He ended with the pleased smile of one who has negotiated successfully a complicated sum, and got it out right.

I knew I should never see my money again, and further fuss seemed pointless.

"All right," I said. "But what you must do is make me a small table like this one you have here, and then we'll stay planks, we'll call it quits."

"Very well pues. In that we stay. Many thanks, señor," said Robustiano.

"Many thanks," said his wife, taking courage to emerge from the back room. "May it go very well with you, señor."

But I am still waiting for the table.

"What do you think has happened?" cried Candelaria, following Rafles and my breakfast into the room. And, without waiting for an answer, she told me. "Paz, you remember the girl, the so pretty girl who was here the other day. Paz climbed out of the window last night when everybody was asleep, and there was Primitivo waiting for her in the street, and they went to Primitivo's parents' house. When I heard it I could hardly believe it, I thought it must be a case of Cayetano's knee. And even without her shawl! But it's quite true."

"And what will happen?" I asked.

"Pues, now they'll have to be married. The mother of Paz is in a state, but imagine to yourself, Paz jumped out of the window! And went off without even her shawl! And I wanted to ask you, you haven't anyone invited to lunch in these days?"

"I don't think so. Why?"

"Because it would be good to kill the old cock before he gets too tough. The young one is treading the hens nicely already. That is, of course, unless you're afraid that it would make your guests quarrel with their amphitryon."

"Why should I quarrel with them?"

"Pues, they say that people who eat cock together get quarrelsome."

"There are people in the world," I said, "who think that if you eat the heart of a lion you become brave. And once it was thought that if you ate your rival or some admired predecessor you absorbed his virtuous qualities."

"Really?" said Candelaria, to whom the idea was obviously quite unsurprising. "Pues, who knows."

I wondered what she would say if I were to pursue the theory in connection with the Christian sacraments. No doubt she would be neither shocked nor surprised. After all, the pre-Conquest Indios practised the ritual eating of victims sacrificed to their gods. And in Mexico one always has the feeling that nothing has ever stopped. More things have started happening but nothing has ever left off.

"But where's Cayetano?" I asked. For Cayetano is very jealous of bringing my breakfast, and doesn't like to leave it to anybody else, unless something really serious intervenes, such as the escape of the fawn. This happened once, and kept Cayetano away all morning. But that day he kissed my hand later on.

Candelaria giggled, and said, "Pues—"

"Well, where is he? Hasn't he come?"

"He's in prison, at least, they say he's in prison," she said.

"In prison? Whatever for?"

"Pues, he had the evening off last night."

"D'you mean he got drunk?"

"Yes, puesen. He put himself a tremendous drunk. He was singing in the street, and the comisario told him to go home, and at last he had to take him and shut him up."

Toward noon Cayetano appeared. He looked very sheepish. He isn't a drunkard, but most of the lads of the village get drunk occasionally. When they are obstreperous or a public nuisance, the comisario shuts them up for the night in the jail and lets them out in the morning. There is no legal procedure and no record is kept of the imprisonment, and it isn't much of a disgrace. It is a patriarchal scolding, like being sent to bed without any supper. It is a good system for a policeless village, where disputes are often argued out before the comisario, who composes the case without invoking the law.

"Well, Cayetano?"

Cayeano looked at the floor, twisting his foot and fingering his sombrero.

"What shall I say to you, señor?"

"Best not say anything. But tell me, has this happened to you before?"

"No, never."

"But it happens to a lot of men here?"

"That yes yes. Nowadays, that is. Five years ago we didn't have a lockup."

"Really?"

"No. Marcelino built it when he was comisario. He got the money for it, and he finished it just before his term was up, and he was very proud of it."

Cayetano sniggered as he said it, and I looked at him questioningly.

"You see, señor, just after finishing his term as comisario, his friends made him a fiesta. And he got so drunk and noisy that the new comisario shut him up for the night in the jail that he had built himself. He was the first person to go there."

The lesser of the two chief shops in the village is quite small. It sells earthenware bowls and pots, baskets, sewing thread, mercerized cottons and DMC, embroidery frames, bottled soft drinks, buttons, onions, candy, brooms, goat cheese, and so on. Anything the owner may have from her garden, such as coffee or peanuts, is seasonally on sale too. For the owner is a woman of property. She and her sister, Lupe of the fierce duck, each own a house on the lake front. The houses are side by side, and Bernardina does not live in hers but behind her shop. She often rents it. Lupe does for the tenants of Bernardina's house if they want her too.

Bernardina is small and elderly and gentle and vague, and her eyes are neighbors that have fallen out. She comes into her shop from the little room at the side and looks to right and left of you, bracketing, you suppose. She is very uncertain as to what she has in stock, and when you ask her whether she has black thread or a white button, she says, "Who knows. Let's see."

She is also very uncertain about adding up the bill. She writes down all the items on a tiny piece of brown paper, not, as often happens here, the paper she is going to wrap your parcel in. When she has done something really difficult, such as adding up three buttons at seven centavos each, one reel of thread at eleven centavos, and five saucers at two for nine centavos—you would have bought six but she only has five—she presents the result to you to verify, and each of her eyes wears a different expression. The one looking slightly to your left is full of doubt as to the success of her summing, but humble and expecting mercy, while the one looking slightly to your right, equally conscious of incompetence, seems to fear that it will be visited with wrath. When you assure her that the result is correct—it usually is—she sighs deeply, the eyes relax their double vigil, and the smallest purchase is wrapped in a scrap of paper. Now, the rapids of business passed and social millponds reached, is when she inquires after the health of any friends she may know you to have.

"And how," she says, "is the señorita who—it makes now many months—bought the two little yellow buttons?"

Across the lake, down toward the east, it was raining, a chance storm most unusual at this season, but we were in sunshine. The rainstorm moved out over the lake, a compact rolling storm, and the sun reconquered the stretches of the farther shore, beyond and behind the storm. Then suddenly a rainbow shone out, very bright and perfect, one arm reaching down into the water. As it blazed brighter, beyond it a second arch appeared, wider and paler, fading into nothing high above the lake. It too shone gradually more clearly, and then a third arch, of dim and fainting colors, sweeping a yet vaster circle, spanned out across the mists. This is not an uncommon sight here, and I have seen moon rainbows too, sheens of ghostly metallic pallor, curves of spun glass between darkness and darkness.

Slowly the rain swung across the lake and reached shadows over Ajijic. Outside the mirador there are two large earthenware jars. The raindrops falling on them made long dark streaks. But only for a second or two. Then the moisture was absorbed, and the jars were ready for another raindrop. Watching the raindrops splurge and vanish, I had been hardly conscious that I was flicking my cigaret lighter.

"Let me try, señor." And there was Cayetano beside me.

He made me start. And yet he often appears at my side suddenly like that. When he is not working he will come down to the mirador and, whether I am alone or not, stand a few yards away or squat under the mango tree. It is not at all unusual for the mozo of a house to sit down on the edge of a group of people. He won't join in the conversation, but he will laugh at a joke. There is nothing disrespectful in his behavior, and it is very convenient, for you never need to ring for anything, the mozo is right there. Occasionally I have asked Cayetano if he wanted anything. He always answers, "No, señor, but does anything offer itself?"

He took the lighter, and, at his first first flick, it worked. A pleased smile lit his face.

"I caught it tired," he said.

As the storm passed and the sun flowed round us again, I heard a frenzied crying from the top of a tall pecan tree. There two Derby flycatchers have nested. They have young. From the mirador I have watched them for days, flying back and forth with food, their elegant black backs and sulphur breasts brilliant against sky and leaf. I saw a big raven circling round the top of the tree. Through field glasses I could see the raven peering down at the nest. Then he settled on the topmost branch, a little above the fledglings. By now the parent flycatchers were flying round and round, making darts at the raven. They were quite madly valiant. The raven didn't take the least notice of them. He sat and looked down into the nest. Then, in a leisurely way, he flopped down, stood on the edge of the nest, and helped himself to a baby flycatcher. The parents' cries were quite heartbreaking. Still they circled and still they made darting ineffectual attacks on the murderer. But nothing availed, and the tragedy continued to its ending. Satisfied, the raven flew slowly away. The flycatchers pursued him a little way, and then flew back to their devastated home. After a little, the wailing cries died down, and I had an idea that perhaps they had found one chick alive. But, though I watched the nest day after day, I never saw a sign of a fledgling. And then one day the parents were gone, and I never knew whether or not a young flycatcher went with them.

Holy Week is the greatest fiesta of the year, not only religious but national. Often enough the state has had the sense to make religious feast days into national holidays. The two seasons of the year when Mexicans get a few days' vacation are Holy Week and the week that surrounds the Sixteenth of September, the festival of independence. Of the two, Holy Week is the more important. In Ajijic, Don Pedro, who was last year's comisario, has begun to build a shelter of beams and boughs and banana leaves, under which he is going to install a bar, selling beer, soft drinks, and tequila. He does this every year on the part of the beach near the mole, which is necessarily and automatically the center, where excursions arriving by launch spend the day. Usually he borrows money to do it, or he gets drinks on credit, and then he borrows chairs and tables from everyone who will lend. He invariably makes a loss. But Don Pedro no doubt has his vision fixed upon the future, when Ajijic will be a resort with conveniences, and year by year he backs his vision, hitherto always unsuccessfully. As a final touch of amenity the big eucalyptus tree nearest the mole has had a notice nailed to it. The notice says: "Within a hundred meters each side of the mole it is forbidden to bring cattle or women to wash."

The church, too, is a scene of great activity. The usual quantities of cut paper garlands are draped, and the chancel is being hung with lengths of gleaming blue and white mirror cloth. The big chandeliers are clean and set with candles. From each of the vaulted domes that line the nave swings a chandelier. They are heavy and decorative. I have avoided standing under one since I first went up onto the roof. Up there you see that at the apex of each dome is a small hole, through which comes the chain supporting the chandelier. This should be attached to an iron bar which rests across the hole. Thus the chandelier can be raised. Some of the chandeliers still have iron bars. But others have had their bars lost or stolen, and the heavy chandelier and its chain are supported by a very inadequate-looking piece of wood, unsquared and unpainted.

This year Holy Week is unusually splendid, for the corn mill has acquired a dynamo and offers electric light. The plaza, several streets, and the church have been fitted, as well as a number of private houses. The charge is made per bulb per month, and the light is on from sundown till eleven o'clock. There are even two light standards on the beach, and if they go on early they effectually spoil the sunset.

I had taken five lights, for the kitchen, bathroom, patio, dining room, and sitting room of my present house. A light that goes out at eleven is useless to me in a bedroom. The lights were installed one day when I was in Guadalajara, and Candelaria had everything ready for my return. The bedroom and the patio were ablaze with hundred-watt bulbs, unshaded, and the remaining three lights had been put in the huerta, so that the orange and banana trees were theatrically floodlit, while kitchen, bathroom, and dining room remained in darkness.

"Now," said Candelaria, "now Remedios would like Ajijic."

Candelaria has been very perturbed all week by the scarcity of fish. Middlemen buy a whole catch from the fisherman, and for many the week has indeed been one of fasting. Even the little charales have been scarce. In Guadalajara you can get frogs, which ordinarily are obtainable only on Fridays. They are big fellows, and fry to a crisp gilded lightness that no chicken can attain.

Candelaria has also been upset by the rise in prices. All prices rise in Holy Week. Hotels accustomed to charge eight pesos a day jump to twenty. Even in Ajijic one notices the change. Eggs, for instance, went from six centavos to fifteen, and then became unobtainable. All available eggs were taken to Chapala. Old women walked the five miles there and the five miles back to sell a dozen eggs at holiday prices. We had no eggs in the house. No small boys came with single eggs warm from the hen, and Refugio, from whom I often bought above market prices because she was so very poor, did not come any more. No doubt she too went to Chapala. At last I decided to go out in the car to look for eggs. I set out toward San Juan Cosalá. In the farthest parts of Ajijic village I inquired, but nobody had any eggs. At last I found myself in San Juan itself, fifteen kilometers on. I asked for eggs.

"Pues, yes," they said, "the señor in the house down there has them, the house with the door."

All the houses had doors, but this door was a new one studded with big nails, handmade and very handsome. In front of the house was a truck, into which crates of fruit were being loaded. As I approached a man greeted me warmly.

"And how are you?" he said. "A long time since I saw you. And how have you been?"

I could not for the life of me remember having seen him, but it appeared that at some time or other he had known me.

"Eggs?" he said. "You've come to the right place. I have all the eggs in San Juan. I send them to Guadalajara."

And he showed me cases of eggs.

"Then perhaps you don't want to sell any?"

"Yes, how not, as many as you want. But come in and see my huerta. How many eggs do you need?"

I asked for two dozen, which seemed a very small order for him. I I had a basket with me.

We went through the house to the huerta, which was full of well-tended trees. A mozo brought chairs, and picked fresh limes for us and brought a bottle of tequila and salt and small glasses. We had a very agreeable conversation, but I got no clue as to where I had seen the man before. And when at last I rose to go he allowed me only to pay the San Juan price for my eggs.

"They've been put in the car," he said.

They had. In the back of the car were also several big papayas, and a pile of limes and oranges, a welcome present, for both the latter were scarce.

We took cordial farewells of one another.

I have still no idea who he was or where or when I had known him, and I haven't seen him since.

Now that Paz had run away from home and gone to Primitivo's home, it was her family that was anxious for the marriage. They wanted her to marry him at once, but of course that was not possible during Lent. Primitivo's parents did not offer any opposition but they got their own back for being high-hatted by Paz's family. They said Primitivo could do as he liked, that no doubt Paz was a nice girl, and that nobody could deny she was pretty.

All this Cayetano told me.

"And you see, Primitivo wants me to be padrino at the wedding."

Padrino is the nearest thing to best man. But the padrino has certain obligations. He must first officially ask the parents of the girl for her hand. At the wedding, all expenses, including trousseau, are the bride-groom's, everything except the coins given to the bride and which she keeps as good-luck tokens and never spends. The parents of the girl are not required to spend anything, though of course they can give as handsome presents as they wish. Many Mexicans do not like their brides to bring with them any garments they have had before, they like them to owe everything to the husband. The padrino, how-ever, is expected to provide the music, and the coins given to the bride.

"Won't that be expensive for you?" I asked.

"Pues," said Cayetano. "How much have I got in the bank?"

He had twenty-three pesos something.

"And remember you were saving up for a leather jacket."

"I know. But you see, Primitivo is a great friend, he's my twin."

He paused, figuring in his head.

"Twenty-three pesos and seven for this week, and perhaps you would let me have next week's in advance?"

Twice Cayetano had brought his savings to over thirty pesos, and I had been hoping that when Señor González de la Comarca came in May he would have done it again, not in order that I might win my bet but that the old gentleman would have to admit that Indios could save. But it was not fair to try and influence Cayetano, and I agreed that that way he would have nearly forty pesos.

"And I hope you will ask me to the wedding, Cayetano."

"That yes yes, how not, señor. Paz is going to have a very nice dress of white satin. Primitivo's father has sold a cow and it will be a very nice wedding."

Just then Rafles called him, or I should probably have heard every detail of the wedding feast. I heard them together down below in the patio.

"But it's quite easy," Cayetano was saying. "And whatever are you bringing a match for? Imagine a match to put on the electric light!" He laughed mockingly.

"If it's so easy, pues, do it yourself," answered Rafles crossly. "You say you've seen the señor do it."

I looked over the parapet. They were hovering about by the electric light, which goes on at this time.

"Last night," said Cayetano, "I saw it go on by itself, but I think that was because the señor forgot to turn off the switch the night before."

Suddenly Rafles darted forward, turned the switch and leaped backward.

"Silly," said Cayetano, who had done nothing. "It's not dangerous, nothing of dangerous.'

Then he caught sight of me.

"I was going to say, señor, Don Pedro sends to say, if you would buy two cases of Coca-Cola and a case of beer which he got for his cantina and which he now has to pay for, but which he didn't sell?"

The fawn got sick.

"It's got worms," said Cayetano.

We dosed it with castor oil, but it went on having worms. It got very thin and excretion seemed to hurt it.

Cayetano brought Venustiano to look at it, and Venustiano took a bucket of water and crioline, mixed very strong, and doused the fawn's anus. For a day or two it seemed to get better. But then it got worse again. Cayetano mixed more crioline and water. This time the fawn didn't react. In a few days it didn't stand up any more.

It lay there in its corral and wouldn't eat anything. We brought warm milk and a little brandy with the milk. But it wouldn't drink. I put minute amounts of milk and brandy on its tongue, but it didn't swallow any. Then Cayetano tried.

"It knows me," said Cayetano. "It knows me as it doesn't know you, señor, if you pardon me. When we went to the beach we always turned to the left. But one day I turned to the right, and the fawn had gone a little way before it gave itself count it was not with me. It turned, and looked, and its legs trembled, and then it saw me and came running."

The fawn was devoured by worms. You could see them now in the passage of the inflamed anus. It was devoured by worms and it was dying.

"D'you think it's in pain?" I asked Cayetano.

"Now yes yes, I think that yes," he said. His dark fingers ran through the soft white fur of its throat. "Another time, when that Candelaria had left the corral unlatched, it came to my room, and I woke with a start, hearing in the dark loud breathing. And it was the fawn and its nose touched my hand."

It was dying and it was suffering. When your pets have to be put away, it is brutal not to stay with them till the end. It is brutal to send them alone to a veterinarian, to a stranger. The fawn looked at us out of its big gentle eyes and it licked my finger once. Then Cayetano shot it. The Indio has always lived close to pain and death and violence. There was a gleam of tears in Cayetano's eye, but I felt ready to vomit. The big eyes still looked at us. Until they had ceased to see we had been there.

MAY

THIS is the hottest month of the year, and the dustiest. The earth is so dry that one can hardly believe that in six or eight weeks everywhere will be green. The land is in all the tones of off-white, ivory, and sere yellow, in the dancing heat it has the glimmer of nicotine-stained mother-of-pearl. The trees are silvered over with dust and looking across any valley you see great columns of dust, quite large enough for Jehovah to travel in, which means that cars are going down distant dirt roads. Of all the months of the colorful Mexican year, May is perhaps the least colored. It seems to be almost the month of no color. But that is illusory. It is easy to miss the nuances of the parched. An oyster and its shell, at first glance pale and drab and slightly boring, include a whole orchestration not only of grays and pearls and ivories but in fact ghosts of all the rainbow. So here in May the countryside has every tint, in minor keys, as it has in summer in Umbria. The dust itself is pale gold or tinged with carnation. On white plastered walls hang shadows of forget-me-not, and the shadows on the flanks of the hills are milky lilac, the lilac that stripes a peeled onion. The vine, which was stripped in February, is now again covered with foliage, and my patio swims always in a cool luminous green. It is not colorlessness, it is not pallor that is everywhere. Rather, everywhere the spectrum has been transposed from stridency to delicacy.

Not that Mexico is ever quite without stridency of color. This year there are no jacaranda trees to carpet the plaza with blue-mauve. But here and there the flamboyant blazes orange-scarlet, and in front of the church the big primavera tree is hung with clusters of yellow blossom. And you can find all the splendors that spilled down all the sunsets by simply cutting a fruit, the pitahaya. It is a cactus fruit, with a dull green prickly outside. Inside it is soft, with soft dark seeds. Like the loquat, it must be eaten very soon after plucking. It tastes pleasant and cool, of nothing in particular, and is better eaten with honey. But peel a basketful, and your dish will brim with color; one fruit will be scarlet, another crimson, a third greenish yellow, another butter color, another white, another orange, and another magenta.

Yet these royal tones only offset the tender ones, for it is these that are at one with the mood of the season. It is the time when everything seems to go slowly, the men and the animals and the hours. Rightly, the still lazy weather is called the Calms of May. Everything seems to retire, to recede into a luminous waiting, a waiting that only the rains will break. Day by day the lake goes down, and the wine-glass willows, stranded now, throw compact round shadows, shadows that lie as still, in the windless air, as those who seek them. It is nearly twelve months since I came to Ajijic, and it seems as if the extremes of the year, the fantastic lights and the fantastic darknesses, the joys and and the annoyances, were resolving into a coda, slow with an Indio cadence.

The nights are warm but not hot, and they have this month a peculiar distinction of beauty, for up in the hills they have started burning off the tillage. It is a wasteful and destructive way of clearing the ground, and has helped the charcoal burners to their melancholy success of deforestation. But it is extremely decorative. By day, only pale plumes of smoke smear the hills. But at night long snakes of fire glitter all round the lake. Here a ridge is rimmed with orange flame. There a glowing S curves up a dark shoulder. There a zigzag of sparkles elbows down a slope. Shapes with the foreign grace of Persian letters are written on the darkness. And night after night I sit on the terrace watching these costly illuminations, enjoying them and regretting them.

May brings three fiestas in its opening week. The first is, as everywhere, Labor Day, and the fifth commemorates the Mexican victory over the French at Puebla in 1862. These are two national holidays, but in Ajijic national holidays are never quite so important as church festivals. So it is the third, the Day of the Cross, that is the most interesting.

Behind Ajijic, on a knoll about a third way up the mountain, stands a cross under a simple roof, and each of the four divisions of the village has a cross at some crossroads. The village crosses are decorated with flowers, and so is the one up the mountain. It is a stiffish climb, but the band and practically the whole village go up there. The band plays there almost all day, and they let off rockets from the cross, too.

And there is another celebration. In each of the village divisions there is a tree hung with bread and with fruits, including hunks of watermelon carved into grotesque faces. Men and boys climb to them, and he who first seizes one prize is entitled to the lot.

Cayetano had the afternoon off and when he came back I asked him whether he had tried for the fruit and bread.

"Oh, no," he said. "I didn't make the struggle. I wouldn't like to win."

"Why not?" I asked, for the total is worth some pesos.

"Pues, I wouldn't want to have to provide the party next year. And that's what happens if you win, you have to spend a lot of money next time. So I didn't try."

"But then aren't there lots of people who don't want to win? I wonder anyone wins at all."

"Sometimes there's somebody rich, who doesn't mind giving the party next year, and then he wins on purpose. Or else somebody has had some drinks, and his friends dare him, and then he climbs up and wins. He's usually sorry afterward."

"And who won where you were?"

"Oh, César won. But then he's rich, señor, he can afford it."

I tried to imagine César climbing into a tree after a piece of bread.

"Of course," added Cayetano, "he didn't do it himself. He sent his boy, Pedrito, into the tree."

I went out in the late afternoon with Primitivo, who having been a haircutter and a builder is now doing a little fishing again. He was going to put some setlines out in midlake. The heavy boat slipped easily through the satin water. These boats are virtually unsinkable. I have often seen one at anchor, full of water, with only the slight lift of the prow and the rowlocks visible, surviving thus for days. Primitivo and his young brother, who is twelve or so, were rowing, using short choppy strokes. A rowlock here is usually a single pin, and each man wields only one oar—a square blade on the end of a pole.

"You should come with me sometime and make the round of the lake," said Primitivo, flashing white teeth in the sunshine. "A gringo gentleman, a very nice gentleman, made the round with my father once, and he was so pleased that he bought a canoa, one of the big sailing canoas, and then he arranged it all very comfortably with a bed and a stove—he even put in an excused, a toilet—and lived on it. A thousand pesos he spent to make it over. My father and my uncle went with him to work the boat. They'd stop at a place and then my uncle would go ashore and buy whatever they needed."

"That sounds fun. What happened when they got becalmed?"

"Nothing," shrugged Primitivo. "Nothing. They just waited. They could make a fire and cook and the gringo gentleman fished. He was like us, he didn't have to be doing something all the time. He knew how to sit still."

About a mile out Primitivo stopped jabbing at the water with his oar. The boat slid on, losing way. He and his brother made a short job of putting out the setlines. They would leave them there all night and fetch them in the morning. Then we drifted for a little, while Primitivo smoked a cigaret I gave him. It was very peaceful, because we all knew how to sit still.

The sun made its last-minute hurried dive behind the mountains and we rowed back, and the lake round us drained of blue and turned to brass and platinum. A tortoise, sitting on the uncovered summit of a rock inshore, looked at us gravely and dove as we went by, and Primitivo and his brother sang in high strained voices.

"There's my little mother," cried Primitivo. For little mother is quite an ordinary term of affection between lovers. And there on the beach was Paz, her rosewood skin glowing against a dress of reseda green, waiting for Primitivo. I remembered how Cayetano had told me they loved each other much much.

When we reached land I saw that there was a captured grebe on the shore. There are many of these lovely birds on the lake. They are the stately white-throated grebe, Aechmophorus occidentalis, which they call here pilili. Their eyes are hot scarlet and each flattened toe has an individual web. They are almost as persistent fishermen as the Indios, and so, though it is forbidden to shoot them, they are sometimes shot. They cruise in shallow water, and then suddenly dip their swanlike necks and dive, appearing yards away from where they went down. But sometimes one is caught within the circle of a great seine net, and drawn slowly inshore as the net is hauled. Then the fisherman takes it by its proud white throat and puts it on the beach. The grebe's legs are set so far back on the body that it can only move very clumsily on land and cannot take off for flight, and even rising from the water it must speed along splashily, treading the water, till it gains the momentum to rise into the air. On land the grebe is a grotesque and pathetic sight. Often, they tie the bird by one leg. And then they bait it. It is not humble in captivity. It hisses furiously at anyone who approaches, and if you approach too near, you will get a nasty bite. Today several fishermen and a group of small boys were teasing the grebe and prodding it with sticks. It had tired, and was no longer making clumsy darts at stick or hand, but still its hot red eyes glittered royally, though it could do nothing but endure. It was an ugly sight to see.

I asked the fisherman why they were treating the bird so cruelly. But nobody had an answer, nobody knew. The Indio is affectionate to animals, but the Indio's ancestors were ruthless in torture.

"Will you sell it?"

Yes, they would sell it. They asked three pesos for it. This was absurd, for its little down could not fetch that and it had no other value. Finally I bought it for one.

If I had felt I could control it, I would have taken it down the beach and loosed it in private, for fear that catching grebe and selling them to me might become a lucrative business. The fisherman undid the string, and I got the bird by the throat and took its body with my other hand. It was a heavy bird and it struggled, and its eyes, clear and lambent as fire opals, looked closely into mine. I can't say I let it go. It would be apter to say I dropped it, into the shallow water. But it had recovered itself in a moment. I watched it as it sped away. In a few minutes it was cruising around and fishing at the end of the mole, as if there were no danger in its world.

Now, in the warm weather, everybody goes down to the beach more, not only for business but for pleasure. In the hour before sunset, boat-loads of girls in brilliant dresses often cruise slowly a little offshore. The men gather and gossip under the trees.

I was strolling one evening when I met Venustiano, who was water-ing his two cows and his horse. He drives the three animals down every late afternoon. All four go very slowly. The horse takes his drink quickly and noisily, the cows, knee-deep in the lake, slowly and almost distrustfully. Meanwhile Venustiano stands and looks. When the ani-mals have finished drinking, they stand and look too, and often all four will spend twenty minutes or so in contemplation.

"What a nice evening," said Venustiano, when I greeted him, and the horse and the cows moved their heads as if to say that they were enjoying the glitter and the azure and the splashing too.

A little way off a man was sitting under a willow. He had his back against the trunk and his knees were hunched up under his chin. His hat was pulled down, and he had his sarape round his shoulders. Venustiano indicated him with a shake of the head.

"Poor Nacho," he said.

In that melancholy figure I had not recognized plump cheerful Nacho who played in the band.

"Why? What's happened to him? Some disgrace?" For in Spanish that means not a disgrace but an accident, giving one the agreeable feeling that disgrace is not earned but an act of God.

"Haven't you heard?" said Venustiano. "Pues, he had a terrible experience."

He paused for a moment and made a clucking noise at the smaller cow, which had strayed a little. It returned slowly.

"You know Nacho's wife Cuca. A very good woman, a good mother, very hard-working. But ugly, very ugly. A big mouth with one tooth in it. Pues it seems that for some time Nacho has been having ideas about how nice it would be to have a pretty young wife instead of Cuca. From time in when it happens that men abandon their wives, and go to another village, and find a pretty girl and live with her. Nacho had been thinking things like that pues. And one night as he was coming home he was thinking very much on that. He had almost decided he would look for a way to leave Cuca. And then suddenly, as he was walking, a large black animal, perhaps like a dog but a very big dog, came rushing along and passed between Nacho's legs and Nacho was hoisted onto the animal's back and carried two blocks, quick like that, and then there he was on his back in the road, and the animal had vanished. You can imagine, puesen, that gave him quite a shock. He thought at once that it had to do with his thoughts about Cuca, because he knew they were wicked thoughts. So the next day he went to the padre and confessed. He confessed the whole thing, his thoughts about Cuca and all. And the padre told him that it was certainly the devil and a warning to him to behave decently and be a good husband to Cuca who was the mother of his children. Poor Nacho. That's why he's so depressed."

And Venustiano gave the smallest chuckle, as if he thought it was very bad luck that now Nacho was condemned to stay with a wife who had a big mouth with only one tooth in it.

"And the padre used the story for a sermon," went on Venustiano. "Without mentioning names, of course. But everybody knows who it was. The padre said everybody should be very careful because the devil often appears in Ajijic."

"Really? And does he always appear like that, like a big black dog?"

"That yes no. The padre said he himself had seen him. He said that one night, coming out of the parochial house, he had suddenly seen a great black coach advancing straight upon the church. He knew it was the devil, so he made the sign of the cross, and as it was reaching the entrance to the church the big black coach swerved away and disappeared into the night."

I knew the new priest very little, but he was a man of education. He had made good use of Nacho's sad experience. And I could not help remembering how, some time before, some friends of mine, leaving late at night for Chapala, had, as they afterward told me, mistaken the turning of the main road and driven clear up to the plaza, so that they had had to double back past the church. They had a big black sedan.

Venustiano was looking at me sidelong. Was there, among the countless wrinkles of his face, under the rugged gray bristles of his mustache, a little grin?

"I often get back late," he said, "when I have been working at my vegetables. I wonder what I should do if I met a big black coach.

"Poor Nacho," he added, and clucked at his animals.

He took off his hat to me, and the horse and the two cows followed him slowly up the beach.

When I got home it was obvious that something had happened. The volume of talk from the kitchen was much greater than normal. Candelaria, Rafles, and Cayetano were all speaking at once excitedly. I caught a few sentences, and called to Cayetano.

"Who has been killed?"

"A young man called Sebastián. I knew him. He was working at the mill when I was there. Then last night they killed him."

"Do they know why, and who did it?"

Cayetano shrugged. "He was a great taker, he drank a lot. Anyone might have done it. Nobody liked him, nor much less."

"Had he enemies?"

"No, no enemies. But nobody liked him. Probably they were all drunk. They say it was two of the workers at the mill. But who knows."

That evening Rafles asked leave to go to the funeral. It appeared that the murdered boy was her cousin.

"Very sad for you."

"Pues," she said, "we were quarreled with him, we had had a disgust. But still I must go to the funeral. They're going to bury him with his feet tied together."

"Whatever for?"

"Pues, because then, you see, his murderers won't be able to run away. They'll have to come back to untie his feet before they can run away. Then they'll be caught, even if they're brave enough to stand the wailing spirits."

So Rafles went to the funeral, and when she came back she could not find her dustpan. She was very upset, for the dustpan has been her pride. I had brought it from Guadalajara, and she had never seen such a thing, having been used to gathering up sweepings with her hands. A Mexican servant will empty ash trays and wastebaskets onto the floor, sweep everything to the door, and there, on hands and knees, transfer all the sweepings by hand to a box or a piece of paper. The dustpan was of blue enamel, and every day, after using it, Rafles washed it in soap and water. It was gone.

It was found later in the day, round at my new house, Merced had lacked something to carry mortar in, and, coming round early, had taken the first suitable object he saw. The dustpan was restored to Rafles. But the mortar had hardened, and it was irretrievably ruined. She washed it and scraped it and did get most of the mortar off. But the beautiful blue enamel was spoiled. For Merced it had been the most natural thing in the world to take the dustpan. When you have very few tools or utensils, each must be put to a variety of uses. The next day he was using a chamberpot.

Rafles had been with me since December, had worked very well, and, like the other servants, had put on weight. She seemed perfectly happy, had never complained or been out of temper. Suddenly, two days after the funeral, she said she wanted to go.

"But why? Aren't you happy here?"

"Yes, how not." And if she had said, "No, how not," the expression of her face would have been just the same.

"You earn well and you eat well. What's wrong?"

"I want to untire myself," she said.

The Spanish for to rest means literally to untire oneself. Effort being unnatural, after it you untire yourself. Mexican servants, when they want to rest, will throw up a job without thought of getting it or another one after the rest. They can go to their homes, there will be a tortilla for them. So Rafles is going to get untired, but of course she knows of somebody to take her place.

That afternoon Nieves, who had been my first maid, came and greeted me.

"Well, Nieves, good afternoon, how are you, and how have you been?"

"Regular, señor," she said, which means so-so, rather better than worse. She smiled, and, after months of Rafles' blank round face, I found myself glad of the smile and the sharp Indio bones of Nieves. "Regular. And you?"

"Very well, thank you."

"Rafles told me she was leaving," said Nieves.

"Yes."

"And so I come."

"D'you mean you'd like to work here again?"

"Yes."

Mexican servants are like that. Not only after leaving with good will all round, but after leaving in a temper, or wounded to the quick, or insulted, or anything you like, they will turn up again one fine day, as if nothing had ever happened.

"I could start right away," said Nieves. "And of course I know the work."

I wanted my sitting room in the new house washed pale gray. In this brilliant light I find white always too dazzling. Sometimes in Chapala the white houses hurt the eye, and I wish they would make a rule such as the Dutch have in Curaçao, where the one color you mayn't paint your house is white. Nowadays you see a few Indios wearing dark glasses, but many of them have trouble with their eyes. In Mexico, the gray days are if anything harder on the eyes than the sunlit ones. I explained to Don Bernabé that I wanted a very pale silver-gray, using the word gris. But that is a word that is very seldom used.

"Ah, you mean leaden," he said.

Spanish, in spite of its enormous vocabulary, is poor in color terms. Brown, for instance, must be called coffee, which is an indifferent substitute.

"Light leaden," added Don Bernabé. "I imagine to myself most exactly the tone. Light little leaden."

On the whole Don Bernabé is receptive of ideas. Anybody who knows Mexico has noticed that door handles are always put on in such a way that you cannot open or close a door without grazing your knuckles. They are often, if provided with a lock, put on upside down, for no obvious reason. I was quite determined to be able to open and close my doors painlessly. Don Bernabé listened attentively to what I had to say about door handles.

"What a most well-thought idea! Many times I have hurt my fingers like that. That is what is wrong with us Indios, we don't think of things." He shook his white head sadly. "No, we don't know anything. Merced! Come and listen to what the señor has projectated about the doors! Yes, señor, little light leaden, like silver."

A young man got out of a launch and came up to me on the beach. He said good morning using my name.

"As I was going to stay in Chapala, my uncle Carlos asked me to visit you and see how you were," he said, in English. "Luis González de la Comarca, at your orders."

We shook hands, and I asked him into the house. He was tall and had hay-blond hair, as if his ancestors had come from northern Spain. He was in English-looking tweeds, and had the same courtly manners as his uncle, but with a touch of pompousness that spoiled them.

"You know," he said, "my uncle thinks you are a little mad to like living here, in Ajijic, in this old house."

"But I do like it."

"Yes, I would like it too. If I had something to do, of course. If one had land. If we still had our haciendas, that is the life I would choose, to live on one."

"And where do you live?"

"I have been living in Mexico City, studying. I have nearly finished now. I have just completed my social service."

"And what's your line?"

"I'm an architect. There's a lot of building going on in Mexico, and there'll be more. That's why I chose it."

It is unusual for Mexicans of the class of the González de la Comarca to think in this practical way. Some of them have managed to save something from their ancient fortunes, and salted it away in the United States, or bought valuable city real estate, on the rents of which they live. But others hang on in their old once elegant houses, watching the money go, while the younger generation, beautifully dressed, does nothing but help it go.

"What does your uncle think of that?"

"Oh, he approves. He has come to see that we can't go on forever as we used to."

"And the rest of your family?"

"Would you believe it," he said, "of all my family—and it's a big family—I'm the only one of my generation who has studied a profession? The only one."

"I think you're very wise."

"Well, I'm almost through now. As I said, I've done my social service. They sent me to make a survey for a possible road down in the south of Jalisco. It was pretty rough living, but it's over now. My uncle tells me you are building a house here. I should like to see it."

When I started to build my small house with the help only of Don Bernabé I had not bargained to have to show it to what the old man called an archichitect, let alone before it was finished. But there was no help for it, and we went round to the land.

Don Bernabé, when I presented him to González de la Comarca, performed a ballet of bows and courtly gestures, greeting the "nephew of Don Carlos, with whom I am well acquainted." And when he learned that the young man was not only himself but an architect as well, he was delighted.

"Then you will appreciate the works of construction, señor," he said, as between compeers. "You will notice the measures we have taken and the improvements that the señor has inventated."

The pompousness that often spoiled the young man's manner vanished, and he accompanied Don Bernabé everywhere and listened to everything that he had to say, complimenting him on his work.

"And do you," he asked, "find the cement we get nowadays as good as the old?"

He was, I realized, back in time past, he was the hacendado being gracious to the peons. It suited him. But then dispossessed aristocrats always retain their graciousness where respect is automatically accorded them, and when it is not, become pompous.

We completed the tour of the land and left by the beach.

"You will have to have all theses people moved away," he said, pointing to a fisher family's camp that had grown up beside my boundary wall. The fishermen often make semi-permanent homes on the beach, tents or mere shelters such as the one I had eavesdropped on. You look into such a tent and see hanging from the roof pole coat hangers laden with mirror-satin dresses, and outside, against some convenient rock or dry wall, an open-air kitchen has been arranged, while washing dries on any hand rail or coping (or often on barbed wire, which, though it may tear the clothes, indubitably prevents them from blowing away).

"Why, this is an installation in every form," said González de la

243

Comarca, in Spanish. "You'll have to get the comisario to turn them out."

I had been worried about the installation, for I have also seen that, with time, a few rocks are piled into crosswalls, jutting out from your garden wall, and then a roof is added, and then a door, and in no time the inhabitants probably have squatters' rights. Such habitations are unhygienic, and for that unpleasant neighbors. But I hadn't made up my mind what to do, for I cannot but feel that the native Indios have first right to the shores of their own lake. But I avoided discussing the matter with González de la Comarca, and we went back to the house for lunch. We sat on the roof.

"I am looking at this old house," said González de la Comarca, "and thinking how nice it could be if it were made over. Perhaps I shall ask my uncle to let me do it. Using the village labor as you are doing. I imagine it comes out cheap like that."

"D'you know," I said, "I shall never know how much the house has cost. Too many things are bought at odd times in odd places for me to keep proper account. But nothing is expensive. I hope you won't want the house before mine is ready."

"Of course not. So long as you wish it, this is your house. And there's no question of my doing anything like that at present. Not till I have been received."

"And when will that be?"

"In four or five months from now. I have a position waiting for me. And as soon as I have started my career, I shall be married."

"My congratulations," I said.

There was something un-Mexican about this energetic planning and performance. I began to have hopes for the Mexican upper class if it could produce a young man like this.

"Yes," he said. "She is a nice girl. Not one of the modern ones with gringo manners. For of course I would not want my wife to go out unless she went with me, and I should expect her to go to Mass every day. My fiancée is a very nice girl. She would never do anything without asking my permission."

All old Mexico came back as he spoke, and I thought how strange a mixture he was of new and old. There are many husbands like Luis González de la Comarca. So it is not surprising that a Mexican hus-

244

band can divorce his wife for adultery committed anywhere, but she can only divorce him for adultery provided it has taken place in the home.

He left soon after lunch. I went down to the launch with him.

"Please tell your uncle," I said, "that he has lost his bet. My mozo has twice saved up as much as thirty pesos in his bank. He will know what I mean."

"I know too," he said. "My uncle told me. I'm glad. I was to pay you if my uncle had lost. Twenty-five pesos, isn't it?"

"Yes. We bet twenty-five on the condition that, if I won, five were for Cayetano." I decided not to give Cayetano his money until after Primitivo's wedding, so that he would not be centavoless.

"One can make something of these people, you know," said the young man as he handed me the bills. "They're not all hopeless. But of course my uncle is old-fashioned. I am not."

I made my farewells, and gave him my best wishes for his marriage.

"Thank you," he said. "I intend that we shall have many children."

I drove to the western end of the village, to the part they call the Beehive, where the houses and the people are poorer, and everyone looks more farouche. Aurora lives down there, and she had told me that her ten-year-old son had got a poisoned foot. Of course, she had said nothing about it before. Ten days previously, climbing a dry wall, he had dislodged a rock which had come down and torn his ankle. There was a filthy bandage round the boy's foot, and under it a cut some five inches long, over the Achilles tendon. The wound was suppurating, and he had a little fever. I had first seen the boy the day before, and I had come to change the dressing. I had told Aurora she must boil each day the bandage I had taken off. This is not the acme of hygiene, but if here you gave out fresh bandages daily for every wound, you would spend a fortune. I changed the gauze, and used the old bandaging. Aurora brought it to me, neatly folded, when I had cleaned the wound. The boy was very brave.

"And are you sure you boiled it?"

"Yes, yes, my little Trini boiled it, didn't you?" She turned to her daughter, who always stood by me, dumb and staring, when I was there.

245

"No, I washed it," said the child.

"There, what can we do?" said Aurora, with her martyred smile. "What can we do pues?"

"I washed it like you told me," said the girl inexorably.

Aurora just sighed and her hands fell to her sides, with a gesture of going down valiantly in face of fearful odds.

I hadn't brought any fresh bandages with me, so I had to use the washed one. When I had done, Aurora followed me to the door.

"Will he die?" she asked.

"Certainly not, if you see to it that the bandages are boiled."

"How not," said Aurora, "that's very easy."

On the way back I passed César's potrero. A potrero is a garden devoted to small things like tomatoes and peanuts, as distinct from a huerta, which has fruit trees. César himself, solid, prosperous, and beaming, was at the gate, supervising the loading of his truck with cases of tomatoes. I stopped and talked to him.

"You've been to the Beehive?"

"Yes," I said. "How different it is down there. And such swarms of children. What is the population of this village anyway?"

He thought for a little and then said, "Well, perhaps two thousand. But God knows how many children. I'm sending you those young banana trees you wanted this evening, and, of one time, some of those pink oleanders you liked. They are a present. But put much care for they grow like weeds. The children die a lot, you know."

The Beehive had depressed me. It seemed all dirt and poverty and neglected children and death. César's neat wooden cases were of a different world. Down the path between some nicely growing corn came two of his children, a boy and a girl, as neat and healthy-looking as you could wish. I wondered whether César in his own childhood had been as well cared for as his own young were now. There is a new Mexico.

I wanted to have my huerta planted in orderly fashion. You often see huertas and gardens full of splendid trees and flowers all growing in such a tangle that not only can you not see them, you can hardly find your way among them, let alone tend them properly. But then they have not been planned. A little mango? We'll put it in here. Six oranges? Well, there's room for one over there, and another there between the coffee bushes, and, let me see, another could squeeze in there between the cauliflowers and the lime tree. And so on. The fact that the mango will grow enormous and the cauliflowers soon cease to exist is irrelevant. Everything is calculated on the moment of here-now. Last week was something, and next week may be something else, who knows, but here-now is here-now. So leave as much room for the cauliflower as for the lime tree. Every time I acquired a tree or bush for my garden the same situation arose.

"We could put the pomegranate there," said Cayetano. "It's quite a long way from the papaya tree."

"But I'm going to take all the papayas down."

"Oh, yes, so we are," said Cayetano, and relapsed into baffled silence.

"Now if we have plumbago all along the wall, and in front of the plumbago hibiscus bushes, where would this oleander look nice? How high does it grow?"

"So of high," said Cayetano, reaching above his head.

"In that case it wouldn't look well in front of that wall at all."

"No, it wouldn't, it's true," said Cayetabo. "We have to think it carefully."

At this point Don Bernabé came along and confused the issue by telling us that he had a plant like that and it grew best near the well.

"Should we put it by the well?" asked Cayetano.

He and I went down the huerta together and on the way we passed the little strip of land I had given him to grow what he liked in. When I first gave it to him, I asked him what he was going to plant.

He thought for a minute, and said, "Pues, in each of the little mounds of earth I have made I shall sow tomatoes. I shall put in two or three seedlings in case one or two of them die. And I think there would be room for a few peanuts as well, and why don't I put in some squashes between them? Then if the tomatoes don't give, I have the others."

I told him he would do far better to put in one tomato seedling in each mound. But the idea that everything might flourish was too attractive.

"And my uncle has given me some carrot seed. Carrots always do well here, señor."

So he put the carrots too, and, just for luck, some zinnias as well. Of course, what little came up was weedy and undersized. Now, his little garden was neat and orderly, each variety of plant in a small section, and not overcrowded.

"Why don't we put in several pomegranates?" suggested Cayetano.

Candelaria and Nieves came frowning over the kitchen account book. As Nieves can write, the book is kept by her at Candelaria's dictation.

"Please, señor, look at the book. We cannot understand what has happened."

"Well, what has happened?"

"We have put down everything quite correctly, except that this girl put down eleven little centavos for little onions, when it should have been fourteen, but we have corrected that now."

"Then what's wrong?"

"Pues, as I say we've got everything down right, and look!"

Candelaria held out her hand. In the brown palm lay two pesos and a pile of chicken feed.

"Well?"

"You gave me four pesos, pues, and the account adds up to three pesos eighty-eight centavos, and that leaves twelve centavos, and I've got them here."

With the air of a conjuror, Candelaria opened her other hand to show me twelve centavos lying in it.

"Then what is all that?" I asked, pointing to the pesos and chicken feed.

"But that's what we can't make out."

I looked through the account. The items and prices were normal and the addition was correct.

"But why have you bought cheese, Candelaria? You know I don't like the cheese we get here."

"Because the cheese you brought from Guadalajara has finished itself, and I shall want cheese for the spaghetti tonight. I'm going to get it now."

"You've not bought it yet?"

"I'm just going."

248

"But you've put it down in the account."

"Oh, yes, I've put down everything I'm going to spend today. Everything—"

I had shut the book and was looking at Candelaria without saying anything. As when she had first come to work for me, Candelaria's accounts were closer to fantasy than figures. Suddenly it dawned on her what had happened. She snatched the book from me, and flung her apron over her face as a Roman must have covered his humiliation with his toga. From beneath the apron came muffled cries of "What a silly I am! What a silly!" as she rushed back to the house, followed by Nieves. When I went up half an hour later they were still explaining to each other how they had gone wrong.

But just then Cayetano came in with news that claimed the attention of the kitchen for some time. That afternoon the soldiers who had been sent from Chapala shot the probable murderer, a worker at the mill who had disappeared directly after the murder. They found him a little way up in the mountains and shot him "while trying to escape," under the law of flight. Candelaria is convinced that he had gone no farther owing to the binding together of the dead man's feet.

"You see," said the comisario with pride, "that it is very little just to say that this is a savage village, nor much less."

The building is held up again. Don Bernabé told me, very respectfully, that on the following Wednesday he would not be able to work, or Merced either.

"Why? What's happening?" I asked.

Don Bernabé drew himself up, all five foot three of him. "I am getting married, señor."

He had been about three months widowed, but, after all, the Emperor Francis I waited no longer, unable at an age greater than Don Bernabé's to support a longer period without sin or marriage.

"Congratulations. And whom are you marrying?"

"I am marrying that Sebastiana, the niece of Don Vicente."

I knew Sebastiana. She was not more than twenty, and a nice girl. But she was not pretty. I suppose Don Bernabé, with his several-roomed two-story house, his little property, and no doubt some money saved, apart from his earning capacity, was quite a catch.

Don Bernabé worked up till the day before his wedding, and he worked the day after it, but not much. He came along when I was down at the house, which now looks practically habitable. We talked about the patio. It will be very small. It lies behind the house, with the kitchen on one side and the garage on the other. The fourth side I have had walled. I hesitated, wondering whether to leave it open to the garden. But as it is I have the view of the mountains above the wall, and the little tiled space is quite enclosed. There is no door from patio to garden. You have to go through the house to get from one to the other. But then that way it is easy to roof the whole patio with screening, so as to be able to sit there at night with a light.

"I consider," said Don Bernabé, staring at me hard out of his pale old eyes, "that it would be practicable to roof in that manner a part of my yard. My wife does not like flies. How much a meter is cloth of wire?"

A boat came in bringing watermelons from San Pedrito, down at the other end of the lake. There aren't many watermelons in Ajijic. I wanted one, for I had finished the last pineapple. Pineapples, of course, don't grow at this altitude. In Guadalajara, however, you can get superb ones, for a short season. Very white of flesh, they are not fibrous and have a delicious aroma. Watermelons were rather a come-down, but taken with plenty of salt and a squeeze of lime they are tolerable, and their strawberry-scarlet is at least a feast for the eye. I have often been warned that watermelons are dangerous because of the risk of typhoid. This is probably true, but I have eaten them for years without ill effect.

Cayetano came with me to the beach where they were being sold. He loves to bargain, and I always enjoy hearing him do it.

"I told the Señor who had the tomatoes that at twenty-five centavos a kilo they were very dear, so he said he was keeping them for seed, and I said who knows if you sow them maybe they won't be born let alone give, and he thought and said he would let me have them at twenty, and I said eighteen, and in twenty-one we stayed."

While Cayetano was chaffering, I leaned against the dry wall at the end of the huerta and listened. I have learned the Indio tricks of conserving energy. I never walk farther than I have to, and if I must wait somewhere where there is no seat, I prop up a wall. I happened to look down the wall where my left arm was resting. I jumped. There, wedged between two loose stones, was an alicante. Only the tail was showing, marked with black and white diamonds not unlike a rattler's. Alicantes are poisonous, but very lethargic. I prodded it with a stick. It didn't move, and for a very good reason—I have never seen such a perfectly sloughed skin. Cayetano tried to exchange it for a watermelon.

When we got back to the house there was a young girl sitting in the patio.

"It's Modesta, señor," said Cayetano. "You know, the daughter of the sister of the señor who sells us kindling who lives up by the Eye of Water."

Modesta came shyly toward me. Round the ends of her fingers she was twisting the beard of her shawl into tight little knots, which she then put into her mouth and sucked. Finally I managed to understand what she was saying.

"Mamma said she asked herself if you didn't have one of those nice little bottles like my uncle has and if you didn't want to sell it to her." Then she giggled, glanced at Cayetano, and ran into the kitchen.

I am always being asked for my old bottles. By pouring the dregs of one bottle into another, I managed to find a nice little bottle for Modesta.

"Many thanks," she said. "Very many thanks. It isn't quite like the one my uncle has and how much is it?"

"Well," I said, "your uncle is a friend of mine, and so is your mother, and now I know you. So I'll make you a special price. Twenty pesos."

Modesta shrieked with laughter and rushed to ask Candelaria whether she had heard what the señor had said and repeated the whole thing to her, giggling all the time. After that, I asked Modesta what her mother wanted the bottle for. She had lost her shyness after the joke, and suddenly spoke in a breathless spate:

"Pues, you see, señor, we had another but unfortunately I let it fall very lightly and it broke itself to me but before that you see my brother Chucho used to take it half full of milk when he went to work at the mine and then when the little kid was sick we used it to feed him and when we had the wedding last month we put flowers in it and they looked very pretty and then I let it fall and it broke itself to me."

Raúl Bonilla had written to say that he was in Chapala again. The next day he arrived in the late morning. In the front seat, sandwiched between Raúl and a friend, were a huge gun and a great Dane. The friend was introduced to me as Alfredo Something. I don't know to this day what his surname is.

"And he lives here because he likes it," said Raúl, introducing me. This often strikes not only the villagers, but educated Mexicans, as extraordinary. "What! You could live in Chapala, or in Guadalajara, or in the Capital, and you choose to live in Ajijic!" they cry and look at me wonderingly.

Alfredo was plump and pasty and his English was very scattery. Later Raúl told me he was a lawyer and a very cunning one.

"Now we speak the other language, so my name is Alfred," he said, shaking hands with me all over again. "What is your name in my language?"

Motzín pretended not to see the great Dane, and slipped prudently into the kitchen to sit under the table. But Tippet, who likes new faces, was all over him. In no time she had taken him down the huerta to play in her favorite lettuce bed. After a little Motzín followed them.

We had drinks on the terrace. Raúl tried several times to get the conversation into Spanish, but Alfredo was determined to speak the other language. Fortunately he was not a person who knew how to sit still, and before long he disappeared with his gun in search of duck.

Raúl told me his dog-breeding business was doing well, and that he was going to try other breeds besides Dackels. He was studying veterinarian's work too.

"There are many ways of living," he said, "and this is one."

For lunch, Candelaria had made gaspacho, iced tomato soup with cucumber and avocado in it. After that we had fried charales with chicory salad, and panela, the excellent Mexican cream cheese. A hot-weather lunch.

"I suppose," said Alfredo, "you cannot get meat here. Oh, boy, give me a steak of three inches."

"What a pity you didn't shoot a duck," said Raúl gently.

Over coffee, Alfredo, who moved very clumsily, spilled all the matches from his box. Raúl stooped to retrieve them.

"With permission, señor," said Cayetano, already on his knees and gathering the matches deftly. Raúl helped him.

"That's all Indios are good for," said Alfredo, in Spanish. "Things like that. To put matches in a box. And now they have the power." He spoke as resentfully as Señor González de la Comarca, who probably would not have consented to know him.

"Alfredo is very political," said Raúl, with his slow lazy smile. "He often changes his politics, but he feels them very strongly."

Alfredo snorted, and his pasty puffy face set into the Caesarean lines to which so many sham Caesars have accustomed us.

"And you, Raúl, you do not like to choose. That is what is wrong with us Mexicans, we do not like to choose. But now it is necessary to choose."

"Alfredo is very rightist," said Raúl. "I know it is not well thought of nowadays, but I, I prefer the middle of the road."

The dogs came running in, Tippet snapping playfully at the great Dane and Motzín a step or two behind, polite but not effusive to his guest.

"You know," said Raúl slowly, "to the extreme left and right of most roads there is a gutter."

In the end I did not go to the wedding of Paz and Primitivo. I had caught a chill. At this season, the difference between sun and shade temperature is treacherous. I had walked in the sun and sat down in the patio without putting on a coat, and as a result was running a fever.

Cayetano had the day off, and the village car, its broken down condition somewhat disguised with white bows, had been ordered to drive the pair the block and a half from the church to the bride's home. They had acquired a house, whose one room had been fitted with window frames but not with glass, and, after consultation with Cayetano, I had given them some blankets. On the way from the church a special detour was made for me to congratulate them and

253

Cayetano brought them in with a proprietary air, as if the whole thing were his doing. Primitivo was hardly recognizable. I had only seen him in overalls, huaraches, a sombrero. Now, in a dark city suit, shirt, tie, and shoes, he was transfigured. Paz wore white mirror cloth, yards and yards of it, smartly cut, and a lavish veil. She really looked very beautiful, her rosy copper skin glowing against the pallor. Cayetano had been forehanded, and whisked a charged shaker out of the icebox for the bridal health. They stayed a few minutes, and then went on to the party. This would be a long meal, with many drinks, and the music playing as loudly as it could in a small confined room. I heard afterward that it had been most successful.

I lay in bed, wondering what was happening to the building. We had had so many delays recently, for one reason or another. And now that I was laid up it seemed not unlikely that no work would be done. While I was feverish and depressed, everything seemed insuperably difficult, everything seemed bound to come out wrong. I had sent Cayetano to ask Don Bernabé to come and see me, and he had not come. In mid-June I was supposed to vacate the house I was living in now, and we had little time left to make my two rooms habitable. And what with the money I had put into the land and the building materials, I could not go on paying workmen and running a rented house at the same time indefinitely. I still had to plant the garden and the huerta, if the land was ever to give a return. In the modern world, it is good to feel that, if need be, you can live on your corn and fruit and maybe keep a cow. I imagined all sort of setbacks and disasters, all of them translating themselves into expenses which ended in uncertain but excessive numbers of noughts. So I kept myself awake worrying and kept myself worrying by not going to sleep. May ran on into June. It was hot and hotter, and I had the bedroom door left open till late, and bats came in. They swooped and fluttered, and then they perched on a beam and squeaked at each other. Outside the hissing bird hissed maddeningly. I changed my pajamas three or four times a night and lived on gallons of brine and fruit juice, giving myself injections while Candelaria, like a witch over a caldron, brooded over the boiling syringe, and Cayetano hovered, all helpless good will. None of the servants left me to go to the fiesta at San Antonio

Tlayacapam on the thirteenth, a fiesta of which it used to be said that if there wasn't at least one man killed "the fiesta doesn't serve."

"The fever doesn't want to cut itself," said Candelaria, shaking her head at me in a graveyard way. All night the flittering fluttering bats went like witches through my half-dreams.

Two days later I got up, and, feeling too tired to walk, took the car the few blocks to my land. I turned in at the gap in the wall where Don Bernabé will build the gate with the little roof of tiles and bumped over the tracks which will one day be a drive. The huerta was a desolation of bricks and adobes and tiles and lime pits and builder's rubbish. The house looked just the same as when I had left it, except that the front door was in. There were no workmen to be seen. I got out of the car, opened my front door, and went into my house.

Suddenly, everything had been finished. Both rooms, whose floors had been earth, were tiled. The windows were in place, and the Venetian blinds, one a little crooked. Walls and ceilings were plastered. The shelves were in the book alcoves. There was really only painting to be done. The kitchen was whitewashed, clean and welcoming. I went into the bathroom and turned a faucet. Water flowed. In the bedroom, the closet shelves were in too. I pulled up the blind on the door to the terrace. It was roofed, and half the floor was covered in tile. Down at the other end, Don Bernabé and his workmen were filling the rest of the earthen space.

I opened the door and went out, onto the new tiles with their splashed reds and yellows. The lake was pale blue glass, glittering with a million twinkles that rebounded from the dust-green willows and the gray rocks of the dry wall, from the back of a black cow and the white billow of a big square sail and from the water in the little bath of birds. Opposite, set in the center of the view, the long quiet curves of Cerro de García were tawny mauve behind veils of haze.

Then Don Bernabé saw me. He put on his hat and doffed it with great gestures. His inquiries and courtesies flowed round me. I congratulated him on his achievement.

"The week that enters," he said, "we shall commence the eight little columns for the octatagonal mirador on the roof."

Merced and the workmen came after him. One of them found a little chair, and, all at once tired, I was glad to sit down. The dancing lake broke up the sunshine and tossed it everywhere like confetti. Suddenly we were all smiling.

It was the hour before sunset, always the most beautiful and often the warmest of the day. The pale blue sky was not of the gauze of winter, but of opaque stretched flannel. Only the limits of the long eastward distances were smudged where air and water merged without horizon line. Southward, at the crest of its long gentle curves, Cerro de García sported a little plume—the first cloud. But the rains will not break just yet. The afternoon was hot and the heat beat like a slow heart, in a sure but languid rhythm. Movements were in slow motion, sight pierced a golden warm curtain, the sun-shot ripples lazed in air and water. The fishermen leaned on the rope as if their weight alone, the weight of bodies seeking rest, and not the strain of muscle, would bear in the seine and set its wooden floats atwinkle. A steer trod slowly, and, as slowly, a fresh-water crab side-stepped the descending hoof. Even the lizards seemed to move more slowly. On a hot stone a little frog panted, its palpitant flanks hurrying, hurrying, with a hurry that did not fray the thick still air any more than the splashing, chattering gesturing of the people. For half the village seemed to be on the beach. All along the water's edge women were washing clothes, and behind them the beach was a flower garden of many-colored garments. Here and there groups of girls bathed, and there were knots of screaming splashing urchins, the little ones naked, the bigger ones in white drawers. Young men were bathing from several anchored canoes. Some of them swam and dove well, and the small boys endlessly climbed into convenient boats and jumped back into the water. Even members of the older generation, who seldom risked immersion, were taking baths with the complete three soapings. Doña Arcelia of the corner shop, in a vast colorless tentlike garment, advanced majestically into the water, her hair streaming down her ample back, her hand clenching a cake of soap. Bernardina of the other shop was undressing with ingenious wriggles, slithering her clothes downward underneath a flowered cotton dress, while her eyes looked anxiously and simultaneously to right and left. The three dressmakers, in satin slips of scarlet, cyclamen, and violet, minced into the lake daintily with little screams. A little way removed from other bathers, Primitivo and Paz, she in a flowing pale pink nightdress, stood waist-deep and soaped quietly, on their faces a look of drugged content. The grandmother of Nieves, her head a bird's nest of straggly gray, in a slip of yellowed darned patched calico, squatted on a stone and laboriously lathered her knotted cocoa-colored limbs. Elpidia, plucking her gown from her big round body, came tottering out of the water, seized little Silvanito, who had written in furrows, and soaped him mercilessly. The mother of Cayetano was washing one of his coats. Aurora rose from her scrubbing stone and sprinkled all the white things with water, so that they might bleach well, and all the time kept up a flow of corrections and reproaches to little Trini, who, with her hair pinned up on her head, was rubbing herself with much diligence and little soap, in four inches of the dirtiest water. After washing body and hair, the women splashed noisily, pretending to swim, with their hands on the lake bottom and their legs lashing the water and their rumps jolting like a school of porpoises. It was an animated scene, and attractive, for whereas a beach covered with bathers of the so-called white race resembles a pork butchery, all streaky hams and lardy chops with patches of salami, the tones of Indio skin, all the way from amber through beige through rosewood to mahogany, glow richly against sky and lake, making air more blue, water more silver.

Now César's truck came snorting and bouncing down from the plaza, and César himself, that busy man of affairs, climbed out, taking time out to smoke a cigar on the beach in the pleasant sunset hour. He chatted affably with a group of villagers, his gold teeth flashing. He was wearing blue denim trousers and a faded sombrero, but all the same he exuded an air of big business and prosperity. Even Don Bernabé, who seldom took a stroll, was walking along, dwarfed by his great hat and blood-red sarape, beside his young wife, Sebastiana. Doña Florencia, who had an independent income, paraded slowly up and down, dressed in unrelieved matt black and carrying a very floral sunshade. Nacho, who had had such a disagreeable encounter with the devil, was asleep flat on his back while on his stomach his sombrero rose and fell gently to his breathing. Chui, looking, as always, cheerful and slightly tight, was with a group of friends under the farthest eucalyptus tree. One of them plucked at a guitar and sang in a high strained voice, "One day with another—" At one limit of the beach the herd of black sheep with white topknots trotted down to drink, at the other, a herd of pale beige goats capered to the water. Motzín and Tippet chased a lizard fruitlessly.

A fisherman tilted the straw cartwheel of his sombrero and threw a whitefish, its cellophane scales streaking a blinding arc, into the tall basket held by a lad with a red kerchief knotted round his head. The bark of a swimming dog kept time over the water with the slaps of a flung stone. A flight of the black birds that exercise at sunset rent the air and was gone. At their accustomed place near the wine-glass willows, Venustiano, his two cows, and his horse were contemplating the view. I left my new small house, into which I shall move next week, and walked along the beach.

"I've finished the volume of Carlos Marx," said Venustiano, as I went by. "Not worth the three pesos I paid for it." Then, each of his myriad wrinkles a shade deeper, a tone more morose, he added: "But who knows."

A hummingbird whirred, and a guitar string caught the high vibrant note. The two daughters of the new comisario came onto the beach. They wore full flowered robes and under them two-piece swim suits, and the elegant Javier swaggered down the mole to meet them, in his royal-blue trunks.

"One day with another,
The luck will surely change,"

sang the guitarist, as if to greet the moderns. And behind the music, distantly, beyond sight, a speedboat hummed. For the luck has already changed, and Ajijic, with all Mexico, is on the way. It doesn't quite know where it is going, but then that is a state not confined to Mexico. And if progress comes first bearing as gifts face powder and movies and swim suits and trumpery, well, that is a way that progress has. Nothing will change very quickly, and many novelties will be adopted and adapted so thoroughly as to result almost unrecognizable, molded to a rhythm of living that is ancient and not unsensible and satisfactory to those who practice it. And the people, earth-colored and close to the earth, springing from it and returning to it as adobes do, will not change but will remain kind and generous and good-tempered, quick to laughter, quick to quarrel and quick to forget the quarrel, in some things utterly careless, but not easy to deceive in things that lie nearest to here-now, that moving point which, although it is allwhere and anywhere, comprehends the whole real world.

Tiburcia was going home. She had a huge basket of washing on her head, her small boy was tugging at her apron, and in one hand she carried a live pigeon.

"The boy's got a little fever," she said. "I'm going to put him to bed and split open the pigeon and put it on his stomach."

At the door of the huerta sat Candelaria, who had followed the pre-vailing fashion and had a bath, her drying hair spread over her shoulders. She was combing it and putting the combings carefully into an old cornflake carton.

"When I have enough," she said, "I'm going to make a little cushion to send to Remedios. And if I don't have enough hair of mine I'll ask Moursi for some of his. You will give it me, won't you, Moursi, Moursi?" And she picked up Motzín with her hands in the pits of his forelegs so that he yelped.

Nieves came up the beach from the water. She too had been bathing. Her damp hanging hair and her small eyes were seal-black against her tobacco-golden skin. She picked a spray of bougainvillea and tucked it behind her ear. She looked very aristocratic, an Amerindian princess.

"Would it be possible to have the day off tomorrow?" she asked. "I want to help my mother kill a pig. What do you think?"

In the huerta, under the banana trees, shadows were smoothing the rough ground with lilac dimness. Cayetano was watering a tray where we had sown some green peppers.

"Look," he said, "almost all we sowed have been born."

He finished spraying gently among the points of green. It is not so long since he learned to use a sprinkler, instead of sloshing water in gallons out of a gasoline can. He had on an old pair of flannel trousers of mine, miraculously cleaned, altered, and renewed.

"Señor," said Cayetano, "I have one peso fifty that I want to give you for the bank. It is what I didn't spend on the wedding. With that and the five pesos you gave me that the nephew of Don Carlos left for me I can start to save up again. I would like a leather jacket. And that Merced, Don Bernabé's son, has got a very nice clock, with a waker, that cost him seven pesos, and I would like to get one too, because I have learned to read the hour. The clock is a very pretty blue, just like Javier's bicycle. And do you think I could gather enough little centavos for a bicycle for me?"

I reached the patio and it was still and calm and empty, all green shadows, cool and vacant. Even the swallows, who were tending a last brood in the rafters of the zaguán, were still, one on the nest, and the other perched on the conveniently bent twig of the bamboo roofing. Seated in a low chair by the entrance was an old woman half asleep, with a hen in her lap.

There was a knock at the door, and as I was alone in the house I went to answer it. In the street stood a man I did not know.

"Could you tell me where Don César Ramos lives?"

"Oh, yes," I said. "He lives over there. You go along the street, straight straight, till you come to the corner where the big mango tree is, just beyond that brown cow, and then you give a turn to the right past the house with the red door—"